Table of Contents

Design

cation
Oriented
Techniques

Kevin Mullet
Darrell Sano

SunSoft Press
A Prentice Hall Title

The publisher offers discounts on this book when ordered in bulk quantities. For more information, contact:

Corporate Sales Department
Prentice Hall PTR
113 Sylvan Avenue
Englewood Cliffs, NJ 07632
Phone: 800-382-3419 or 201-592-2863
Fax: 201-592-2249
E-mail: dan_rush@prenhall.com

CREDITS
Editorial/production supervision: *Lisa Iarkowski*
Manufacturing manager: *Alexis R. Heydt*
Acquisitions editor: *Phyllis Eve Bregman*
Cover designer: *Jean Orlebeke*

Printed in the United States of America.

10 9 8 7 6 5 4 3 2

ISBN 0-13-303389-9

SunSoft Press
A Prentice Hall Title

Foreword

I recently tried out a spreadsheet package that was installed on the corporate-wide computer net accessible through my workstation. Immediately after firing it up, I was struck by its primitive visual appearance. It spoke "stone-age design" and I simply couldn't get myself to use that ugly-looking a program. Admittedly, I was in a somewhat unusual situation since I had just started using a networked computer with access to a myriad of different software that had already been installed. If I had bought the package myself as part of a small set of tools, I would obviously had invested more time in exploring its possible hidden charms.

As software gets closer to achieving commodity status, users can be expected to make very rapid choices between the huge number of offerings available on the net, and just as I did, they will immediately discard any interface that looks boring, obsolete, or too confusing. Think of home users flipping through 500 channels of cable TV and then multiply by a factor of several thousands to match the smorgasbord of options on the Internet, commercial subscription services, and major corporate nets. Alternatively, to mention a current commercial product, think of Apple's Software Dispatch CD-ROM, which is distributed to large numbers of home computer owners with demo copies of 75 applications: Each of these applications would at best have a minute or two in which to seduce the customer. Intuitive appeal will thus be essential for the survival of software products in the future. In fact, we may not even talk about software as "products" any more if the model turns out to be more that of service provision through subscription and browsing.

Graphic design is the first and the last part of the user interface observed by the user. Immediately when novice users start up a new software package they are confronted by its visual design and the possibility of a profusion of icons, windows, panes, and dialog boxes. Even after having graduated to the expert user stage, people still have to look at the icons and other visual design elements of their favorite software every day. Would you want to live in a house where the bedroom was painted in an ugly combination of brown and purple? Probably not, but you may spend more time looking at the visual interface elements of your favorite software than you do looking at your bedroom walls.

In the bedroom wall example, people might buy the house anyway and then paint over the wall with a more agreeable color. This example leads me to consider an excuse some developers have for not providing a satisfactory visual interface to their products: "the user can just customize the design to his or her individual taste!" Leaving the design to the users is the ultimate abdication of the designer's responsibility to provide a quality product, and many studies have shown that users are in fact very poor designers and often customize their interface in ways that are detrimental to their productivity (e.g., by using color combinations that are known to cause reduced readability of screen text). Even though there are often reasons to allow users to customize some aspects of their environment, it is absolutely essential for the designer to give the users a carefully thought-out set of defaults to start out with. Also, users will be much more likely to end up with an appropriate customized design if they are given some pre-specified (and well-designed) options to chose from as done, for example, in the Pantone®ColorUP™ set of recommended color combinations for presentation slides.

This book gives many systematic steps one can go through to improve the visual design characteristics of an interface. Mullet and Sano succeed in demonstrating that graphic design is not a black art but a very engineering-like discipline with its own rules. Also, just as in other types of engineering, the rules sometimes conflict and one has to make appropriate trade-offs to arrive at the design that best satisfies the needs at hand. One thing I particularly like about this book is that it makes it clear that graphic design in the user interface business is not just a matter of aesthetics. There is much more at stake than simply pretty pictures, and good graphic design can significantly improve the communicative value of the interface, leading to increased usability.

System usability has many components, including ease of learning, efficiency of use, memorability, reduced number of user errors, and subjective satisfaction. Good graphic design can improve all these quality attributes, though of course graphic design is only one element of overall user interface design, and one should employ systematic usability engineering methods in addition to the principles of graphic design discussed in this book.

It is amazing how much software gets released with horrible interfaces because the developers did not bother to apply a few simple graphic design principles like those explained in this book. For example, I recently saw a system where the concept of a "queue" was represented by an icon of a billiard ball ("cue ball," get it?). Such visual puns may be fun to throw around in a design session but they are often detrimental to the novice user trying to make sense of a new visual environment. Also, of course, this product would be dead on arrival if it was ever exported to a non-English speaking country.

There is no substitute for having "real" graphic designers involved from the beginning in the design of any important interface with major visual elements. Given this fact, other user interface professionals are still often called upon to get involved in graphic design. This book makes it possible for the larger community of interface designers to improve their graphic design skills and understanding of graphic design concepts. Not only will this enable them to communicate better with their visually trained colleagues on interdisciplinary teams, but it will also enable them to do some designs on their own. Face it, we will never bring in enough professional graphic designers to fine tune every last dialog box in all the interfaces in the world, but at least there is no excuse any longer for leaving those dialog boxes to the tender mercies of people with zero understanding of graphic design.

Jakob Nielsen,
Mountain View, California
May 1994

Preface

This book describes a set of fundamental techniques used routinely by practitioners of communication-oriented visual design. With a little practice, these techniques can be applied by anyone to enhance the visual quality of graphical user interfaces, data displays, and multimedia documents. Because all graphical user interfaces (GUI's) are communication systems, their design should be held to the same standards of functional and aesthetic relevance that have evolved over the centuries for traditional print media. While the new electronic media differ greatly from print in many important ways – they are inherently dynamic, for example, and their raster displays provide lower resolution but greater freedom to manipulate color and contrast – there is nevertheless a significant static component to all interactive displays, and much of the knowledge gained from centuries of print design is directly applicable within this domain. Our focus is on optimizing the static displays that provide the building blocks for any dynamic, interactive system.

The approach we describe has its roots in the rational, functional aesthetic seen in modern *graphic design, industrial design*, and *architecture*. We believe that the orientation, process, and training of these *visual design disciplines* are especially well-suited to the problems of visual interface design. Unfortunately, the typical software developer, development manager, or human factors engineer receives little or no formal training in these areas. *Designing Visual Interfaces* attempts to address this problem by describing a number of important design rules and techniques internalized by every visual designer through coursework and studio experience. While we don't mean to imply that readers of this book will be instantly transformed into expert (or even proficient) visual designers, we believe there are nevertheless valuable insights that can be exploited with minimal training in a few basic "tricks of the trade." Although *mastery* of these techniques depends on a heightened sensitivity born of extensive practice, the guiding principles are not overly difficult to understand and most can be applied immediately – even imperfectly – to produce noticeable improvements in real-world product development.

This book is a direct outgrowth of a tutorial (*Applying Visual Design: Trade Secrets for Elegant Interfaces*) we have presented at various professional conferences (the X Technical Conference, INTERCHI'93, and CHI'94, among others) over the past several years. Feedback from tutorial attendees confirms that practical applicability is a reasonable claim. Numerous non-designers have credited the tutorial with stimulating their interest in further study as well as their successful application of the techniques we describe to produce a visible impact on their user interface designs. While we do not mean to suggest that professional design talent is unnecessary, we would be delighted to see the book fill precisely this role. In addition, we have been particularly surprised and pleased with the positive response from graphic designers who have taken the tutorial. We welcome this endorsement of communication-oriented design principles and we hope that graphic designers will find the book equally stimulating.

The basic plan of the course is reflected in the arrangement of chapters in the book, the choice and structuring of the examples, and the presentation of the techniques themselves. Because the typical reader is engaged in commercial product development, we strive to keep the focus on visual phenomena as they are manifested in current software products. Instead of the usual organization (e.g., color, typography, layout) seen in the typical academic design curriculum, we present our topics in an order that relates them to the specific problems of GUI design. Following the *Introduction*, in which we characterize the discipline of visual design and qualify our own particular niche within it, we present six chapters addressing the major visual concerns in present-day GUI's: *Elegance and Simplicity* addresses poorly scoped or overly complex designs; *Scale, Contrast, and Proportion* describes ways to establish clear yet harmonious contrasts within a composition or coding system; *Organization and Visual Structure* explains how to exploit characteristics of human perception to structure displays more effectively; *Module and Program* describes how to extend the structure of an individual display to produce a unified system spanning many displays; *Image and Representation* provides guidance on the production and effective use of abstract and concrete imagery; and finally, *So What About Style?* considers common GUI standards and cross-platform design issues. Each chapter begins with an overview of several important *Principles* governing the phenomena in question and concludes with a description and step-by-step summary of three or four practical *Techniques* relating to the phenomena just described. Marking the boundary between these discussions in each chapter is a catalog of *Common Errors* drawn from existing GUI applications and environments to illustrate problems to avoid.

Designing Visual Interfaces will be useful to anyone responsible for designing, specifying, implementing, documenting, or managing the visual appearance of any form of computer-based information display. Software engineers and development managers, in particular, are our primary audience, both because these groups may have little exposure to the ideas we present and because successful interface design is impossible without their active participation and support. Readers from the psychological and human factors communities should be more familiar with the principles and effects we describe, but visual design – particularly its aesthetic component – will still be unfamiliar territory for most. Practicing graphic designers will be familiar with most of the techniques we describe, but they too should find the application to interface design both interesting and informative. We hope every reader will gain a new perspective on product development as well as an appreciation for the contribution visual design can offer their products and users. Whether you're doing the work yourself, participating in a design team, or directing the work of others, this book should help you understand your communication problem, establish reasonable design goals, and evaluate your progress toward them.

The principles we describe – and the examples we present – are truly generic in that they are equally applicable to any of the existing GUI standards. While the implementation of a particular design goal may vary from widget set to widget set, the principles of effective visual communication do not. Many of our examples happen to have been drawn from the OPEN LOOK GUI–an open GUI standard found primarily in UNIX environments–which may be unfamiliar to some readers. There are two reasons for this. First, as employees of Sun Microsystems, much of our own work has been in OPEN LOOK during the past several years, so examples of both good and bad design were readily at hand. More importantly, OPEN LOOK remains the only GUI standard attempting to address–however imperfectly–many of the communication oriented principles we describe, so it is in many cases the only available example of a particular design goal. To learn more about OPEN LOOK, see the Functional Specification (Sun, 1989) and Application Style Guide (Sun, 1990).

Like any large project, *Designing Visual Interfaces* would not have been possible without the cooperation and support of many individuals and organizations. We are deeply indebted to all those who offered their time, their material, or simply their advice and encouragement during the development of the project. Without their help this book would not have been possible. In addition to the many we cannot thank individually, we would like to explicitly acknowledge the following friends, associates, and colleagues for their generous contributions.

For help in selecting examples of good design and/or permission to reproduce copyrighted work, we thank: Deirdre Quinn, Melinda Maniscalo, Neil Shakery, and Sarah Haun at Pentagram; Erik Spiekermann, Terry Irwin, and Bill Hill at MetaDesign, Mark Johnson, and Mark Goldberg at The Understanding Business; Peter Spreenburg at IDEO; Stephanie Harwood at Clement Mok designs, Inc.; Craig Syverson and Julian Schmidt at frogdesign; Josef Müller-Brockmann; Armin and Dorthea Hofmann; Rudi Rüegg; Paul Rand; Inge Druckrey; Phillip Meggs; Linda Meyers at the Division of Publications, US National Park Service; Martin Fox at RC Publications, Inc.; Lynn Briber at Michael Graves Architects; Eric P. Chan and Jeff Miller at ECCO Design, Amy Edelson at Swatch US; Audrey Hirschfeld at Sony, Bob Panzer at VAGA, Professor Emeritus Shozo Sato, Northern California Center for Japanese Art and Aesthetics and the University of Illinois at Urbana–Champaign.

For artwork and examples from various hardware and software products, we thank: Debra Coelho at Sun Microsystems Computer Corporation, Tony Hoeber at Go Corporation; Lorraine Aochi at Apple Computer, Inc.; Heidi Bollan at NeXT Computer; Steve Anderson at Hewlett–Packard, Todd Fearn at Visual Cybernetics, Gabriella Pacini of Regis Mackenna, and Alesha Marie Guyot of Sunnyvale, California.

Many people provided helpful comments on earlier drafts. We are especially grateful for comments, suggestions, and insight provided by Diane Schiano, Mihai Nadin, Rob Mori, Jay Guyot, Jarrett Rosenberg, Sean Curry, Jakob Nielsen, Rolf Mölich, and Stacey Ashlund.

Phyllis Bregman at Prentice-Hall and Karin Ellison at SunSoft Press showed patience and encouragement throughout the often arduous publication process. Management support from Bob Glass and Rick Levenson in SunSoft and from Nancy Yavne and Kevin Whiting in SunPro was also invaluable.

Finally, we extend our special thanks to Jakob Nielsen for the Foreword and to Jean Orlebeck for the cover design.

Introduction

1

> To design is much more than simply to assemble, to order, or even
> to edit; it is to add value and meaning, to illuminate, to simplify, to
> clarify, to modify, to dignify, to dramatize, to persuade, and perhaps
> even to amuse.
>
> **Paul Rand,**
> Design, Form, and Chaos

This book is about visual design for graphical user interfaces. We have found
the orientation, process, and training of the visual design disciplines to be
especially well-suited to the problems of graphical user interface (GUI)
design. When we speak of the *visual design* disciplines, we include communication-oriented graphic design (often described as visual communication
design), industrial design, and architecture (including interior space design).
These are the professions concerned most directly with the user's experience
of a *form in the context of a specific task or problem,* as opposed to its functional or aesthetic qualities in isolation. Other *visual* disciplines – such as
painting, sculpture, illustration, filmmaking, or photography – while they
have much in common with the visual design disciplines, typically adopt a
more specialized focus or a less applied orientation. Other *design* disciplines
– including most branches of engineering – also have substantial overlap,
particularly in process and methodology, but they tend to focus largely or
even exclusively on functional issues, often at the expense of aesthetics.
Visual design attempts to solve *communication* problems in a way that is at
once functionally effective and aesthetically pleasing.

By *communication,* we mean the full process by which the behavior of one
goal-seeking entity comes to be affected by that of another through the recip-
rocal exchange of messages or *signs* over some mediating physical channel.
Research in communication theory (see Cherry, 1978) has investigated the
statistical properties of communication channels, the structure of language

systems, the psychological and social characteristics of message senders and receivers, and the effectiveness of various coding techniques. All of these factors must be considered in communication-oriented design. Even more fundamental is the field of *semiotics* – the general theory and practice of signs (Peirce, 1931, Morris, 1938) – which we review briefly in Chapter Six. The goal of communication-oriented design is to develop a message that can be accurately transmitted and correctly interpreted, and which will produce the desired behavioral outcome after it has been understood by its recipient.

We refer frequently to *visual language*, by which we mean the visual characteristics (shape, size, position, orientation, color, texture, etc.) of a particular set of design elements (point, line, plane, volume, etc.) and the way they are related to one another (balance, rhythm, structure, proportion, etc.) in solving a particular communication problem. Any *language system* defines both a universe of possible signs and a set of rules for using them. Every visual language thus has a *formal vocabulary* containing the basic design elements from which higher-level representations are assembled, and a *visual syntax* describing how elements may be combined within that system. We will return to these topics shortly, but first we must review the state of the art.

The Mess We're In

With a few notable exceptions, present-day GUI applications leave much to be desired from a communication standpoint. The arrival of GUI technology has opened up new degrees of freedom in the use of color, typography, and imagery. Most of the world's character-based applications are rapidly being ported to Microsoft® Windows™ (hereafter denoted simply as *Windows*), the Macintosh, or OSF/Motif (a GUI for UNIX workstations). The results are reminiscent of the early days of desktop publishing, when computers first gave people without the appropriate background and skills the *mechanical*

1: Imagery that distracts, confuses, or simply bewilders the uninitiated user is all too common in the current generation of graphical applications. (Palettes from Builder Xcessory by ICS.)

2: Non-standard graphical elements intended to differentiate an application from its competition undermine the opportunity for transfer of learning offered by the GUI environment. Do you want users thinking about *their* work or *your* sliders?

capacity to produce "realistic" printed materials. While the technical level of production was indeed impressive, the aesthetic quality left much to be desired simply because powerful tools had been placed in the hands of people without the training needed to use them correctly. Today's GUI applications suffer from exactly the same problem, as shown in Figures 1–4.

> The public is more familiar with bad design than good design. It is, in effect, conditioned to prefer bad design, because that is what it lives with. The new becomes threatening, the old reassuring.
>
> **Paul Rand**
> Design, Form, and Chaos

Ironically, given the graphical nature of the GUI revolution, imagery is one of the biggest problems. The Windows user, in particular, has been "blessed" with a hieroglyphic outpouring of *tool bars, icon bars, button bars, help bars, QuickAccess bars, SpeedBars,* and *SmartIcons.* The vast array of icons needed to satisfy this burgeoning demand (it is now customary to provide a configurable toolbar with an icon for each function in one's application) combined with the need to support low-resolution 16-color displays has led to an astonishing proliferation of low-quality images (1, see also 212–218, *Note: our convention is to cite figures parenthetically by number only, with multi-part examples labeled from left to right: (a), (b), (c), etc.)* that sacrifice

Batch Save

New...   Edit...   Delete

List: Drag & Drop Images ▾

● Open   ALL ▾
○ Acquire

□ Don't go into subfolders

For each image in List:
● Do Script: NOTHING ▾
● Display: Pause for 2 seconds ▾
● Save: Auto Naming Options...
   ● To: Set... Scammer :Utils :DeBabelizer :
   ○ To: Folder image came from
   ○ To: Manually select
   Type: PICT2 ▾ normal
   Colors: 256 (8 bits) ▾ ☒ Auto set
   □ Slice...   ☒ Verify replace
   □ Picture Preview □ 1 image/file
   □ Picture Icon   □ 1 animation/file
      ☒ Bypass warning messages
      □ Hit OK in unattended dialogs

DO IT Cancel Exit with settings Help...

3: Reducing the number of dialog boxes may improve the organization of your application, but there will be little net benefit to the user if the dialogs are this crowded and disorganized as a result.

valuable communication bandwidth in a well-intentioned pursuit of graphical glitz and "fun." Unfortunately, many of these images are so poorly designed as to be practically unintelligible, even when (as is rarely the case) there *is* some degree of consistency across (or even within) applications.

Even in a well designed and fairly well standardized environment such as the Macintosh desktop, it has proven difficult to stem the tide of application-specific styles, arbitrary mappings, and idiosyncratic imagery (2). Flexible authoring environments such as HyperCard extend the "naive desktop publisher" phenomenon to the design of even the GUI primitives themselves. The situation isn't much better in the Windows world, where at least four major "house styles" are now evident among mainstream applications (Berst, 1992 a-b). In fairness to application developers, existing user interface toolkits have provided very little support for communication-oriented visual design. In fact, most toolkits impose unnecessary design restrictions as a side effect of their own implementation or internal architecture.

Another problem that has been around as long as the GUI itself is evident in the haphazard, devil-may-care arrangements of controls in windows and dialog boxes (3). In fact, the typical application interface was probably structured more effectively in the days of character-oriented displays, since the limited number of positions in a character-mode screen had to be managed more carefully – and permitted less variation in the first place – than today's high-resolution raster displays. Basic principles of visual organization developed through centuries of experience with print media have rarely been applied to the on-screen media, and communication has suffered as a result.

Graphical interfaces have generated a prodigious body of research (Shu, 1988, Eades and Tamassia, 1989, Myers, 1990) leading to dozens of commercial products based on visual programming, program visualization, and graphical data display. A wide variety of scheduling tools, project management systems, and personal information managers, not to mention visual programming environments (4) employ visual representations to help users make sense of complex serial dependencies and interleaving or concurrent processes. Despite their commercial success, these applications are plagued by the generally low quality of their visual displays. There appears to be a tacit assumption in each of these areas that simply using a graphical display will automatically confer all the benefits of effective visual presentation on a

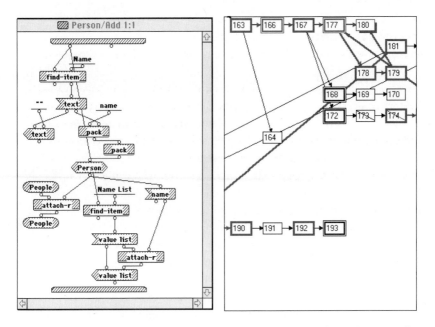

4: Existing "visual" applications have generally made surprisingly poor use of visual language and spatial organization in their graphical displays. Both this visual programming environment (a) and this graphical project manager (b) do a poor job of making the essential information obvious "at a glance."

complex problem domain. Unfortunately, a spatial representation must use visual (and non-visual) language *effectively* for the potential of graphical displays to be realized. The fact that it takes a very *good* picture to be worth a thousand words has rarely been appreciated within this domain (one notable exception can be seen in the elegant BALSA algorithm simulation environment [Brown and Sedgwick, 1984]). The use of color has created similar problems. The limitations of a small color palette have long been compounded by the tendency to fill the color table with colors that are easy to

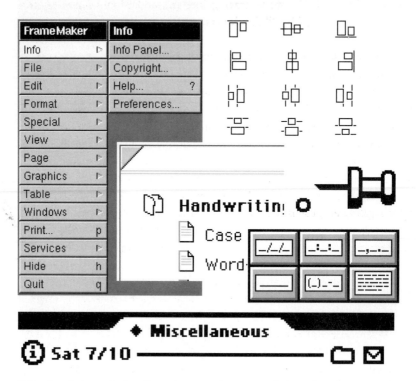

5: Excellent design *can* be found in modern GUI environments – albeit mostly at the system software level – as evidenced by this collage of effective graphical elements (each described in greater detail in the chapters to come) from various graphical applications and GUI standards.

describe digitally. This practice inevitably produces the familiar range of intense, over-saturated colors that still predominates in many computer displays. Eventually, the problem should diminish as displays with higher color resolution become the norm, but better solutions will only arise if the problems with current displays are recognized. As with any dimension of visual language, color can enhance communication, but only if it is used correctly.

Of course we don't mean to imply that the industry has been completely without success in the area of visual design. On the contrary – a number of successful products have led the way with excellent visual solutions. Most of the familiar operating environments, for example, employ some visual elements, and occasionally a comprehensive visual language, that are effective for their target markets (5). These elements succeed from a visual design standpoint largely because their sponsors have made the commitment to involve professional designers. For large system software vendors, the investment is easily justified by the leverage gained in standard *user interface toolkits* that can be re-used by all developers.

Unfortunately, development organizations have rarely shown the same vision at higher levels of the software food chain, and much of the momentum provided by standardized toolkits has been squandered as a result. Today, simply using the low-level toolkit components does little to ensure a high quality (or even a style guide compliant) application because the *way the pieces are put together is usually as important as the pieces themselves.* The remainder of this book will describe ways in which these higher level issues can be addressed. We expect that real success will only be achieved through close collaboration between system-sensitized visual and conceptual designers and design-sensitized software engineers and managers. The rest of this introduction describes the field of visual design and the contribution that a competent visual designer can make to the development team.

Design is not something that can be applied after the fact, when the fundamental organization of the product has already been determined – though this is indeed a common misconception. To be effective, design must be an integral part of the product development lifecycle. The process employed by visual designers is comparable to the typical engineering methodology. An initial understanding of the problem based on thorough background research is followed by an iterative cycle of generation and evaluation until the solution that best meets the requirements is selected for production. The designer serves typically as a planner, coordinator, and orchestrator of many specialist subcontractors. Areas of direct responsibility typically include background research and problem definition; high level design and concept/program development; planning, coordination, and design specification; production supervision and quality control. Some designers produce their own copywriting, illustration, photography, or pre-press production, but more commonly these tasks are contracted out to production specialists.

What Visual Designers Do

6: The painting, *Number 1A*, by Jackson Pollock, illustrates the concern of the fine arts for pure form – divorced completely from functional or representational criteria – as a direct expression of the personal aesthetic vision of the artist. © 1993 Pollock-Krasner Foundation/ARS, New York.

Art and Design

The designer is not an artist, at least not in the sense in which that term is commonly understood. This remains a point of confusion for many in the software industry. The artist, like the poet, is engaged in the manipulation of the formal qualities of a particular medium to produce an aesthetic response. Aside from the technical ability of the artisan and the limitations of the medium, there are few if any constraints on the forms produced by the artist. That forms can be taken from their original context and experienced on their own terms is a central tenet of modern art. This concept underlies the work of modern artists from surrealist sculptor, painter, and conceptual artist Marcel Duchamp to abstract expressionist painter Jackson Pollock (6).

> The designer is a visually literate person, just as an editor is expected by training and inclination to be versed in language and literature, but to call the former an artist by occupation is as absurd as to refer to the latter as a poet.
>
> **Douglas Martin**
> Book Design

Art is valued for its originality and expressiveness. Its focus is on individual artifacts crafted through the manual and aesthetic virtuosity of the artist. Design, in contrast, is valued for its fitness to a particular user and task. Certainly, design is concerned with producing a life-enhancing aesthetic experience where possible, but the design aesthetic is always related to the intended function of the resulting product. Design is focused on the specification of products intended for mass production and widespread distribution. Whereas art strives to *express* fundamental ideas and perspectives on the human condition, design is concerned with finding the *representation* best suited to the communication of some specific information. The choice and arrangement of elements in the concert poster by Inge Druckrey (7), for example, are constrained by the need to effectively communicate the date, time, place, and event in question. The elegant manner in which this information is conveyed within the context of a formal aesthetic statement that reinforces and enhances the message is a hallmark of good design.

Designers are constantly asked to resolve conflicting demands imposed by the problem, the budget, the schedule, and the desired quality level. As in any engineering discipline, trade-offs must be continuously identified, evaluated, and decided on the basis of the best information available. Among the most common sources of contention is the apparent opposition of functional and aesthetic criteria. Communication-oriented visual design views these forces not as irreconcilable opponents, but as symbiotic components of every high-quality solution.

**Functional vs.
Aesthetic Concerns**

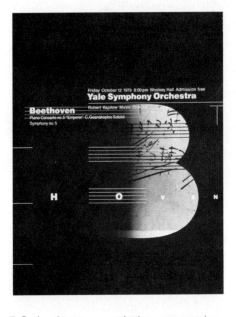

7: Design elevates communication over expression, but without forsaking aesthetic values. Design by Inge Druckrey for the Yale Symphony Orchestra.

Some of the best examples of the synergy between form and function can be seen in the dynamic compositions and active constructivist typography of the so-called *Dutch Constructivists* – including Piet Zwart, Paul Schuitema, and Gerard Kiljan, among others – in the 1920's and 1930's. Faced with the need to produce visually interesting advertising material for some rather ordinary-looking industrial equipment, telephone cabling, and public utilities, these designers turned the problem on its head by celebrating rather than obscuring the formal characteristics of the products being advertised. Unconventional orientations and viewing angles and dynamic graphical devices – including photomontage and superimposition – were used to underscore relationships among elements throughout the composition.

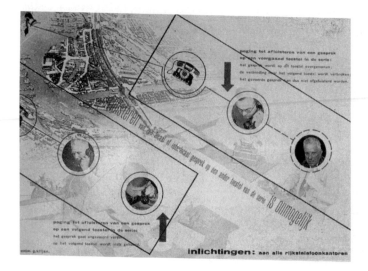

8: The striking formal juxtaposition of both long distance and close-up photography, active typography, and unifying graphical elements plays a clear functional role in this advertisement created by Gerard Kiljan for the Dutch Post Telefon Telegraff.

Gerard Kiljan's poster for the Dutch PTT (8), for example, uses diagrammatic elements and close-ups of callers superimposed in multiple layers upon a dramatic aerial view to show the telephone's ability to transcend physical distance. Note how closely the elements in each layer work together to convey the message of the poster while at the same time producing an aesthetically delightful statement. Similar effects can be seen in the advertising materials and catalog spreads produced by Piet Zwart and Paul Schuitema (9). Unusual framing, scale, and viewing perspectives are in each case used to produce images that are visually arresting and yet intimately related to the product itself. Superimposed graphical devices (the square on the left; the circle on the right) are again used to draw the viewer's attention to a particular area of the display and to relate elements to one another. By drawing attention first to the advertisement as a whole, and only secondarily to the image of the product, the formal aesthetics of the design complement the information content of the advertisement.

Good design defuses the tension between functional and aesthetic goals precisely because it works within the boundaries defined by the functional requirements of the communication problem. Unlike the fine arts, which

9: Unconventional viewing angles and dynamic composition – in which superimposed graphical elements play a critical role – play a functional role (by highlighting the product) in these industrial posters by Piet Zwart (a) – © Piet Zwart/VAGA, New York 1993 – and Paul Schuitema (b).

exists for their own sake, design must always solve a particular real-world problem. Functional criteria govern the range of possibilities that can be explored; aesthetic possibilities that are not compatible with this minimum standard of usability must be quickly discarded, if they are considered at all. Fortunately, there is almost always a wide latitude for aesthetic expression within these bounds, and experienced designers realize that solving a problem in a manner that is uniquely appropriate brings an aesthetic satisfaction all its own.

10: Good design is timeless, if not universal. Grace, economy, and fitness of purpose can be seen in both the monumental Roman inscription from Trajan's Column (a) and the modern Japanese gardener's *secateurs* (b).

Form, Function, and the Question of a Universal Aesthetic

The timeless quality of a classic design is immediately apparent. From the majestic capital letterforms of the Roman inscription (10-a) to the towering grace of the cathedral's apse to the simple, natural forms of traditional Japanese craftsmanship and design (10-b), the human race has delighted in forms reflecting widespread agreement on basic qualities of scale, rhythm, proportion, balance, harmony, and craftsmanship. The same formal characteristics have been appreciated in advanced civilizations throughout human history and they are central to any coherent philosophy of design. An elegant solution is both an artistic and an intellectual achievement that – while it may come to be taken for granted – never becomes trite or irrelevant.

Modern design arose out of the Arts and Crafts movement of the late 19th Century, which in turn had its roots in the depredations of the early years of the industrial revolution. In the torrent of manufactured goods that followed the introduction of mass production, there was little concern for the quality of the design, the integrity of the materials, or the humanity of the production process.   The resurgent concern for quality – in materials and construction as well as design – fueled a manufacturing explosion that has continued ever since. Phillip Meggs (1992) writes that, "*the history of design is the his-*

11: Shaker cabinetry shows the simple elegance of even a purely utilitarian application when natural materials are used with integrity. Does a woodgrain-printed vinyl dashboard really project the same image of quality? Photography by Michael Freeman.

tory of technology and craftsmanship." While design today remains grounded in mass production, the technology of manufacture is viewed as a means rather than an end. The ultimate focus is on the appropriateness of the design in relation to both the function the product is intended to fulfill and the materials from which it is constructed.

An appreciation for the inherent beauty of natural materials is unavoidable for anyone who has taken the time to reflect on the fine grain of properly finished hardwood, the texture of cleanly cut stone, or the fit of a well made artifact. Objects constructed from genuine materials are always valued more highly than those that use a cheaper substitute. The imposition of simulated woodgrain on aluminium siding or simulated leather on vinyl upholstery reflects not a preference for these *surrogate* materials, but rather, a deference toward the cost or availability of the genuine article. Compare the typical false wood dashboard of an American automobile to the delicate grain and careful seamless construction of Shaker cabinetry (11). The irony in this dishonest substitution is that the natural material qualities of the plastic or vinyl themselves – which often hold their own fascination (cf., Tecce and Vitale, 1990) – are prevented from revealing themselves.

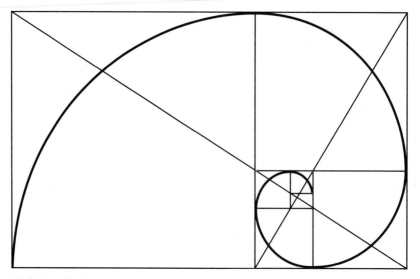

12: The logarithmic spiral can be constructed geometrically, yet it provides the basis for countless beautiful forms produced by the growth of living organisms throughout the natural world.

Design and Rationality

Is design fundamentally a rational or an intuitive endeavor? The great international design movements arising since the end of the 19th century have all advanced the belief that good design is a reflection of some higher truth, whether in form, method, or materials. From the beginnings of the Arts and Crafts movement, through the Vienna Secessionists and the Deutsch Werkbund, the De Stijl movement in the Netherlands and Constructivism in the emerging Soviet Union, through the Bauhaus and on to the rest of the world following the rise of National Socialism in Germany – modern design has been predicated on the rationalist belief that all design decisions should in principal be justifiable on objective grounds. While Modern design has occasionally been charged with mistaking post-hoc rationalization for functional determinism (cf., Banham, 1960, Margolin, 1989), there can be no serious question that the *intent* of these pioneering design movements was to promote appropriate design solutions that addressed the needs of the modern consumer as well as the requirements of mass production.

As to our initial question, of course both approaches to knowledge are essential. Modern design movements have emphasized the rational dimension, without rejecting completely the use of intuition as an important generative element. As with most classic dichotomies, there is value on both sides of the equation:

Without minimizing the value of intuition as a problem solving tool, we propose that systematic design programs are more valuable *from a communication standpoint* than are *ad hoc* solutions; that intention is preferable to accident; that principled rationale provides a more compelling basis for design *decisions* than personal creative impulse. When designing for human-computer interaction, communication is the overriding concern and creative expression is simply one means to this end. This is the orientation we consider most effective for designing visual interfaces and the perspective we adopt throughout this book.

The following pages describe some of the most important design rules and techniques learned by all students of the visual design disciplines that apply directly to GUI design. Most of the techniques we describe can be easily mastered and applied to your next product. We have tried to formulate the rules as crisply as possible, both to distinguish them from more general principles or guidelines that frequently conflict with one another, and to make them as useful as possible for addressing real-world problems. We do not mean to suggest, of course, that any of these rules should never be broken. As designers have realized for centuries, all rules are made to be broken – at least by the experienced practitioner.

We maintain that a rational approach to design is not only possible, but that it is essential, if high-quality design skills are to be replicated and transmitted across the generations.

Elegance and Simplicity

2

In anything at all, perfection is finally attained not when there is no longer anything to add, but when there is no longer anything to take away.

Antoine de Saint Exupery

The term, *elegance* derives from the Latin *eligere*, meaning to "choose out" or "select carefully." The same Latin root gives rise as well to terms such as *elect* and *select* – both of which carry a similar implication of reflection and careful decision. More recently the term has acquired the familiar connotations of refinement and grace, reflecting thoughtfulness and good taste. Achieving the latter, of course, depends upon the former. Visual design is intimately concerned with careful decision making and judicious selection of formal elements. Visual design decisions extend beyond the surface to the very heart of the product concept. The visual designer enhances communication by carefully selecting the elements to be emphasized – and this may involve selecting the elements to be *included* – and ensuring that they are presented so as to be perceptually salient.

Elegance in design is seen in the immediately obvious success of a *novel* approach that solves a problem *completely yet in a highly economical way*. The importance of simplicity can hardly be overstated. In fact, the sheer simplicity of an elegant solution is often its most startling and delightful aspect. Elegant solutions reveal an intimate understanding of the problem and an ability to ensure that its essence is grasped by the consumer as well. Economy of expression – the ability to cut directly to the heart of the matter – provides the basis for aesthetic evaluation in art and science alike. Simplicity abounds in the beauty of nature, from the laws of physics, to the symmetrical growth of crystals, to the structure of living organisms.

13: The Belmont Radio features clean lines and simple, approachable controls. The radio's basic forms are tightly integrated with the circular dial that serves as its focal point. From *Radios: The Golden Age* by Philip Collins ©1987, published by Chronicle Books.

Simplicity plays a central role in all timeless designs. We appreciate solutions that – all other things being equal – solve problems in a clear, economical, fashion. The most powerful designs are always the result of a continuous process of simplification and refinement. We will return repeatedly to simplicity in the chapters to follow, as many of the other design goals depend critically on simplification as a means to their own particular end. Before you do anything else to improve the quality of a design, make sure you have reduced its formal and conceptual elements to the absolute minimum. The benefits of simplicity are functional as well as aesthetic in nature:

Approachability. Simple designs can be rapidly apprehended and understood well enough to support immediate use or invite further exploration. The Belmont Radio (13) includes only three sets of controls – the volume knob, tuning knob and dial, and station presets. The functional relationships of each control group are readily apparent in the absence of competing elements. Anyone can tell "at a glance" how to operate this simple design.

Recognizability. Simple designs can be recognized more easily than their more elaborate counterparts. Because they present less visual information to the viewer, they are more easily assimilated, understood, and remembered.

The function of the Belmont radio is a readily identified by its tuning dial and louvered speaker enclosure, both of which are emphasized by the absence of competing formal elements.

Immediacy. Simple designs have a greater impact than complex designs, precisely *because* they can be immediately recognized and understood wit a minimum of conscious effort. The radio's simple color scheme ensures that the eye is drawn immediately and involuntarily to the bright white controls. The most powerful symbols in human culture are always reduced to their absolute minimal form.

Usability. Improving the approachability and memorability of a product necessarily enhances usability as well. Simple designs that eliminate unnecessary variation or detail make the variation that remains more prominent and informative. In fact, it is nearly impossible to operate a simple design like the Belmont radio incorrectly.

Principles

Understatement can be a difficult quality to grasp through conscious effort. Apart from the obvious focus on economy, or *minimization of component parts and simplification of the relationships between parts*, simplicity in design depends upon three closely related principles. The elements in the design must be *unified* to produce a coherent whole, the parts (as well as the whole) must be *refined* to focus the viewer's attention on their essential aspects, and the *fitness* of solution to the communication problem must be ensured at every level.

Unity
Refinement
Fitness

14: Traffic signs depend heavily on over-simplified, highly schematic imagery to alert the driver to potentially dangerous situations. Each sign refers to a general class of hazard, with a corresponding set of plans and precautions, rather than the specifics of any particular roadway.

15: The elegant Japanese *chasen* whisk is created from a single piece of bamboo whose fibers have been split, formed, and rejoined.

Unity

Elegant tools and utensils such as the Japanese *chasen* tea whisk (15) possess a unity that derives from the intimate relation of a minimal set of parts in pursuit of a common goal. Whenever a single part plays more than one role, the unity of the overall design is enhanced. Elegant solutions produce a maximum of satisfaction from an absolute minimum of components.

16: Circle and star are fused together in the classic identity symbol for Mercedes-Benz. Image courtesy of Daimler-Benz, Stuttgart.

British poster designer Abram Games recognized the key to communication-oriented design in his philosophy of *"maximum meaning, minimum means"* (Livingston, 1992). Visual identity programs, like posters, must be very concise to cut through the torrent of competing messages encountered in everyday life. Identity symbols have evolved over the centuries from the highly pictographic trade-marks of the medieval shopkeeper to the more abstract, symbolic marks used in today's brand and corporate identity programs. The classic Mercedes Benz identity symbol (16) is a familiar example with a strong symbolic quality. Its unity derives from the powerful integration of the three-pointed star with the center of the circumscribing circle. The axes of the star focus the viewer's attention on the origin of the ring. This convergence maximize the integration of the basic forms and the unity of the resulting design.

The EC2 phone from ECCO Design, Inc., (17) displays a similar unity of form in the common curvature of its handset and cradle. Instead of resting in a cavity carved into or molded onto the surface of the phone, as in most contemporary designs, the handset is held in place by virtue of its integration with the contours of the base itself. The relationship of the two elements was clearly planned from the beginning rather than a tacked-on as an afterthought. Visual unity in product design ensures that all of the individual components work together toward a common purpose. The role of the housing is to provide not merely an enclosure, but also a visual field within which control elements and visual displays can be properly related.

17: The unified form of the EC 2 Phone from ECCO Design Inc. is most apparent in the shared contour of handset and cradle. The mechanism is designed-in not tacked on as an afterthought. (See also color plate 1).

18: A common design language can be seen in the NeXTStation hardware and the NeXTStep GUI. Regardless of which came first, the coordination of on-screen imagery and physical product underscore the impression of a total solution.

Visual unity in the human-computer interface may take many forms. The foremost consideration is the integration of the visual language elements used throughout an application. Ideally, the same visual language should be apparent in the system software as well, and indeed, throughout the entire end-user environment. NeXT pursued this ideal to its logical conclusion by using a single design language to unify even the hardware with the system and application software (18, 19). This elegant design contrasts sharply with the colorful workstations from Silicon Graphics (e.g., Indigo, Crimson, Onyx), which awkwardly share the same egg-shell colored monitor. With the demise of the NeXT hardware business, this admirable unity will disappear for most NeXTStep users.

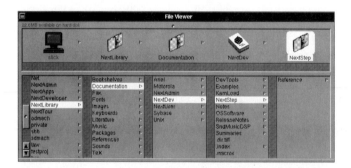

19: By matching the visual qualities of the hardware, NeXTStep transformed the original grayscale display from a marketing liability to a high-style asset.

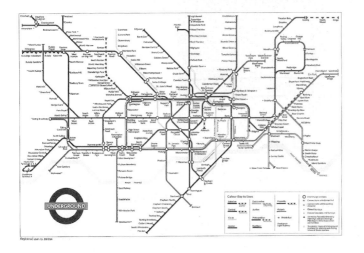

20: The network diagram for the London Underground reflects a problem-oriented refinement of the area's physical geography. By radically compressing the distances between outlying stations, this diagram became the first "fisheye" view. Design by Henry C. Beck, 1935. (See also color plate 2).

Reduction through successive refinement is the only path to simplicity. To create an elegant solution, anything that is not essential to the communication task must be removed. Public transportation maps have for years applied this principle to present complex routing information in an understandable way. one of the earliest and most famous examples is the route diagram for the London Underground system (20), which has retained its basic form since 1935. Instead of maintaining the geographically correct position and orientation of each line, these diagrams maintain *topological*

Refinement

21: The representation of a single line permits even further refinement of the diagram's form, since travellers who are already aboard the train need only concern themselves with the sequence of stops and the availability of connections.

accuracy while introducing simplifying generalizations that regularize the positions and orientations of lines, stations, and transfer points. In addition, the diagram provides a primitive *fisheye* view (Furnas, 1988) by compressing physical distance in outlying areas. By reducing and regularizing the spacing between stations, the diagram can accommodate more information in the same physical space. The same approach is used in the route diagram for the London Underground's Victoria Line (21). In this case, however, the generalization is even more extreme, since the orientation with respect to the surrounding geography or even the relative distance between stations is not important to riders who are already on the train. All that matters is the sequence of stops and availability of connections.

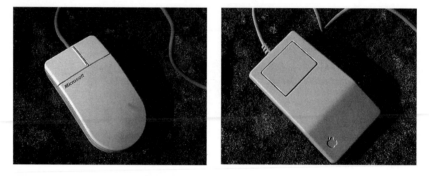

22: Simple, refined, forms convey the basic functionality of the these pointing devices from Microsoft (a) – (design by IDEO Product Associates) and Apple Computer (b). The aesthetics and ergonomics of each design are superior to their recent replacements.

Refinement of physical form can be seen in the original Microsoft Mouse and Apple ADB Mouse (22). The elegance of each design surpasses that of competing designs created before and since. Both designs feature button elements integrating tightly with the basic curves or planes of the mouse while still retaining a distinct identity. In the Microsoft Mouse, the left button (the primary control in the Windows environment) is half again as wide as the right button. This simple visual cue for button targeting is supplemented by a tactile cue in the form of a subtle ridge separating the two buttons.

The external appearance of GUI software has changed very little over the years. Researchers have experimented with minimalist interfaces that reduce the prominence of window borders, scrollbars, and other familiar GUI controls, but few tangible results have been obtained. One problem is that hiding "distracting" controls also removes the *visual affordances* (things that suggest interaction possibilities) those elements provide. The scrollbar itself, for example, reminds the user of its *availability* as well as its operation. Removing visual cues is disorienting, particularly for beginning users, but also for experienced users who can be disrupted by the abrupt transitions as controls materialize and disappear again.

An alternative approach can be seen in PenPoint, where some controls were replaced with simple gestures. PenPoint's elegant notebook metaphor (23-a) eliminates all extraneous details (note the absence of spiral bindings, perforations, rounded corners, ruled lines, etc.), depending largely on its vertical orientation and, of course, the tabs that have inspired a whole new genera-

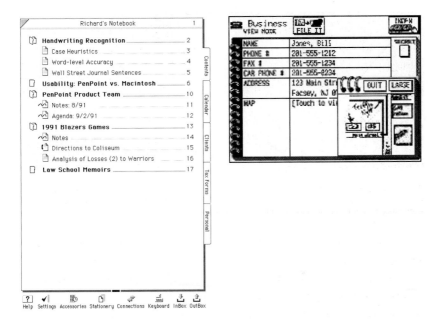

23: The elegant, highly refined interpretation of a paper notebook in the PenPoint user interface (a) contrasts sharply with the intrusive, overly literal "notepad" cues provided by the Sharp Wizard (b). The former conveys a global impression of notebook-ness, while the latter depends on crude "labels."

tion of notebook-builders. Compare the elegant PenPoint display to the busy Sharp Wizard screen (23-b) with its bulky spirals and axonometric rendering showing the dimensionality of the pad. Note how the spiral must sometimes be shortened due to space constraints. How interesting that this product, with its much smaller display, chose the more costly (in terms of screen real estate) route of a highly detailed literal representation.

24: The frugal design of this Shaker sewing desk makes full use of the many small enclosed spaces while providing constant access to the work surface. Photo by Michael Freeman.

Designs are never evaluated in absolute formal terms, but rather, succeed or fail on the basis of how well they solve a particular problem. Solutions can be more or less appropriate in their method, their process, or their outcome. Elegant solutions solve problems with maximum effectiveness through avenues that are desirable in their own right. In addition to its fine construction, the Shaker sewing desk (24) reveals a design of remarkable compactness and

25: The Japanese *kanban* sign identifies the type of goods or services offered by this establishment while blending naturally with traditional building materials used in the facade.

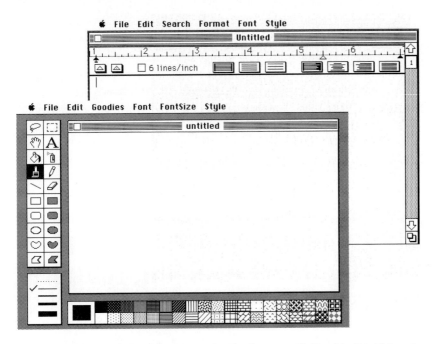

26: The modest design goals and focus on core functionality apparent in the original MacWrite and MacPaint applications reflect the commitment to an appropriate balance between capability and complexity seen in the first wave of software created for "the rest of us."

economy. The maximum use is made of the space consumed by the desk. The depth and accessibility of the drawers, as well as the leg-room under the desk, are all increased by allowing the drawers to open to the side, rather than the front. Tiny storage compartments throughout the desk reflect the need to accommodate materials and supplies. In short, every element reflects the practical concern of supporting the task of sewing.

The traditional *kanban* sign on many Japanese storefronts (25) reveals a similar sensitivity to the qualities of the material. In Japanese architecture, the concepts of subdued beauty (*shibui*) and elegant simplicity (*wabi*) are seen in the refinement and natural character of the buildings themselves. The *kanban* is an art form in its own right, but its fitness as a signage element is apparent in its visual compatibility with the surrounding material context.

In user interface design, the material choices are typically much narrower, but the digital medium can still be presented more or less appropriately. The original MacPaint and MacWrite applications (26) exemplified (and in some sense, defined) the philosophy of the early Macintosh software environment. These simple, straightforward, and highly graphical applications were appropriate for the technical level of the target user as well as for the limited capabilities of the original machine. The presentation in each case is concrete and explicit, with visual affordances or reminders to help users recognize the tools available to them. Simple mechanisms such as the memorably vivid "Fat Bits" magnification mode in MacPaint helped users understand the novel technology while exposing them to some of its power and flexibility. As simple as they were, these two "bundled" applications met the needs of many early users all by themselves.

abcdefghijklmnopqrstuvwxyz ABCDEFGHIJKLMNOPQRSTUVWXYZ $1234567890(.,'"-;:!)?&

27: The Chicago screen font was designed with the limitations and requirements of the low-resolution Macintosh display in mind. The thick vertical elements ensure that each character remains visible when dimmed with the standard 50-percent gray pattern.

The Chicago screen font used for widget labels throughout the Macintosh system software (27) provides an even better example of matching a design to the material qualities of the medium. The font was designed to ensure adequate legibility and contrast on low resolution (72 dots per inch) video displays. The thick vertical elements provide characters that remain legible even when some of their pixels are removed by the standard fifty percent gray pattern used to indicate the inactive state on the Macintosh. The Chicago font's unique typographic character and fitness to the display task helped make it a defining feature of the Macintosh interface from its earliest days on. The original design continues to thrive even as the technological limitations it was designed to accommodate have begun to disappear. Apple's recently introduced TrueType fonts include a scalable, outline-based version of Chicago even though the need for the pixel-level tuning seen in the original bitmap font is largely eliminated by the higher resolution output devices for which scalable fonts are intended.

Common Errors

Common errors related to elegance and simplicity can usually be attributed to poor planning, poorly communicated structure, or attempts to go beyond the scope of a coherent, focused design. The inevitable result is visual or conceptual complexity and confusion. The mistakes described below are all too typical in today's GUI applications.

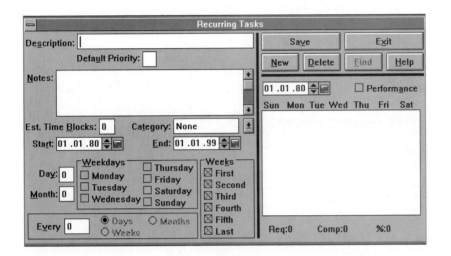

28: *Clutter and visual noise.* The advent of the GUI has meant more, not less visual clutter in most computing environments. Today software products are designed, marketed, evaluated (and all too often, purchased) on the basis of their aggregate feature set, even though many features are used rarely, if ever, by the vast majority of users. The only way to deal effectively with this unfortunate reality is to logically structure the presentation so that each display contains a manageable amount of information. Applications that try to pack as much information as possible into each screen create problems that rival the worst character-based displays. This window from a personal information manager is crowded, confusing, and almost impos-

sible to scan. The window contains so much functionality that the usual 1-pixel lines were not prominent enough to divide the layout into multiple regions. Instead, the design uses heavy 4-pixel horizontal and vertical dividers that do more to attract attention to themselves than to create meaningful higher-level units. In addition, the window's gray background turns a series of carelessly positioned text fields (with their bright white interiors) into a distracting pattern snaking randomly through the left-hand side of the display. While functional overload is clearly a problem with this design, effective use of visual language and display structure would bring a noticeable improvements.

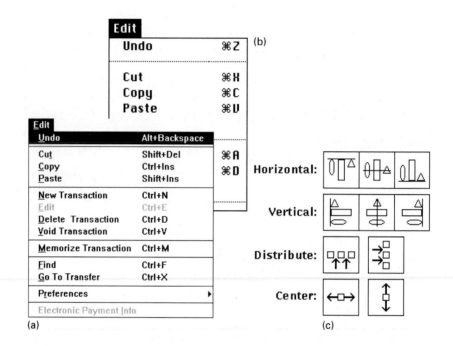

(a)

(b)

(c)

29: *Interference between competing elements.* Menu accelerators (i.e., individual keyboard shortcuts that invoke menu commands directly) in Windows (a) use purely textual cues for both the *qualifier* (e.g., Ctrl, Alt, Shift – the keys you press to indicate that the next key should invoke a command) and *accelerator* keys. These alphabetic qualifiers – along with the "+" symbol used to separate qualifier and accelerator – interfere with the accelerator characters, and sometimes with the menu items themselves. Contrasting these accelerators with their Macintosh counterparts (b) demonstrates the effectiveness of the simpler approach, in which a single graphical symbol is used as the qualifier for all accelerators. Because the "propeller" symbol is not confusable with the al-

phabetic characters, and because there is less visual information in the surrounding area, the Macintosh accelerator characters are far more readable than their Windows equivalents. They can be noticed in peripheral vision while choosing items with the mouse, which makes the logic of the accelerator scheme more apparent and incidental learning more likely. The same kind of visual interference is apparent in the Alignment icons from the OPEN LOOK Developer's Guide (c). The readability of these images suffers from an irrelevant variation in shape within each icon that serves to obscure the relevant variation in alignment.

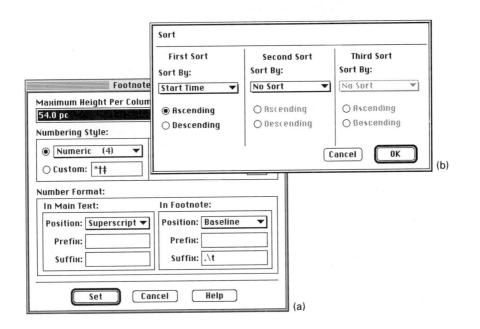

(a)

(b)

30: *Using explicit structure as a crutch.* The presence of nested bounding boxes is usually a symptom of a poorly organized layout. Packing information as densely as possible and surrounding the resulting groupings with explicit borders is never a good substitute for structuring the layout effectively in the first place. Bounding boxes interfere not only with the scanning of the items they contain, but with the surrounding items (including other bounding boxes) as well. Note, for example, how the gaps between bounding boxes, border lines, and textfield boundaries form a mesmerizing pattern at the bottom of the Foot-

note dialog above (a), where a single textfield is surrounded by *four* levels of boundary information. When proper spatial relationships and sufficient margins are maintained, explicit structure is rarely needed to ensure proper visual separation. Unfortunately many applications include structuring devices even when they are completely unnecessary. The Sort dialog (b) would have reasonably effective spatial grouping based on vertical alignment alone if the vertical dividers were simply removed.

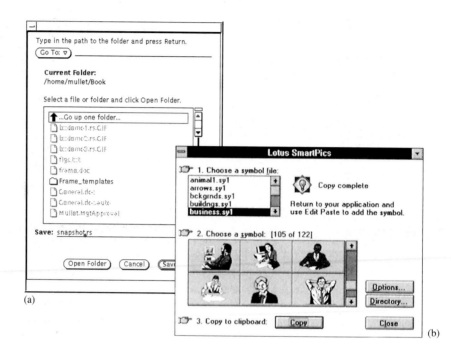

Type in the path to the folder and press Return.

(Go To: ▽) _____

Current Folder:
/home/mullet/Book

Select a file or folder and click Open Folder.

⬆ ...Go up one folder...
bzdemo1.rs.GIF
bzdemo2.rs.GIF
bzdemo3.rs.GIF
figs.txt
frame.doc
Frame_templates
General.doc
General.doc.auto
Mullet.MgtApproval

Save: snapshot.rs

(Open Folder) (Cancel) (Save)

(a)

Lotus SmartPics

☞ 1. Choose a symbol file:

animal1.sy1
arrows.sy1
bckgrnds.sy1
buildngs.sy1
business.sy1

Copy complete

Return to your application and use Edit Paste to add the symbol.

☞ 2. Choose a symbol: [105 of 122]

Options...
Directory...

☞ 3. Copy to clipboard: Copy   Close

(b)

31: *Belaboring the obvious.* Users of GUI applications remain totally unfamiliar with the application functionality only for a relatively short period. Unnecessary navigational aids that might be useful the first time a user sees a product quickly get in the way as soon as even a basic familiarity with the application has been established. Excessive "assistance" doesn't just slow semi-experienced users down – it can also prevent users from understanding the application in the first place, if it obscures the underlying structure of the window. The excessive verbal prompting in the file selection dialog above (a) consumes valuable space to tell users something that should have been obvious from the organization of the window and a basic understanding of the ubiquitous task of opening a file.

Like the presence of taped-on instructions in the physical workplace, the presence of help text in the interface is itself a reliable indicator of flaws in the underlying design. As many as five additional items could have been included in the list (or the window made smaller) simply by removing (perhaps optionally) the redundant text. Similarly, the pointing hands in the Smart-Pics dialog box (b) merely lead the eye along a path it would have followed naturally in any case. Such self-consciously "helpful" feedback does little more than parrot the viewer's natural movement through the dialog. In fact, it may well impede performance by interfering with otherwise obvious spatial relationships.

(a)

(b)

32: *Overly literal translation.* Even if the metaphor can be realized completely, presenting a software artifact as a direct analog to a physical object almost always imposes unnecessary visual and conceptual restrictions on the design. Most GUI calculators, for example, simply replicate the heavily moded, poorly labeled, and difficult to manipulate designs of existing physical designs. The model on the left (a) even goes so far as to replicate shifted functions (deg, oct, hex), even though dedicated software buttons could have been provided within the same space. While they may be familiar (to experienced users of the physical analog) these designs do little to leverage the power and flexibility of their computational host. The uncritical acceptance of the material constraints of a physical calculator prevents these calculator designs from focusing on the essence of the *problem of calculation* in any meaningful way. PentaCalc (b), in contrast, is only loosely patterned after a physical calculator (why shouldn't every GUI calculator provide the valuable tape feature, which is trivial to implement?). While perhaps less similar to "real-world" designs, it has been more carefully adapted to the capabilities and limitations of the GUI. It features flexible display modes, closely spaced buttons (which minimize mousing), and provides an excellent keyboard interface.

Lotus Organizer

(b)

Quit	Device Select
Report	Quick Test ▼
Error Report	Preferences

(a)

OK   No

OK   No

KPT Gradient Designer

(c)

33: *Excessive detail and embellishment.* The siren song of photographic realism is difficult to resist, particularly given the natural human receptiveness to visual stimulation. In the GUI, as in any new medium, more effort has been expended on faithfully replicating familiar themes than on uncovering the unique characteristics and qualities of the new electronic medium itself. Electronic media allow us to focus to an unprecedented extent on the essential elements of a design, but only if the available bandwidth is not squandered on graphical clichés and self-conscious ornamentation. Graphical embellishments that serve only to underscore the "realism" of the design such as the sheen of simulated brushed aluminum buttons (a), the sparkling splash screen (b) or the specular reflections on spherical plastic buttons (c) eventually grow tiresome despite the initial "oohs" and "aahs". These qualities rarely add to the long-term visual appeal of the product because they subvert rather than enhance communication. The extent to which this quest for graphical *pizzazz* has replaced concern for effective communication can be seen in the subtle highlighting of the spherical "OK" and "No" buttons (c). The buttons change *color* when pressed (woe to the user with color-deficient vision), but otherwise provide none of the essential visual feedback that provides the illusion of manipulating a tangible object.

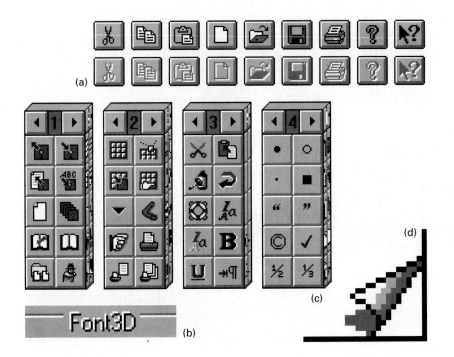

(a)

Font3D (b)

(c)

(d)

34: *Gratuitous dimensionality.* Most people love the sense of tangibility imparted to a widget set by the popular *pseudo-3D* rendering technique in which highlighted and shadowed borders simulate a physically raised surface. It can even be argued that this visual treatment plays a valuable role in identifying "pushable" controls. The increasing use of 3D in situations that do not take advantage of the added dimensionality, however, is more difficult to defend. In the examples above, the chiseled "inactive" feedback in the toolbar icons (a) and the 3D treatment of the textual label (b) both impede the legibility of the resulting signs. Legibility is also reduced by the unnatural foreshortening of the sides of the 3D palette (the Button Cube) (c). This 3D structure actually completes a complex

(and *slow*) animated rotation whenever the user switches to a different set of tools. While the obvious efficiency and scalability concerns (how do the design handle more than four palettes?) are serious enough, the design has problems even as a static display. The view of the "next" palette is too narrow and distorted to be very recognizable, so the complexity introduced by the third dimension provides little additional information over its 2D equivalent. Like the upturned page corner in the bottom of a "book" window (d), it is simply decoration attempting to woo the consumer with its seductive splendor.

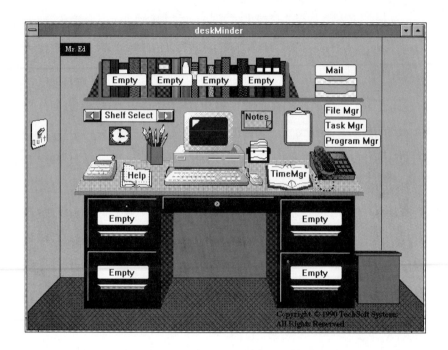

35: *All of the above.* The most spectacular failing of simplicity is often seen in those products trying most earnestly to simplify the GUI for non-technical users. Applications – even whole environments such as MagicCap from General Magic – attempting to leverage users' knowledge about the physical world through a "3D Office" (or 3D world) metaphor are beginning to reach the marketplace. This approach has always been something of a rite of passage for GUI designers. While many would admit (when pressed) to having *their* version of the 3D desktop tucked neatly away in their files, its basic flaws are widely recognized. The extremely literal translation of the "real" world seen in all such attempts, for example, virtually ensures that users will find the resulting environments cumbersome and inefficient, and probably just as cluttered as their real-world office. Interestingly enough, the 3D office nearly always suffers from both an *unnatural point of view* and an *awkward rendering style* that effectively eliminate the impression of being in a real physical space. Ironically, this phenomenon can be traced directly to the 3D representation itself, since accurate perspective conflicts with effective use of display space wherever two-dimensional editing tasks predominate. When the standard File Manager, Task Manager, and Program Manager appear in front of the virtual desk, as in the Windows desktop replacement shown here, any illusion of true three-dimensionality that might have arisen is quickly shattered.

What is simple should be treated simply, what is difficult should be reduced to the simplest terms.

Josef Müller-Brockmann
The Graphic Designer and His Design Problems

Techniques

Reduction
Regularization
Leverage

Elegance cannot be easily summarized in a few rules of thumb. It depends heavily on taste, and taste can only be developed through prolonged exposure to a series of high quality examples forming the benchmark against which subsequent solutions can be judged. Because complex designs rarely seem elegant, simplification is an important step in the development of any elegant solution. Three basic techniques can be used to simplify a design solution:

- Reducing a Design to its Essence
- Regularizing the Elements of the Design
- Combining Elements for Maximum Leverage

To the extent that the overall approach is appropriate to the task, the elegance of the resulting solution will be enhanced as these techniques are applied. With practice, these techniques become second nature. You will begin to apply them – almost unconsciously – to every emerging solution.

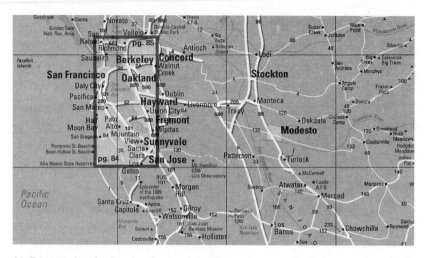

36: This map of the San Francisco Bay area from USAtlas shows use of reduction to produce a level of detail appropriate for the intended audience. The simplified design speeds orientation and facilitates reading at a glance. Design by The Understanding Business. (See also color plate 5).

Reducing a Design to Its Essence

The most fundamental design technique is *reduction*. An elegant design must be reduced to its essential elements and each element reduced to its essential form. The travel maps produced by The Understanding Business (36) make extensive use of reduction as part of its distinctive visual language. This map of San Francisco and the surrounding area of Northern California eliminates any detail that is not likely to be needed by someone traveling through the area (the audience for the atlas in which these maps appear). The result is a truly elegant solution in which the simplified presentation solves the navigation problem for its target user in a way that makes the maps aesthetically effective on purely formal grounds as well.

37: Reduction plays the critical role of emphasizing canonical features in these public information icons developed for the U.S. Department of Transportation (DOT) by the American Institute of Graphic Arts (AIGA). Design by Cook & Shanosky Associates.

Good design is simple, bold, and direct. It ensures that significant design elements will be noticed by removing insignificant elements wherever possible. The familiar public information signage (37) developed for the U.S. Department of Transportation (DOT) was commissioned by the American Institute of Graphic Arts following an extensive study comparing the legibility and aesthetic qualities of 28 existing signage programs (AIGA, 1981). The pictographic signs focus on elements typical of an entire class of objects rather than on the details of any one instance. All visual details except those needed to identify the object's category are removed. This *reduction of iconicity* makes the images more portable across cultural and linguistic boundaries.

Even "essential" elements can often be removed to good effect. Images are often more visually appealing – and just as identifiable – when portions of the image are suggested rather than explicitly depicted. This technique is especially common in visual identities and signage systems where impact and recognizability are critical. The partial contour of the "A" in the identity for London's Victoria and Albert Museum (38-a), for example, is easily completed by the viewer, thanks to graphical cues provided by the serif of the ampersand and the top of the partial letterform. Similarly, the upper portion of the wheel of the wheelchair in the DOT pictogram set (38-b) is only suggested, with no loss in clarity. Viewers are not only *able* to fill in "missing" contours. They delight in doing so. The active involvement of the viewer can make recognition easier and communication more effective.

To apply this technique to interface design, the designer must simplify the presentation as much as possible and question the functionality being presented when the resulting display is still too complex. Every aspect of the

38: Even basic contour information can sometimes be removed without impeding communication. When the overall form is clear, the eye is quite willing to supply missing details, as in this identity for the Victoria and Albert Museum, London (a) – design by Pentagram – and the DOT's access icon (b).

39: Simplified iconic imagery is a necessity at the small scale required by the eNote workgroup pop-up messaging system, from Visual Cybernetics. Reducing the images to their essence and eliminating unnecessary variation helps the icons communicate clearly even at this small scale.

eNote pop-up messaging system (39) is devoted to conserving display space so that the window to remain open on the screen most of the time. The simple, elegant, imagery used for the button labels communicates effectively without a need for verbal labels and the additional space they would require (the process of reducing an image to its essence will be discussed at length in Chapter 6). But the designers did not stop there. Most of the product functionality has been off-loaded into separate, task-specific dialog boxes. This design keeps the main window small and simplifies its window management tasks: since the window need not be resizable, even the window header and borders can be reduced to a simple outline.

An even more ambitious reduction can be seen in the Macintosh start up screen. Instead of a stream of cryptic and often confusing textual status messages, the Macintosh operating system displays a simple image (the "happy Mac" icon in 40-a) that conveys the system status while introducing personality and occasionally even a little humor into a potentially stressful situation. A textual error message (and the "sad Mac" icon in 40-b) is displayed only if a problem is encountered during the start up sequence.

40: The minimal feedback provided during the Macintosh boot sequence simply identifies the system status as normal (a) or abnormal (b).

Simplicity does not mean want or poverty. It does not mean the absence of any decor, or absolute nudity. It only means that the decor should belong intimately to the design proper, and that anything foreign to it should be taken away.

Paul Jacques Grillo
Form, Function, and Design

In all of these examples, the message is reinforced, not weakened, by removing non-essential elements from the design (or by resisting the temptation to add them in the first place). Even experienced designers depend heavily on trial and error to determine which elements are truly essential. The use of reduction as a design technique should be approached as a three-step process:

1 Determine the essential qualities (typically a short list of adjectives) that should be conveyed by the design, along with any fixed formal elements, such as a name or label, an essential control, or a color, texture, pattern, or image.

2 Critically examine each element in the design and ask yourself why it is needed, how it relates to the essence of the design (identified above), and how the design would suffer without it. If you can't answer any of these questions, remove the element.

3 Try to remove the element from the design anyway. What happens? If the design collapses, either functionally or aesthetically, the element must be replaced. Otherwise, consider omitting it from the final solution.

Don't be afraid to remove peripheral features or redundant information. These can always be replaced if users subsequently demand them. Effective design often involves oversimplifying to help make a point. An ounce of inaccuracy can be worth a pound of explanation – if it helps the viewer gain a basic understanding of the message you are trying to convey.

41: In this elegant route diagram for the commuter rail system north of Milan, the orientations of the station labels are regularized along the same diagonal used to govern the placement of the lines themselves.

Regularizing the Elements of a Design

When further reduction is not feasible, the remaining elements can be regularized to further simplify the design. Regularity reduces information by repeating elements according to a discernible rule, principle, or rhythm. Human perception and memory operate more efficiently on regularized stimuli, since the visual complexity of the display is reduced while its structure is enhanced. The predictability of a regular pattern allows the viewer to "scan ahead" more easily to the area of interest when making a comparison or answering a question. Regularity also introduces significant aesthetic benefits, as evidenced by the near-universal human fascination with the decorative effect of repetitive patterns.

Regularity can be achieved by aligning or reflecting elements along common axes, by standardizing or repeating sizes and spacing of components, or by reducing components to basic geometric forms wherever possible. In the diagram in Figure 41, the placement of the station labels on the same 45-degree diagonal used to govern the lines themselves underscores the schematization of the line orientations. Regularizing the weight of the lines throughout the diagram enhances communication by making the one discontinuity – the double width portion in the lower right – immediately apparent.

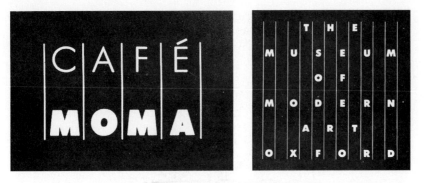

42: The signage program designed by Pentagram for the Oxford (England) Museum of Modern Art utilizes the regular spacing of its vertical rules to modulate the sharp contrast between thick and thin elements in order to create a sense of stability in the dynamic visual identity.

Effective design balances contrast with regularity. The signage program for the Oxford Museum of Modern Art (42) uses regularization to balance the playful contrast between thick and thin forms seen throughout the system. Note how the regularity introduced by the absolutely consistent spacing between characters, lines, and vertical rules creates the *impression* of rigid vertical alignment at the global level (even though characters on two lines fall on different axes entirely), while exhibiting playful variation locally (where the three-letter words can be seen to break the alignment). This interplay between global and local readings produces a dynamic visual identity that is stable, yet active and visually interesting.

43: Regularization is both necessary and apparent in any keyboard layout. This information terminal designed by Pentagram for the Reuters news agency employs subtle color coding to establish functional key groupings that emerge from the rhythmic modular background pattern.

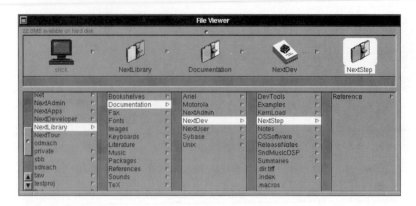

44: The elegant NeXTStep browser displays uniform spacing from column to column. As the window is resized, it "snaps" to the modular dimension to maintain constant spacing.

Effective design establishes a predictable rhythm. The importance of predict-ability in a keyboard layout (43) is obvious, but simpler tools benefit as well. The simple elegance of the NeXTStep browser, like that of a well-designed page, owes much to the regularity of its column widths (44). Columns can be added or removed by resizing the window, but the width remains con-stant throughout. Note how the rhythm is disrupted when the widths of the columns are reduced to the minimum required to display the labels at each level of the hierarchy (45). The irrelevant variation in column widths merely introduces visual noise and distracting apparent motion as the hierarchy is traversed, so the minor reduction in screen space is hardly justified.

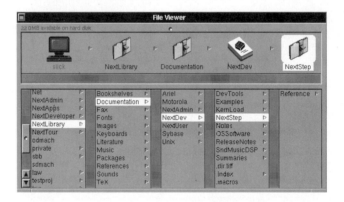

45: Reducing column widths to the minimum needed to display the widest item may seem like a good idea, but the irregular pattern that results is visually disorienting. The impact on the readability of the resulting display more than offsets the minor savings in terms of screen real estate that results.

Continuity is not only the uninterrupted steps from one point to another, but it is also the cohesive force that holds a diverse composition together.

Donis A. Dondis
A Primer of Visual Literacy

Establishing a pattern simplifies the design by moving the viewer's experience to a higher level of abstraction. Thus, a series of black and white rectangles becomes a "checkerboard" when suitably arranged. Design elements must be regularized on many levels simultaneously to produce this effect. Some generally useful strategies include:

Summary: Regularization

1 Use regular geometric forms, simplified contours, and muted colors wherever possible.

2 If multiple similar forms are required, make them identical, if possible, in size, shape, color, texture, lineweight, orientation, alignment, or spacing.

3 Limit variation in typography to a few sizes from one or two families.

4 To reap the benefits of regularity, make sure critical elements intended to stand out in the display are *not* regularized.

Any irregularity will be interpreted as significant by the user, who will cheerfully ascribe to it a meaning even where none was intended. By regularizing non-critical design elements throughout the work, you will be able to attract the user's attention reliably by introducing an obvious irregularity whenever you *do* wish to make a distinction.

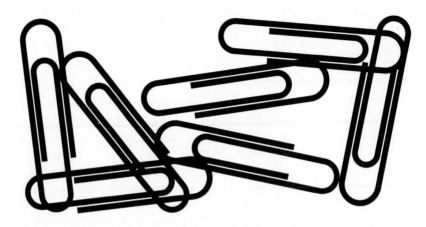

46: The ubiquitous paper clip achieves its marvel of simplicity by combining the tensioning and grasping functions needed by any clipping device within a single wire element. The Norwegian inventor Johann Valer is credited with the original design in 1899.

Combining Elements for Maximum Leverage

The most challenging means of simplification involves finding points of *leverage* at which design elements play multiple roles. When one part does the work of two, the elegance of the solution is always enhanced. The humble paper clip (46) shows that elegant design is not limited to expensive luxury items. The effectiveness of this familiar commodity is not compromised by its incredible simplicity. The clip combines the tensioning and grasping functions needed by any clipping device in a single strand of carefully stressed wire. Though we rarely pause to appreciate this elegant solution (an unfortunate consequence of effective design is that it tends to "disappear" as use of the product becomes transparent), its grace is hardly diminished by its ubiquitous presence and utilitarian role.

47: Individual design elements play multiple roles in these identity marks for the Ohio Department of Education – Office of Sex Equity (a), and the Floral Images florist service.

Effective design is *visually efficient*. Both of the identity marks in Figure 47 incorporate multi-functioning visual elements. The rectangular element in the symbol for the Office of Sex Equity (47-a), for example, forms part of the "E" in *equity* while forming the square that serves as counterpoint to the circular element in the underlying "different but equal" theme. In the second example (47-b), the vertical stroke of the "F" (for Floral Images) curves organically through a transitional flourish to double as the stem of the mark's bird-of-paradise flower.

Leverage is particularly important in user interface design, where screen real estate (the amount of display space available to the application) is a precious commodity that's always in short supply. Successful designs use leverage extensively to simplify standard elements that recur throughout the environment. One of the best examples is a GUI window's title bar (48), which provides not only a place for labeling the window, but also an area for locating

Images			
Name	Size	Kind	Last Modified
Freehand 1	13K	document	Mon, Jan 11, 1993
Freehand 2	9K	document	Mon, Jan 11, 1993
Freehand 3	10K	document	Mon, Jan 11, 1993
Picture 5	17K	document	Mon, Jan 11, 1993

48: Leverage abounds in a window header, which is at once a label, a drag area, and a space within which to present window management controls. The lines used to highlight the active window provide further leverage by affording draggability even as they increase the window's prominence.

window management controls, indicating when the window is active, and allowing the user to drag the window to a new location. Similarly, a scroll bar provides not only a handle with which to scroll the window content, but also an indication of the current location in the document and (in some GUI's) the portion of the document that is currently visible (44, 48).

Leverage is difficult to achieve because it requires *insight* into the user's task domain. When it becomes apparent that two controls or displays are almost perfectly coordinated (or perfectly complimentary) the designer can use the same mechanism to support them both. A clever example of this technique is seen in WordPerfect Office (49). Instead of adding an extra message line to

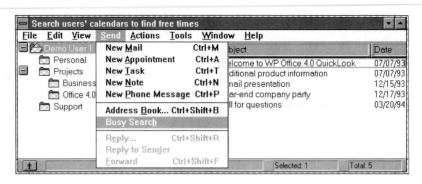

49: Leverage in a GUI presentation is often made possible when two aspects of the user's task are mutually exclusive. In this window from WordPerfect Office, the window title is replaced with a string describing the current function as the user browses through a menu.

each window, the design re-uses the window's title bar to display help information while browsing items in the menu. Because users necessarily choose the correct window *before* they begin looking for the menu command, they are unlikely to need the contextual information provided by the title while navigating the menu system (which is the only time the help display is used).

Effective design utilizes every component to its fullest. While every GUI control requires some form of label, each control doesn't necessarily require a label all its own. Indeed, identification can often be provided by context. When controls have different logical priorities, labeling items uniformly across levels (50-a), obscures the relationship. Combining labeling functions allows the logical relation of the subordinate parameters to be conveyed by their position and "indentation" while making it clear that the higher level labels to apply to the subordinates as well (50-b). The consolidation of irrelevant detail makes the important information immediately apparent.

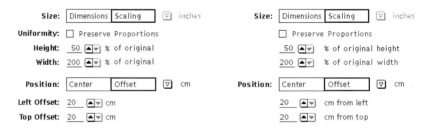

50: Leverage can often be achieved by exploiting contextual information provided by the display itself. Visual interference between adjacent labels (a) can be reduced by allowing each bold label in the left-hand column to set the context for several subordinate controls on the right (b).

> Elegance is achieved when a variety of roles is accepted by each part, permitting the whole to operate at several levels of awareness, with interweaving functions inflecting one to another in a state of equilibrium and flux.
>
> **Krome Barrett**
> Logic and Design

Achieving maximum leverage for each element in your design requires a thorough understanding of both the communication problem at hand and the design elements at your disposal. As a design nears completion, it should be systematically examined to determine if any unneeded redundancy remains:

Summary:

Leverage

1 Review the functional role played by each element in the design. (This information should be a natural product of the reduction phase.)

2 Look for situations where multiple elements are filling (or partially filling) the same role.

3 Question whether an element's role could be filled as well by an adjacent component, possibly after minor modifications.

4 Combine redundant elements into a single, simpler unit or replace the lot with a common higher-level idiom from the target environment designed to address the situation.

Maximum leverage is not desirable in every design. Particularly in user interface applications, too much leverage can cause problems if it introduces complex mappings that must be remembered by the user. The classic example is the digital watch whose multiple functions and modes of operation are accessed through a pair of tiny buttons. The difficulty of remembering which buttons to press (and how many times!) quickly outweighs the aesthetic advantages of the economical design. When leverage can be used to reduce the complexity of the interface, however, it enhances both the usability and the aesthetics of the product.

Scale, Contrast,
and Proportion

3

The subtle interrelationship of scale, contrast, and proportion can be seen in every harmonious design. The effectiveness of a clear composition always depends at least as much (often more) on the *relationships* among the parts as it does on the parts themselves. These relationships, which emerge at the global level of the display, must nevertheless be manipulated locally, by modifying the attributes of the displays component parts. Unfortunately this is one of the most difficult problems in visual design – and the one that requires the most practice to develop. Altering even a single attribute of one part in a complex composition can have a significant impact on the balance, the unity, and ultimately the harmony of the whole. When a single element is too large or too small, too light or too dark, too prominent or indistinct, the entire design suffers. This section describes ways in which relationships between elements can be manipulated to produce the desired global effect.

Scale describes the relative size or magnitude of a given design element in relation to other design elements and the composition as a whole. Grillo (1960) describes scale as, "*the feeling of a design fitting its space and its surroundings.*" Scale is never meaningful in an absolute sense – if nothing else, it is defined in relation to the human viewer. Achieving the right balance between point and counterpoint, between pattern and focus, between figure and ground, depends on careful manipulation of the graphical qualities of each element in the display. The magnitude of the differences required to establish this balance are governed by the principles of contrast.

Contrast results from noticeable differences along a common visual dimension that can be observed between elements in a composition. Contrast provides the basis for *visual distinctions*, which are the building blocks of meaning in a visual message. The dimensions along which visual contrasts can be drawn include *shape, size, color, texture, position, orientation,* and *movement.* Effective visual design consists of selecting – for each part and for the whole composition – the visual treatment that most effectively realizes the communication goal. Visual design, however, is lifeless when its only concern is for communication efficiency. Scale and contrast must be modulated to produce the right balance between interesting visual dynamics and pleasing, harmonious proportions.

Proportion, described by Grillo (1960)as, *"a rapport between two dimensions,"* deals in ratios rather than fixed sizes. It determines the balance and harmony of the relation between elements. Proportion is the metric that guides the choice of scales in a contrast relationship. Classical systems of proportion codify relationships known to please the mind as well as the eye. In practice most designers manipulate proportion on the basis of a highly developed perceptual sensitivity acquired through years of experience, rather than through mechanical techniques, but classical systems such as the *Golden Rectangle* are the inevitable starting point. Regardless of its source, the effective use of scale, contrast and proportion confers many benefits:

Differentiation. Contrast is essential for differentiating elements from one another – for allowing form to emerge from the void. We see Cassandre's steamship (51-a) first, for example, as a large rectangular form emerging from the lighter background. Similarly, the hands in Armin Hofmann's theater poster (51-b) depend on high-contrast contours to differentiate them from the dark background. Their size, weight, and organic form help to further distinguish them from the hard-edged typographic message.

Emphasis. Scale and contrast can be used to emphasize important elements or areas in the composition. In Cassandre's poster, the framing of the minuscule tugboat within the dark mass of the ocean liner emphasizes both the smallness of the tug and the colossal scale of the liner. The name of the ocean liner ("*L' Atlantique*") is emphasized by contrasting its size and value with those of the other typographic elements to make it the most prominent piece of text in the display despite its location at the bottom of the poster. In the Hofmann poster, the high-contrast photography highlighting the contours of

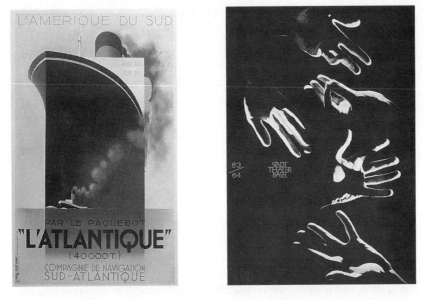

51: Posters often use extreme contrasts to great effect. The poster's image must be sufficiently dynamic to capture the viewer's attention and hold it until the message can be delivered. Designs by A.M.Cassandre (a) (© 1993 ARS, New York/ADAGP, Paris) and Armin Hofmann (b), Basel.

the fingers and hands adds emphasis to their evocative gestures – the orientation of the fingers is more apparent as background detail is removed – and provides a heightened sensation of movement throughout the composition.

Activity. Scale and contrast move the viewer's eye through the composition in a predictable sequence that can be used to support a particular communication goal. Note how the eye is drawn almost involuntarily to the tugboat in the Cassandre poster, *despite* its small size. This tendency is reinforced by the careful merging of the smoke trails from each vessel. The medium value smoke contrasts with both the dark hull and the light sky to provide a prominent path leading the eye from smaller to larger vessel and back again.

Interest. Scale and contrast add visual interest to a composition by juxtaposing elements with strongly opposed visual qualities to create tension, drama, and excitement. In the Hofmann poster the contrast in orientation and gesture of the five hands projects a strong sense of theatrical movement and emotional involvement that draws the viewer in to the point where the poster's message can be delivered. Delivering the message effectively depends on appropriate use of visual language, which we now review briefly.

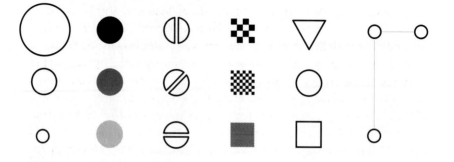

52: Bertin's "retinal variables" form the basis for all forms of visual coding. A visual code can be based on (from left to right) contrasts in *size, value, orientation, texture, shape,* or *position* in 2D or 3D space. *Hue* (chromatic color) provides an additional dimension not pictured here.

Background:
Visual Variables

Effective design respects the capabilities and limitations of visual language, which, at its most basic level, concerns the primitive visual distinctions that are available in human vision. Visual contrasts must be established by manipulating the perceptual qualities (52) of *size, value, hue* (not shown), *orientation, texture, shape,* and *position.* These characteristics are described by Bertin (1983) as the *retinal variables,* because they are perceived immediately and effortlessly "above" the picture plane and across the entire visual field. This *automatic* perceptual characteristic makes the visual variables the fundamental units of visual communication. In the hands of a skilled visual designer, they can be manipulated to structure and enhance the experience of a composition, package, environment, or user interface.

Bertin (1983, 1989) provides a comprehensive survey of the *visual variables* and the rules governing their effective use. All of the material in this chapter depends critically on these phenomena, so we will review them briefly. The information to be represented in a visual display is characterized by the number of dimensions (i.e., the things being measured), their length (e.g., the number of possible values on each dimension), and the scale of measurement (e.g., nominal, ordered, quantitative) for each dimension. The nominal scale supports two kinds of reading, so Bertin's taxonomy considers four styles of perception: *associative, selective, ordered,* and *quantitative.* The visual variables differ greatly in their suitability for the four types of analysis. Learning to use them correctly is essential to effective visual communication.

In using a nominal scale, the user is concerned only with categorizing or differentiating (*nomin* = name) the things being observed. In *associative perception*, the viewer ignores variation on one visual dimension in reading the remainder of the display. A visual variable is considered *associative* if it does not affect the visibility of other dimensions in the elements to which it is applied. We can recognize the hue of an object, for example, regardless of its orientation. Conversely, a visual dimension is *dissociative* if visibility is significantly reduced for some values along that coding dimension. It can be difficult, for example, to determine the hue of a very small dot or thin line. All visual variables except size and value are associative – they can be "overlooked" when necessary. Size and value are dissociative because they dominate perception and disrupt the processing of other correlated dimensions.

In *selective perception*, the viewer attempts to isolate all instances of a given category and perceptually groups them into a single image. The task is to ignore everything *but* the target value on the dimension of interest – to see at a glance where *all* the targets are within the display. A visual variable is selective only if the grouping is immediate and effortless. All of the visual variables except shape are selective (orientation is selective when represented by points or lines, but not when represented by area). The fact that shapes must be identified individually under focused attention while other visual variables can be perceived across the entire visual field explains why a graph is more effective than a table for certain communication tasks.

53: Shape is the only variable that does not permit *selective perception*. The "K" is difficult to locate in (a) because the other characters in the visual field, while differing in shape, have the same size, color, and value, and are formed from lines of the same weight and orientation. When a redundant value cue is added, however (b), perception of the "k" is immediate and effortless because the eye can selectively attend to value differences across the entire display. Although shape coding can be highly effective in *identification* tasks, it is poorly suited to *location* tasks.

In *ordered perception*, the viewer must determine the relative ordering of values along a perceptual dimension. Given any two visual elements, a natural ordering must be clearly apparent so that the element representing "more" of the corresponding quality is immediately obvious. When a variable is ordered, there is no need to consult a key to determine the ranking of the various levels. Position, size and value are ordered in human perception: rankings based on these qualities are immediately obvious and readily apprehended. Texture is also ordered to the extent that value covaries with the granularity of the texture.

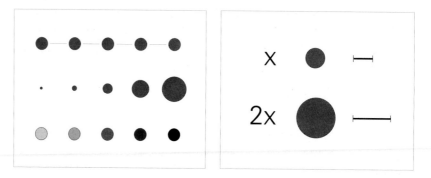

54: *Ordered* (a) and *quantitative* (b) perception. A natural ordering is apparent—the items can be arranged objectively from greatest to least—when objects vary in *size, value,* or *position* (a). Only *size* and *position,* however, permit objective judgment of how *much* greater the difference is (b).

In *quantitative perception*, the viewer must determine the *amount* of difference between two ordered values. When a variable is quantitative, the user does not need to refer to an index or key to determine how *much* more of a quantity is represented by a given mark. The relative magnitudes must be immediately apparent. The viewer can immediately see, for example, that one line is twice as long or half as wide as another. Only position and size are quantitative: they permit accurate approximation of the true ratio from the observed visual differences.

The visual variables also differ substantially in their *length*, or the number of discernibly different measurement levels each can support. Shape is the "longest" visual variable. We can recognize an almost infinite variety of different values along this dimension (i.e., recognizably different shapes), making it particularly well-suited for identification (e.g., "*what* is the thing located *here*?"). Position in two-dimensional space also supports an infinite number of values in theory, but in practice the limits of display size and resolution normally constrain its effective length. Because even small relative differences are easily discriminable, however, position nevertheless supports more fine-grained variation than any other variable.

Orientation is the "shortest" dimension, with frequent visual confusions arising if more than four levels are attempted. The other dimensions fall somewhere in between. Value and texture support fewer than ten levels; size and color can support a few more, depending on the communication task. Bertin's findings are based largely on experience, but they are supported by experimental research on pre-attentive processing in vision by Treisman (1984, etc.) and on graphical perception by Cleveland, et al. (1983, 1984), In addition, two excellent surveys have been produced by Tufte (1989, 1991). A command of these principles is essential for the design of effective information displays, to which we now return.

Principles

Scale, contrast, and proportion are powerful tools in the hands of an experienced designer. If proportion sets the rhythm of the display, then the scale of its components determines its forcefulness and their contrasts determines its excitability. These powerful elements must be used with care, particularly in user interface design, where the goal is rarely to shock, to arrest, or to persuade. Contrasts must be clear enough to convey the intended distinctions, yet subtle enough to produce a harmonious relation between the elements in the display. The dominant contrasts must be strong enough to produce an effective dynamic within the display, yet sufficiently restrained to permit the viewer to remain in control of the experience.

Clarity
Harmony
Activity
Restraint

55: Global shape coding can be effective in situations–such as traffic control and road hazard warnings–where identification supersedes location. Drivers are trained to notice any sign that appears along a roadway. A clear shape code provides a redundant cue to help identify critical situations.

56: A clear typographic hierarchy conveys information in this poster announcing an architecture exhibition at the Bauhaus. Design by Herbert Bayer, © 1993 ARS, New York/VG-Bild-Kunst, Bonn.

Clarity

Contrast, like any other aspect of design, is effective only when it is clearly intentional rather than random or accidental. Clarity of intent ensures that contrasts can be easily perceived and that values can be clearly equated or differentiated. Ambiguity is costly as well as unsettling. When the intent of the designer is clear, viewers don't need to waste valuable time wondering if the subtle distinction they have noticed is relevant to the message being communicated or simply an accident. Herbert Bayer's poster for a lecture on architecture at the Bauhaus (56) establishes a clear hierarchy of information based on the position, size, and orientation of the poster's typographic elements. The subject and date of the lecture are at once the most prominent elements in the display and the most important pieces of information in the message being communicated. Their sharp contrasts with the other typographic elements ensures that the information will be noticed in a predictable order corresponding to the sequence intended by the designer.

Good design clarifies the role of each element in the ensemble. Clarity results from a single-minded focus on communication. It ensure that whatever the message or purpose of the product, its essence is reflected in the physical form of the design. Clarity of form, for example, is used to good effect in the construction of the Kodak Carrousel slide projector (57). This early example of the movement toward externally obvious product semantics shows how contrast in form between the circular elements and the rectilinear housing underscores the function (to rotate) of the circular elements.

57: Clarity of form is apparent in the original design for the Kodak Carrousel projector. The contrasting qualities of roundness in the rotating elements and rectangularity in the housing amplify and reinforce one another and underscore the function of each part. Design by Hans Gugelot.

Clarity is equally essential for effective user interface design. Shape coding is used in the OPEN LOOK GUI (58) to distinguish between commands, which initiate actions, and settings, which reflect state. Controls with setting semantics always have sharp rectangular borders, while those with command semantics are always presented with rounded ends or filleted corners. The strong perceptual cue provided by this distinction improves the global structure of control areas and helps clarify the role of menus, which can contain either type of element.

Contrasts in value can be very useful in helping to segregate the display into meaningful regions. One useful application of the popular "pseudo-3D"

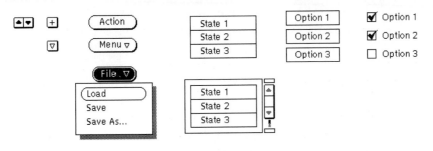

58: Shape coding in a GUI can be used to *identify* different classes of controls. The OPEN LOOK GUI distinguishes between *commands,* which initiate actions and are identified by curved ends or rounded corners, and *settings,* which store the state of an attribute and are identified by squared off sides and ends. Where the primary task is *location* (as in a default button) a stronger visual cue is needed.

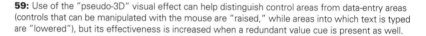

59: Use of the "pseudo-3D" visual effect can help distinguish control areas from data-entry areas (controls that can be manipulated with the mouse are "raised," while areas into which text is typed are "lowered"), but its effectiveness is increased when a redundant value cue is present as well.

look is the distinction this treatment permits between data-entry and control areas (59). In this case, the value contrast is supplemented by a "dimensionality" contrast. In addition to their near-universal preference for the concreteness of this style of imagery, users derive genuine functional benefit from the early and automatic perceptual separation of figure (places to type) and ground. Note the importance of the correlated value contrast, however. When foreground and background have the same color, the clarity of the display is greatly reduced. When the distinction between controls and data breaks down, as it did in the early days of HyperCard (60) users become confused about the intended interaction model.

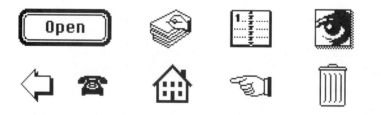

60: The freedom introduced by authoring products like Apple's HyperCard quickly began to break down many of the benefits associated with the standard GUI. Because "Icons" in HyperCard followed the interaction protocol of buttons, the function was no longer indicated by the form.

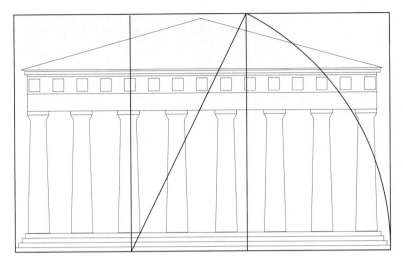

61: The Golden Section was used to govern the overall proportions of the facade–as well as many of the internal structural relationships–in the sacred architecture of classical Greece. The Parthenon is widely recognized as the most perfect example of centuries old tradition.

Harmony describes the effect, seen at the level of the whole, of the *pleasing interaction of the parts*. The Parthenon in Athens (62–a) – and in fact all sacred architecture in classical Greece – was based on an elaborate mathematical canon relating the width, height, and spacing of interior and exterior components to one another. The canon was parametric – the number of columns and overall scale of the temple could changed without disrupting the system – as seen in the Temple of Concorde at Agrigento in Sicily (62-b). While the Parthenon is based on a variety of formulaic ratios, the most famous is the Golden Section, which governs the overall proportions of the facade (61). The Golden Section is formed by sweeping the diagonal from

62: The Ancients' love of rhythm and proportion is still apparent in the Parthenon, Athens (a) and the Temple of Concorde, Agrigento, Sicily (b).

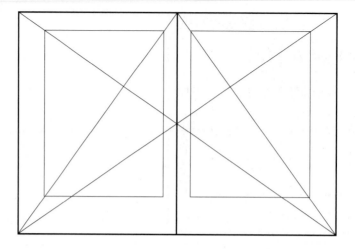

63: Classic layout schemes for book design are carefully constructed to ensure harmonious relationships between parts. This example establishes a dynamic symmetry in which the proportions of copy area, page, and spread are identical.

the lower midpoint of the square to the baseline, where it forms the longer side of a rectangle whose height is the unit square. Research has shown this ratio to be the most inherently pleasing, when viewed as a simple rectangle, of many possible alternatives (Barratt, 1980, 109–113). It shares the property of *dynamic symmetry* with similarly constructed ratios like the "root 2" rectangle used in the classic page layout schemes developed by medieval monks and scribes (63) as well as the modern DIN system of paper sizes. This property allows the rectangle to be recursively subdivided into ever-smaller copies of itself, each retaining the same proportion.

About Microsoft Project		
Microsoft	Microsoft Project Version 3.0 Copyright© 1990-1992 Microsoft Corporation	
	This copy of Microsoft Project is licensed to:	
	Project Microsoft SunPro Serial number: 37864 37864 37864	
	386 Enhanced Mode Conventional Memory: 37864 KB Free Math Co-processor: Present Disk Space: 48368 KB Free	OK

64: An application's most carefully organized window layout is often seen in its "About box," which represents an insignificant portion of the application's functionality by any metric.

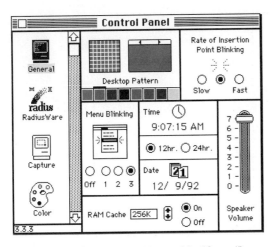

65: In the haphazard, unplanned layout of the "General" Control Panel from the Macintosh System 6.08, control groups appear to have been placed wherever they would fit, with little regard for their effect on the organization of the window itself.

In contrast to these classical composition systems, which evolved over hundreds of years and embodied the craftsman's respect for the integrity of the sacred artifact, today's windows and dialogs are *ad hoc* and highly arbitrary, seemingly thrown together with little thought or consideration for the relation of one element to another, or of anything to the whole (65). This is beginning to change, however, as design firms increase their involvement with large scale, multimedia information systems (66), and as the focus of GUI software moves increasingly beyond the realm of graphical editing tools to the much broader world of content delivery and presentation.

66: The systematic layout scheme used in this multimedia production for Apple Computer relates elements in the composition to one another and to the screen-specific information presented in the headline and right-hand margin. Design by Clement Mok designs, Inc.

67: Sharp contrasts add activity to posters by Herbert Matter (a) and Joseph Müller-Brockmann (b)

Activity

Elements in contrast exert an influence on each other that exaggerates their contrasting qualities. Posters depend heavily on the resulting compositional dynamics to draw the viewer's attention to the focal point of the message. Herbert Matter's travel posters (67-a) exhibit strong contrast between foreground and background elements. The twisting mountain road contrasts effectively with the foreground close-up of the roadway surface as well as with the monumetal Alps in the distant background. In similar fashion, Josef Müller-Brockmann's concert poster (67-b) captures the dynamic ten-

68: The supergraphic sign applied to a building exterior creates dramatic tension through a contrast in scale to both that of the building itself and to that of "normal" signage. From *Basic Typography: Design with Letters*, by Ruedi Rüegg, ABC-Verlag, Zurich, 1987. Design by Giulio Cittato.

sion apparent in the music of these 20th Century composers with the drama of its strongly contrasting thick and thin forms and its disquieting diagonal orientation. Contrasts such as these provide visual interest, especially when familiar elements are presented in unexpected ways. Giulio Cittato's supergraphic building sign (68) is an example of the excitement that can be created by juxtaposing familiar objects at unusual scales. Such monumental signs may be inappropriate in some circumstances, but when used to support an important communication goal, their effects can be powerful indeed.

Graphical user interfaces can exploit the activity generated by effective contrasts to help users maintain orientation and context. In the graded, three-level input focus feedback provided by NeXTStep windows (69), for example, the black header of the active window is easily distinguishable from the lighter headers of the inactive windows. When a pop-up window receives the input focus, the window header of its parent lightens to a medium gray that contrasts with both the black header of the key window and the lighter gray

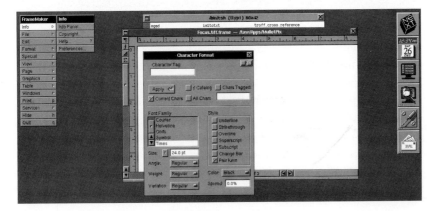

69: The unique, multi-level input focus feedback in NeXTStep uses contrast in value to directly indicate which window is active, and–when a secondary window becomes active–which primary window it is associated with. Because value is an ordered dimension, the mapping is both natural and obvious.

of the inactive windows. Because value is dissociative (Bertin, 1983), the perceptual dynamics of this coding scheme are affected by the medium gray of the screen background and the white of window data panes, both of which can act to disrupt the code in certain window arrangements. When the user's attention is focused on the window headers, however, the naturally ordered perceptual scale allows the gradation from light to dark to map naturally to the semantic relationships among windows.

70: The subtle interplay of positive and negative space in the Japanese *shoji* screen is made possible by the absolute regularity of the spacing between elements along the horizontal and vertical axes and by the lack of distracting variation in the form of the elements themselves. (Photo by Shozo Sato.)

Restraint

Contrasts should be strong, but few in number. When too many contrasts are drawn, when too many scales are applied within the same design, when too many proportional relationships are established among elements, the resulting chaos makes effective communication impossible. The most successful designs rely on a few basic contrasts to establish order and visual identity within the work. The elegant Japanese Shoji screen (70), for example, employs only a few different modules in the thickness of its structural components and the widths of its paper panels. The regularity produced by eliminating all other variation makes the critical proportions more apparent and enhances the transparency of the screen as a whole.

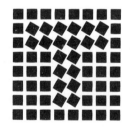

71: Understatement need not impair communication in designs based on subtle contrasts. In each of these examples, a subtle variation of position (a) or orientation (b,c) is enough to convey the intended meaning. (Design of identity program for Tactics cosmetics (b) by Pentagram.)

systemtechnisch	systemtechnisch
Software	Software
anwendungs-technisch	Integration Text/Grafik und Bild

▶ **QUALIFIKATION:**

Mitarbeiter/Setzer: ausreichender Kenntnisstand . . . . ja/nein
Nachschulung . . . . ja/nein
Inhaber/Disponent: gutes fachlich/technisches Niveau . . . . ja/nein
Qualitätsinteresse gut/fundiert . . . . ja/nein
starkes kaufmännisches Interesse . . . . ja/nein
Schulung sollte angeboten werden . . . . ja/nein

72: The restrained use of contrast in this form by MetaDesign ensures that critical orienting elements (e.g., the red triangle and bold headline) will emerge automatically from the page. The red triangle is able to function effectively as an *attractor* precisely because there are no red *distractors* in the display.

Contrast is always most effective when limited to one or a few dimensions. Note how the visual impression of a bunch of grapes can be captured by varying only the spacing between grapes (71-a). There is no internal detail and practically no variation in size. Effective visual identity programs are often based on simple repetition based on translations of the same basic forms. The identity marks for Tactics cosmetics (71-b) and Sun Microsystems, Inc. (71-c) both rely exclusively on the selective rotation of elements in a regular pattern. Eliminating distracting contrasts on other visual dimensions makes the movement and articulation of the basic forms more apparent. When the user can see how the configuration is constructed, the surprise of an unexpected approach adds visual interest to the resulting display.

Effective visual design uses the compositional dynamics produced by effective use of contrast to *enhance communication*, not simply to add variety or interest. Contrasts are conscious, few, and never overwhelming. Gratuitous graphical embellishment are never added as decorative afterthoughts or used simply because the technology is available. The small red triangle in the form above (72), for example, is designed to draw the users attention to a critical area, not simply to entertain. The subtle background texture created through the use of a consistent gray tone for the questions and even the check boxes ensures that the suitably emphasized titles will "pop" visually

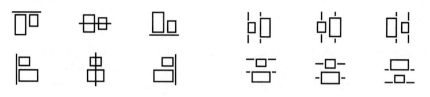

73: Restrained visual coding in these images from Aldus IntelliDraw focuses attention on the most important differences and allows the alignment cues to be perceived more easily and accurately.

from the display and become immediately apparent to the user. This principle has been understood by cartographer for years. The predominance of muted, unsaturated colors in the large background areas of a well-designed map provides the setting needed for the striking prominence of small saturated color elements used to identify important landmarks and other points of interest (Tufte, 1990).

74: The stylized representation of GUI components in the Zinc Interface Library permits the contrast of *distinguishing* features to be maximized even as the contrast of *non-distinguishing* features is minimized within the image set.

The same principles apply to the visual codes used throughout GUI applications and environments. The diagrams in Figure 73, for example, represent various options for aligning and distributing graphical elements in a drawing program. By limiting contrast in the elements being aligned, the relationship between elements (or more accurately, between the elements and the line that indicates their alignment point) becomes clear. (Compare these examples with those in Figure 29-c, where the much greater variation in shape, size, and orientation of the sign elements makes the "reading" of the relationship far more difficult.) The same technique is used in the icons from the Zinc Interface Library (74). By abstracting away non-critical detail elements (text becomes lines, etc.) instead of faithfully rendering every pixel, the icon-set helps users focus on the critical differences between images (such as the various field-specific punctuation characters). In each case, limiting contrasts to those needed specifically to communicate the information of interest works to enhance selective perception and thus simplify the task of extracting meaningful information from the display.

Common Errors

Common errors involving scale, contrast, or proportion typically involve contrasts that are too sharp or not sharp enough, or figures that relate poorly to their ground. Some specific examples include:

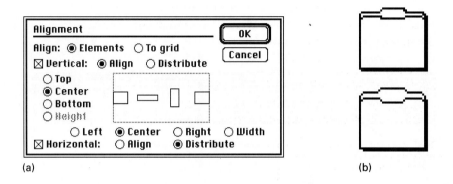

(a)

(b)

75: *Insufficient contrast.* The effects of too much and too little contrast are surprisingly similar. Both make elements difficult to distinguish, resulting in an undirected uniformity at the one extreme and utter chaos at the other. Lack of typographic contrast was a problem in many early Macintosh dialog boxes. Most relied exclusively on the Chicago font, which made it difficult to visually distinguish labels from values and subsidiary labels – both within and across controls. Note the homogeneous "wallpaper" effect that effectively masks the internal structure of this dialog box from Aldus Freehand (a). The word "Align" appears in four different places, with three different meanings, but with no typographic coding to help underscore the distinctions. Very little structural informa-

tion can be called out to help guide the eye through the layout when the typographic uniformity is this dominant. Sometimes contrasts must be exaggerated beyond "realistic" levels in order to have the desired effect (b). In these folder icons, the upper image is more physically accurate, but the impression it creates is weaker due to inadequate contrast between folder height and tab height. The lower example exaggerates the tab to more strongly convey its identity as a folder. In essence, the GUI depends on caricatures of the objects being represented, so this approach is perfectly appropriate.

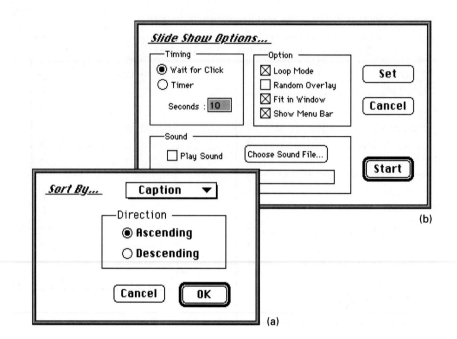

Slide Show Options...

Timing
◉ Wait for Click
○ Timer

Seconds : 10

Option
☒ Loop Mode
☐ Random Overlay
☒ Fit in Window
☒ Show Menu Bar

Set

Cancel

Sound
☐ Play Sound   Choose Sound File...

Start

(b)

Sort By...   Caption ▼

Direction
◉ Ascending
○ Descending

Cancel   OK

(a)

76: *Excessive contrast.* The excessive typographic contrast seen in these dialogs from the Kudo Image Browser is also a problem. This dialog box contains no less than five different type sizes in three different fonts. Note the apparent lack of reason behind many of the typographic decisions – why is the Chicago font used inside the "content area" of one dialog (a) but not the other (b)?, why does one window (b) contain a button with a light sans serif label?, why do the two dialogs use different fonts to label their bounding boxes? To make matters worse, the fonts are similar, but not visually compatible. A cardinal rule of typographic design is that fonts from different families in the same style of face (e.g., serif or sans serif) should not be mixed under any circumstances. Finally, the fonts are *used* incorrectly, since in one window (a), the less prominent typeface serves as a higher level label for its more prominently labeled (in Chicago) subordinate control. Garish color schemes are another familiar example of the same problem. In both cases, so many contrasts are being drawn that none of them can emerge and contribute to the organization of the display.

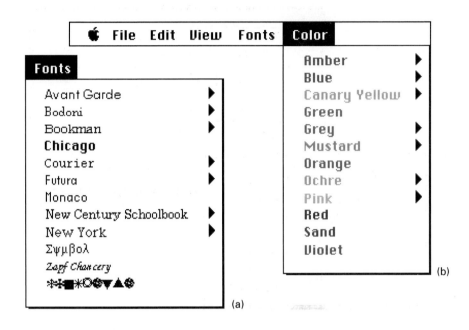

(a)

(b)

77: *Visual interference.* Contrast on one visual dimension often disrupts the processing of visual information on other dimensions. This is the phenomenon termed *dissociative* perception by Bertin (1975) One common example is seen when font names are displayed in their actual fonts (a) or color names in their actual colors (b) or. Aside from the fact that some values (such as the current background color and any Symbol or Dingbat fonts), are inherently pathological, this well-intentioned coding is rarely sufficient to identify the target. The thin, linear elements of typographic labels provide a very poor con- text within which to display subtle variation in color and font. Perception is dominated by both the background and the surrounding elements, and the small size and limited scope of the label rarely provides an adequate preview in any case. The result is almost always a visually disorienting display that makes processing all of the information more difficult.

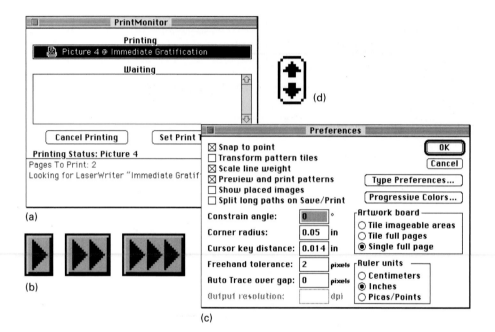

(a)

(b)

(c)

(d)

78: *Spatial tension.* Because screen real estate is always at a premium, the temptation to consume as little space as possible for each window is often overwhelming. Spatial tension occurs when controls (or controls and labels) are placed too closely to one another. It's hard to imagine a better example of this problem than the extremely tight, even overlapping, spacing between labels and controls in the Macintosh System 6 Print Monitor (a). Tension also arises when figural elements are too large to fit comfortably in the available ground, as in the various arrow controls above (b,d). In each case, the arrows extend too close to the border, and the unity of the sign suffers as a result. Miserly windows crowd their contents and make it un-

necessarily difficult to extract information by failing to provide an adequate ground upon which an appropriate global figure can be formed. The Preferences dialog above (c) exhibits this problem as well as interference between its closely spaced controls. Note the contention between the boundaries of the stacked textfields as well as the tension created by the very narrow gaps at the top and bottom of the dialog.

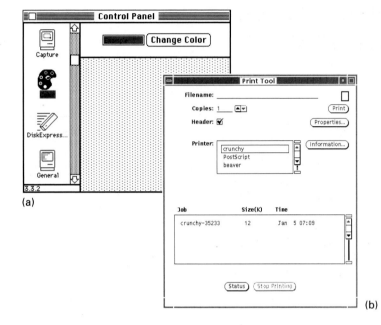

(a)

(b)

79: *Overextension.* A less common, but still serious problem arises when windows are too large for the information they contain. Usually this occurs because the same window is being used to display multiple chunks of information one chunk at a time, as in the original General control panel (a). When the chunks vary widely in size, some are bound to be too small to integrate effectively with the space in which they are displayed. The problem can usually be addressed by reorganizing the information to reduce the variability between groups. Other problems with overextension involve poor use of space within the window. Unless an extravagant – even artistic – effect is intended, the addition of this much space in the margins and between controls is both wasteful and visually discomforting. The extra space does little except obscure contextual information that might otherwise be provided by the rest of the display. In this example (b) a transient textfield can appear in the gap below the first scrolling list, but it is used far too rarely to justify the wasteful layout.

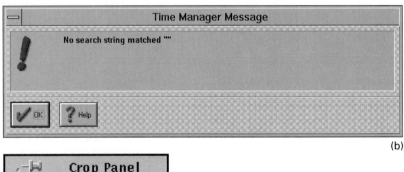

(b)

(a)

80: *Awkward dimensions.* Extremely large or small windows (a) relate poorly to the screen or window context within which they appear. Aside from the obvious functional problem of obscuring the rest of the display, very large windows are visually discomforting because they almost (but not quite) fill the display. They also tend to be visually disorienting, since they obscure most, if not all, of the window from which they were invoked. Very small windows that are similarly unsuited to the context in which they appear can be equally troublesome. They are easy to "misplace" during the normal course of window management and, in a busy display, may never be noticed in the first place. Windows or controls that are disproportionately tall or wide (b) can produce similarly awkward results. Dialog boxes designed to handle very long message strings often introduce this problem. The more general awkwardness of "incorrect" proportions is also seen frequently when familiar objects that differ widely in scale and proportion are forced into a common display unit, as in the case of the widget icons used in many GUI development environments.

Visual ambiguity, like verbal ambiguity, obscures not only
compositional intent, but also meaning... visual forms should not be
purposefully unclear; they should harmonize or contrast, attract or
repel, relate or clash.

Donis A. Dondis
A Primer of Visual Literacy

Techniques

Scale, contrast, and proportion are among the most subtle aspects of design. **Layering**
The popularity of classical systems of proportion reflects both the difficulty **Sharpening**
of these problems and the desire for foolproof mechanical solutions. Three **Integration**
simple techniques, while falling short of an automatic solution, are relevant
to most interface design problems:

- Establishing Perceptual Layers
- Sharpening Visual Distinctions
- Integrating Figure and Ground

Mastery of these techniques requires extensive practice, but the underlying
principles are not difficult. The ability to perfectly balance the interplay of
scale and contrast comes only with experience. The boundaries of insuffi-
ciency and excess, however, are easier to define, and it is here that we begin.

One trick that is especially helpful in all of the following techniques (and **The Squint Test**
many in the subsequent chapters as well) can be described as the *squint test*.
The squint test can be used to simulate the early visual processes that form
the basis for perceptual organization and any coding effects operating across
the entire display. To apply the technique, simply close one eye completely
and "squint" the other eye to reduce the light and disrupt the focus. Looking
at the entire display, try to identify the features of interest using only that
eye. Lean back from the work, if necessary, to make it easier for your eye
take in the entire composition. Anything not readily apparent to the squint-
ing eye it will not be apparent "at a glance" in the finished display.

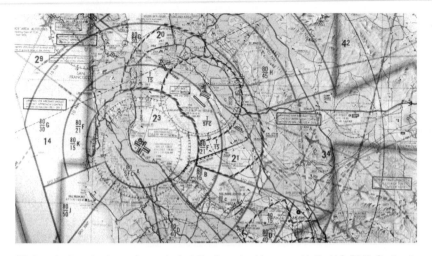

81: Layering based on hue, value, and orientation (curvature) is apparent in the U.S. FAA's Sectional Aeronautical Charts. Such dense information displays can succeed only if contrast is carefully controlled to prevent one dimension from dominating another. (See also Color Plate 4).

**Establishing
Perceptual Layers**

Scale and contrast can be used to divide the display into a few distinct regions or *layers* that are processed selectively or in a predictable sequence. Maps for aeronautical navigation (81) replace most ground detail with additional information relevant to the pilot. Because flight-related and geographical information are often spatially contiguous, an effective layering scheme is essential. Contrasting color, value, and texture are used to segregate geographical from flight-related information. This allows the most important features (airports, radio beacons, altitudes, etc.) to emerge clearly from the dense display. The pilot can then determine the information needed and use the layer that isolates that material to extract it quickly from the display.

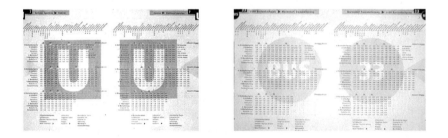

82: Effective perceptual layering is required whenever foreground and background must be read independently. These timetable pages use background elements to establish a global context that identifies the mode of transit for a given page. Courtesy of MetaDesign, Berlin.

Effective layering is essential whenever it is necessary to read overlapping elements independently. The graphical variables involved must be *selective* (meaning elements with this characteristic can be viewed independently, without interference from other variables already plotted in the display) and *associative* (meaning they do not affect the visibility of other elements. The timetable for the Berlin Transit Authority (BVG) (82) uses color to layer a large but lightly screened background symbol identifying the mode of transport (e.g., U-bahn, S-bahn, Tram, Bus, etc.) represented by that page. This allows users to quickly identify the contents of the page while flipping through the book without interfering with the detailed reading of the schedule. Electronic illustration and publishing systems use similar contrasts to distinguish guide lines, margins, and other "invisible" elements from the content being edited (83). In each case, it is easy to ignore a layer you're not interested in.

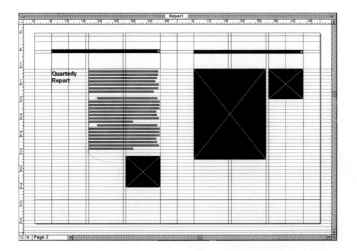

83: Because it is both *selective* and *associative*, color is especially useful as a layering device. In this window from QuarkXPress, color-coded guidelines group easily and naturally according to purpose. (See also Color Plate 3a).

Layering can take place even when elements in the layers do not physically overlap. The classification of Macintosh icons (84), while superficially dependent on shape, actually operates on the basis of orientation cues. The most common elements – documents, folders, and applications – have important orientation tendencies (vertical, horizontal, diagonal) that are quickly learned by all users. The NeXTStep font selector window (85) uses color (in this case white) to group subsets of its information content for

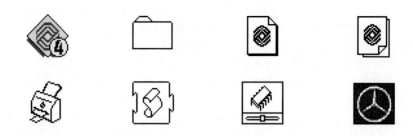

84: Layering based on orientation (e.g., horizontal, vertical, diagonal) in Macintosh Finder icons allows the class of icon (application, folder, document/template, etc.) to be recognized independently of the internal imagery identifying the creator application or even the particular document.

independent processing. The font window uses color in a similar manner to tie the components of the font name together across lists, and to link the resulting font name to the preview area at the top of the window.

Effective design creates no more contrast than necessary. This usually means variation along one dimension at a time. To layer effectively, you must maintain a strong similarity between the elements being grouped within a layer or region. This allows the viewer to easily identify the elements in question as a strongly defined subset of the available information. The visual characteristics of the group can then be manipulated to make the layer more or less prominent than the rest of the information on display.

85: Even when elements don't overlap, layering can bring elements together to be read as a unit, as seen in the NeXTStep font panel.

To apply this technique, you must begin with a thorough understanding of your communication goals. Communication design always begins with an analysis and organization of the information to be communicated. This is one area where the aesthetics of a display cannot be considered in isolation from the purpose for which the display is intended. We will therefore treat this analysis as an integral part of our four-step layering process:

Summary: Layering

1 Group each item of information into a small number (7+/- 2) of categories according to its origin or intended use. A group must be established for any group of items that will need to be processed independently. Each item must be assigned to at least one group.

2 Determine the rank or importance of the various groups and organize them into an even smaller number (e.g., 3-5) of echelons based on this ranking.

3 Use appropriate perceptual variables to establish the layering effect. Size and value can establish clear perceptual hierarchies, while hue is most effective for non-hierarchical grouping.

4 Maximize the perceptual difference between groups while minimizing the difference within groups.

5 Use the squint test to ensure that elements in the same layer group together as a unit, but that group itself can be visually separated from the rest of the display.

Effective perceptual layering allows the viewer to attend selectively to the elements in any one group with a minimum of interference from the others. Layers in different echelons will differ in their perceptual prominence (see techniques under *Sharpening* below), but perceptual coding must be used carefully to ensure that the user can ignore the more salient information when necessary during extended use.

abcdefghijklmnopqrstuvwxyz

ABCDEFGHIJKLMNOPQRS
TUVWXYZ
$1234567890(.,'"'"";:!)?&@#%

86: Its straight serifs and sharpened contrast between horizontal and vertical strokes distinguish Bodoni–the first *modern* typeface–from its subdued, organic, *old style* and *transitional* predecessors.

Sharpening Visual Distinctions

Like all meaningful contrasts, those used in layering must be strong enough to clearly distinguish the elements in question. *Sharpening* is a technique that ensures that contrast between elements is adequate for effective discrimination or aesthetic effect. The classic Modern typeface, Bodoni (86), increases – or *sharpens* – the distinction between horizontal and vertical strokes seen in earlier serif typefaces to produce a powerful and radically different visual effect. Bodoni uses maximum contrast between thick and thin strokes to suggest modernity, tension, and visual interest.

87: The extreme scale contrasts apparent in the typography of the journal cover by Carlo Vivarelli (a), are appropriate for a newsstand, but would be overkill for a GUI. The much smaller difference seen in the NeXTStep file selection dialog (b) provides adequate contrast at typical viewing distances.

Effective design creates meaningful distinctions when it creates any at all. The cover design in Figure 87-a leaves no ambiguity about the relative importance of headline and content. The size contrast in the "headline" of the NeXTStep file selector (87-b) is weaker, but still adequate at typical viewing distances. The minimum acceptable contrast depends on the viewing task, but a useful guideline is available in the standardized type sizes of traditional metal typography. The series made it easy to establish easily discriminable size differences since display type (14 point or larger) was generally provided in even multiples of 12 points. The rule is never to use adjacent values from this series, since this leads to ambiguity. While greater flexibility is provided by digital systems, the same principles of legibility

BlackBlack
BlackBold

BoldBold
BoldMedium

BlackMedium
BlackLight

BoldLight

88: Typographic contrasts based on weight should generally span more than one "step" on the scale to ensure adequate legibility. The contrast between bold and medium or between black and bold, for example, is generally unclear and should be avoided. Better results are obtained using the stronger bold-light and black-medium, or even black-light contrasts.

apply today. Adjacent values often provide inadequate contrast in type weight as well. For the Univers family (88), the minimum contrast needed for effective communication is achieved with medium-black (a) and light-bold (b). Contrasts above the line are weak and ambiguous, while those below the line are adequate.

Effective design ensures that all contrasts are clearly intentional and designed to fulfill a specific communication goal. Sharpened contrasts are especially important for providing critical *state feedback* in GUI's. Selections, the availability of controls or menu items, and window focus are all important examples of sharpening in the Macintosh desktop interface. Active, selected, or focused elements are more prominent (by virtue of a sharp value contrast) then the surrounding area, provided the solid black (or colored)

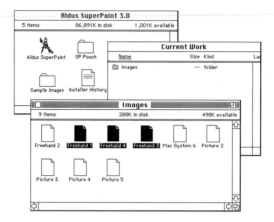

89: Sharpening of visual feedback in Macintosh selection and window focus feedback ensures that users will immediately recognize the scoping of the menu commands they issue.

selection dominates the window borders within the "focus layer" (89). If users are allowed to customize the selection color, the critical visual mapping needed for *ordered perception* may be disrupted.

Sharpened contrasts are affected by the background against which they appear. The common practice of dimming unavailable commands and controls (90-a) makes it easy to tell at a glance what options are available to the user. If the background is colored, however, it becomes more difficult to ensure that a third color can be found midway between those two colors that will make inactive items sufficiently distinct from active items while maintaining their legibility (90-b). The chief goal of the *layering* technique is to limit contrast *within* layers to minimize this sort of effect *across* layers.

90: Effective sharpening provides adequate contrast between active and inactive menu items in every GUI. The effect is influenced by the menu background: maximum contrast is achieved on a white background (a) with progressive weakening as the background darkens (b).

Combining two values in accordance with the laws of contrast changes and enhances the effect of both values. Round treetops look rounder if there are angular buildings near them; a tower looks taller if it stands on a flat plain; a warm color looks warmer if it is combined with a cold color.

Emil Ruder
Typography

Sharpening ensures that the perceptual distinction between two echelons – and indeed between any two contrasting elements–is large enough to permit easy recognition. Once the necessary layers have been identified, the sharpening technique used to ensure their adequate discriminability and proper ranking is straightforward:

Summary: Sharpening

1 Identify the rankings that need to be established across the groups of information (see analysis under Layering, above).

2 Determine the range of variation (e.g., minimum and maximum values or sizes, number of colors, etc.) available and use as much of it as possible in the resulting code.

3 Use logarithmic rather than linear scaling across the visible range to ensure the discriminability of contrasts at large absolute magnitudes. Doubling each successive level is usually sufficient.

4 Use the squint test to ensure that at least the first two or three echelons can be easily recognized "at a glance."

It is important to utilize as much of the "visual bandwidth" as possible. Elements in the first echelon (e.g., the most important information) should be prominent enough to emerge from the design and secure the user's attention almost involuntarily. Less important information may require focal attention and conscious effort to extract, but the layering should work to make this easier to do once the viewer's intent has been established.

91: The *Information* symbol from the U.S. DOT signage program (a) shows perfect integration between figure and ground. Unlike the distorted versions on the right (b), the circle and question mark possess a unity of scale that cause them to be read as one, rather than two objects.

Integrating Figure and Ground

To ensure the impression of a single unified design, the perceptual qualities of the *figure* – the primary formal element – must be carefully matched to those of its *ground* – the visual context within which the figure appears. The symbiotic relationship between figure and ground is apparent in all effective designs. We recognize forms on the basis of their outer contours, which become apparent by virtue of the contrast – normally in terms of value – between the internal (figure) and external (ground) areas. When properly integrated, these internal and external forms complement one another.

92: Figure and ground are tightly integrated in this identity for the 1994 Winter Olympic Games coverage. Design by Pentagram.

The seemingly straightforward *Information* symbol from the US DOT public information system (91-a) is the product of a complex balancing act between the size of the question mark (the figure) and its containing circle (whose white interior portion forms the ground for the mark). If the question mark is even slightly too large or too small, too thick or too thin in relation to the outer circle (91-b), the result is visual tension and discomfort. When not properly *integrated*, the question mark and its containing circle no longer appear to be part of the same unitary sign because the harmony and balance of their relationship has been disrupted.

Visual integration requires that figure and ground be *approximately equal* in terms of their *scale* and *visual weight*. In Figure 91(a), the visual weight – or dominance in human perception – of the symbol's dark and light areas are approximately equal. In the symbol for the 1994 Winter Olympic Games coverage (92) the figure emerges through the implicit closure of the lines forming the mountain tops. In this case the *enclosed* area of the figure – including the symbols for the Olympic Games and CBS, as well as the mountains – is approximately equal to that of the ground, even though the dark-light ratio is biased heavily toward the dark value.

Effective visual integration ensures that figure and ground exist in a state of balance and stability. In GUI design, where some form of bounding structure is normally present, adequate separation between the figure and its containing element should always be maintained. The top row in Figure 93 shows the overly cramped default horizontal and vertical padding for button labels in the OSF/Motif toolkit. Increasing the space surrounding the label (bottom row) enhances both the readability and integration of the visual form.

93: Poor integration often results from improper default values in UI toolkits such as OSF/Motif. The tight padding (upper row) provided by default in Motif (perhaps appropriate for applications such as telephone keypads). Better integration (lower row) can be achieved by increasing these values.

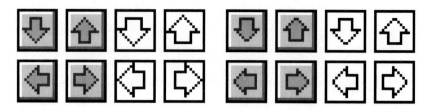

94: These Macintosh scroll arrows suffer from poor integration between figure and ground. The arrows are off-center (and thus asymmetrical with respect to their ground) because their width is an odd number of pixels (note the single-pixel point) while the ground has an even number. "Blunting" and centering the arrow leads to improved integration, albeit of a weaker form.

To maximize visual integration, internal element should be placed as symmetrically as possible within the enclosing space. The Macintosh scroll arrows have always been off-center in their containing rectangles (94-a), because the 16-pixel dimension that is "natural" for the raster implementation conflicts with the arrow's width of an odd number of pixels. Compensating by "thickening" the point of the arrow (94-b) enhances visual integration, albeit at the cost of a lower-quality arrow.

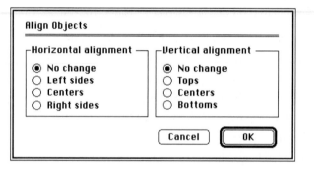

95: Integration is important for higher level GUI objects as well. The effective balance between figure and ground in this dialog from Aldus SuperPaint, for example, make the four element groups apparent.

The same integration issues apply at higher levels of application design as well. While a window may not require the same degree of unification as a symbol, both its appearance and its organization are enhanced by the proper integration of the control groups it contains. The technique applies recursively: this dialog box from Aldus SuperPaint provides adequate margins around the entire content region, and between the four major element groups within the content region, and between the internal labels and bounding contours of each control.

The feeling of a design fitting its space and its surroundings is what we call scale. A design may be good in all other respects, but if its scale does not fit where it belongs, it is wrong while many a design in poor taste is admissable if it possesses the quality of scale.

Paul Jacques Grillo
Form, Function, and Design

These examples show the wide range of situations in which figure and ground must be related to one another. In a GUI, everything – from individual symbols to entire layouts – appears within an explicitly or implicitly defined visual context. Fitting the design to the context in which it appears is usually a four-step process:

Summary: Integration

1 Determine the overall size of the figure/ground combination. Note that designs will usually require adjustment as the overall size is changed, since critical internal relationships are disrupted when a figure is scaled uniformly. Also note that the size of either figure or ground may be adjusted to produce the necessary scale relationships.

2 Equalize the *visual weight* of figure and ground. Use the "squint test" to check that neither the positive or negative space dominate.

3 Provide enough space around the margins of the figure to eliminate unwarranted visual tension. This is often the most difficult aspect of the technique in GUI design, particular since screen real estate is such a precious resource.

4 Position the figure correctly within the ground. The figure should usually be centered within the ground unless communication requirements dictate otherwise. Use the squint test to ensure that the figure still appears to be centered.

Effective integration ensures that figure and ground act to reinforce rather than distract from one another. Because the background in a GUI uses the same visual elements as the foreground, margins must be more generous than in print design. Simply ensuring an adequate margin area around the content region of each window or icon will do much to improve a GUI. With practice, your eye will become trained to recognize exactly how much space is needed to achieve the proper balance between figure and ground.

Organization and Visual Structure

4

The eye travels along the paths cut out for it in the work.

Paul Klee
Pedagogical Sketchbook

Organization and visual structure provide the user with the visual pathways needed to experience a product in a systematic way. Structure affects the visual experience at its most primitive level because it is the first aspect of the display to be perceived as information is extracted and used to guide subsequent interaction. Because they are experienced effortlessly and automatically, phenomena at this level provide critical communication channels that can be used to supplement or interrupt the user's higher level activities.

Organized structure does not occur naturally in man-made artifacts, so it must be consciously induced by establishing relationships among the components of the design. Effective use of structure allows individual elements to work in concert without being diminished in their own right. The eye craves structure and will seek to impose its own organization onto a design whose structure is not readily apparent. This breakdown threatens communication, since the designer is no longer in control of the message.

Without the integrity provided by a coherent visual structure, a design quickly becomes impossible to interpret and understand. The cost is functional as well as aesthetic, since progress toward any goal is continually impeded – even for expert users. Structure introduces several key benefits:

Unity. Visual structure ties even highly disparate design elements together and allows them to work in concert toward a common communication

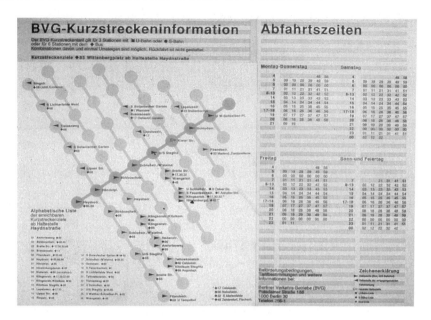

96: Structural elements designed to aid the user engaged in typical reading tasks play a crucial role in organizing the large quantity of information presented in these posters, which explain a special mass transit fare system based on distance traveled. Courtesy of MetaDesign, Berlin.

goal. The lightly screened bars forming the background of the timetable in Figure 96 serve not only to reinforce the tabular structure of the layout at a global level, but also to simplify the local reading of the tabular display.

Integrity. A strong and coherent structure keeps the design focused on the communication goal by creating an emergent form that contributes to the meaning of the ensemble. The strong repeating element of the screened bars helps integrate the design on both the horizontal and vertical axes. On the horizontal dimension, the bars tie the rows strongly together and make it easy to make comparisons across columns. On the vertical dimension, the bars establish a rhythm that leads the eye down the page and makes it easy to scan ahead by a predetermined number of rows.

Readability. Structure enhances readability by dividing the information content of the entire display into manageable subsets that can be processed separately or in parallel, according to the designer's wishes. The discontinuity created by simply removing the screened bars from the timetable is itself a powerful structural element.

Control. Structure allows users to predict areas of interest and eases their navigation through the composition. Control of structure allows the designer to influence this process of exploration and ensure that the information is delivered effectively. The large scale of the timetable's headlines captures the viewer's attention and ensures that no time is wasted in looking at the wrong display. Four smaller labels identifying the denser tabular areas serve the same function at that level of detail as the viewer progressively focuses on the appropriate cell.

Information intensive applications such as timetables for transportation systems are among the best and most familiar applications of visual structure. Although the information they present is primarily tabular, powerful visual cues are used to guide the user to the relevant portion of the display. We turn now to a brief review of the early visual processes that support the processing of these cues and the separation of the display into figure and ground.

Several general principles of perceptual organization were first described in the 1920's by psychologists of the *Gestalt* school. The gestalt psychologists were interested in describing the processes by which individual elements were grouped into *gestalts* (wholes) during early visual perception (Wertheimer, 1958). By describing how the global structure of the whole emerges from the finer-grained local structure of the parts, the Gestalt principles can explain the success of many visual design techniques.

Background: Perceptual Organization

The principle of *proximity* describes the tendency of individual elements to be associated more strongly with nearby elements than with those that are farther away. This phenomenon can be observed on two different levels in Figure 97(a). They eye organizes the dots first into four vertical columns because the horizontal separation is much greater than the vertical separation. Then, because the separation between the middle two "columns" is greater than the outer gaps, the whole figure is seen as two groups of two columns each.

The principle of *similarity* observes that elements will be associated more strongly when they share basic visual characteristics (such as the visual variables of shape, size, color, texture, value, and orientation described previously) than when they differ along these dimensions. Thus, the figure in 97(b) again appears as two groups of two columns each, despite the fact that the inter-element and inter-column spacings have now been equalized.

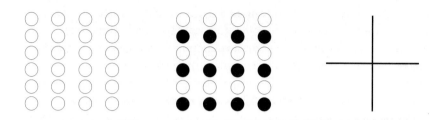

97: Gestalt grouping phenomena: proximity (a), similarity (b), and continuity (c).

The principle of *continuity* describes the preference for continuous, unbroken contours with the simplest possible physical explanation, rather than more complex but equally plausible combinations of more irregular figures. The form in Figure 97(c) is thus perceived as two crossing lines rather than four abutting lines or two (or even four) opposing angles. The related principle of *closure* describes the powerful human tendency to interpret visual

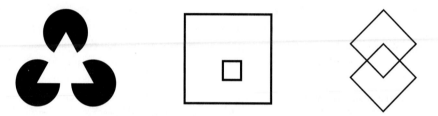

98: Gestalt phenomena in form perception: closure (a), area (b), and symmetry (c).

stimuli as complete, closed figures, even when some of the necessary contour information is absent. Figure 98(a) is easily seen as a triangle superimposed on three complete circles even though neither of these forms is technically present. This example also has the interesting quality of *figure-ground reversal*, in which the viewer's visual attention alternates between the white triangle and notched black circles (98-a). Either (or both) can be viewed as the *figure* – the object of interest – or the ground on which the figure rests. As we shall subsequently see, this phenomenon can be used to great effect in producing engaging graphical identities and effective window layouts.

Returning to the grouping principles, the principle of *area* states that the as a smaller of two overlapping figures will tend to be interpreted as figure while the larger is interpreted as ground. In Figure 98(b), the inner square is perceived as a distinct form in front of a larger square instead of a hole in the larger form. Since these phenomena appear in virtually every design problem, the successful designer must take care to ensure that the emergent structure works to reinforce the function of the display.

Finally, the principle of *symmetry* describes grouping based on the emergent properties of the form instead of the characteristics of its constituent parts. The greater the symmetry of a possible figure, the more likely we are to use it as our interpretation of the gestalt. Figure 98(c) is thus seen as two (overlapping) rather than three objects. This claim has received solid empirical support in recent years (Hochberg and McAlister, 1953, Hemenway and Palmer, 1978). Forms with a high degree of "figural goodness" are rated more highly and perceived more readily than weaker, more ambiguous forms.

Principles

Organization and visual structure are the staples of successful communication-oriented design. Whereas scale, contrast, and proportion can be elusive, unpredictable, even capricious, organization and visual structure are based on steady, reliable methods that can be applied time and again in the same familiar way. Organization begins with classification, which involves *grouping* related elements and establishing a *hierarchy* of importance for elements and groups. When this hierarchy is clear, the display itself can be structured to reflect the *relationships* between the elements while maintaining a pleasing *balance* in the resulting composition.

Grouping
Hierarchy
Relationship
Balance

99: The U.S. Interstate Highway signage program makes effective use of perceptual grouping and information hierarchy. The eye is drawn immediately to the city name and route numbers.

100: The button layout in this Sony Mini-Disc player illustrates effective grouping based on proximity, similarity, and continuation. Some groupings are reinforced by physical borders. Courtesy of Sony Electronics, Inc.

Grouping

The first step in the development of structure is the grouping of display elements into higher-order units. The words in a book, for example, are grouped into columns, sections, pages, etc. By grouping similar elements together, the designer helps the user deal with a complex information display by reducing it to a manageable number of units. Higher level structures orient the user and help them establish a plan for moving the attention to some interesting portion of the display for a more detailed reading.

Several of the *gestalt* effects – including proximity and continuity – are exploited in the Reuters logotype (101), which brings to mind the punched tape motif from the early news ticker. In addition to producing a unique graphical effect, the forms underscore the historical cachet of the well-

101: The familiar logotype for the Reuters news service depends on several Gestalt grouping phenomena (proximity and continuation) that turn a dot pattern into a word. Design by Pentagram.

known firm. Effective perceptual grouping is always based on the Gestalt principles. Powerful grouping of individual elements can be seen in the Sony MiniDisc recorder (100). The controls on this device group naturally due to the high degree of similarity (in terms of shape, size, color, and surface texture) within groups and the generous spatial separation between groups (i.e., proximity *within* groups). The shallow, dished-out "bounding boxes" surrounding each control group serve more as a sensuous accent than a functional grouping device in this product design.

The standards manual for the Berlin Transit Authority (BVG) in Figure 102 also makes heavy use of proximity and similarity (the two most powerful and general grouping principles), but it shows effective perceptual grouping based on continuity as well. The groups break the page up into several regions of interest, allowing the viewer to easily select a "topic" for more detailed examination. Because the types of information in each group are fairly obvious – even at a distance it is easy to recognize groups dealing with color schemes, identity symbols, etc. – there is little need for explicit labeling. The only "added" structuring device is the dark block in the lower left-

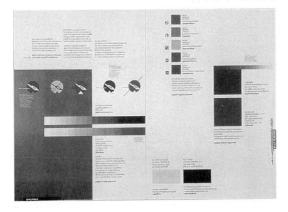

102: Elements group naturally based on similarity and alignment ("common fate") in this spread from a standards manual for the BVG Potsdam lines. Courtesy of MetaDesign.

hand corner. This element shows the effect of the visual identity on a dark background and is exploited compositionally as an important part of the spread's overall structure. Note the operation of continuity in allowing the eye to group the horizontal rows of circular identity marks and the value scales below them as individual objects extending "over" the darker field.

The user interface designer rarely enjoys the luxury of negative space to the extent seen in the BVG standards manual. Proper use of spacing and alignment, however, can produce grouping that is just as effective. This dialog box from Adobe Photoshop (103–a) uses explicit bounding boxes to organize eight vertically stacked controls into four pairs. This arrangement is difficult to scan because the alternating displays cannot be easily isolated perceptually. Because the task may involve comparing adjacent rows or ignoring intervening rows, there is no ordering of the controls that would not produce some interference. The problem, however, is easily solved by simply realigning the controls into a two-column layout (103–b) that puts the image components on the left-hand column and the corresponding alpha channels in a right-hand column. The improved *spatial logic* of this reorganized display allows the bounding boxes to be removed, the secondary labels consolidated, and the group labels moved into the right-hand margin, where they are much easier to scan.

103: This before-and-after example shows ineffective grouping with explicit bounding boxes (a) and effective grouping without explicit reinforcement (b). Spatial logic (i.e., coding based on position) is always more powerful than graphical embellishment at producing effective perceptual grouping.

Grouping in interface design is always used to bind functional units tightly together while distinguishing them from the surrounding controls. The same Gestalt principles can be applied to ensure effective grouping without heavy boxes and borders. When properly established, groupings can be recognized immediately and effortlessly by the user because they depend on visual phenomena operating below the level of conscious attention.

104: Strong scale contrasts in the typographic elements of this booklet cover lead the eye through the composition to create an effective information hierarchy. Courtesy of MetaDesign.

As groupings are established, they must–by manipulating the visual variables described by Bertin (1985)–be ordered in a hierarchy of perceptual prominence corresponding to the intended reading sequence. These examples from the public information system for the Berlin Transit Authority (BVG) show a clear typographic hierarchy reinforced by strong graphical elements. The booklet above (104) uses the monumental scale and oblique orientation of the "B" letterform to set the context for the rest of the design. This is the most important signal identifying the geographical region to which the timetable applies. Other typographic elements in the background support this

Hierarchy

105: Although size contrast is the most powerful tool for creating visual hierarchies, contrasts in position and value (the other *ordered* variables in human vision) can be used as well. In these print collateral (a,b) and signage (c) examples from MetaDesign's BVG program, the prominence of the yellow bar depends on position and value, both of which are superceded by the large "60,-" in (b).

global reading with more detailed information at a lower level of perceptual prominence. The yellow rectangular element at the upper right is a motif recurring throughout the program (see examples in 105 also). It groups visually in the middle of the information hierarchy with the BVG mark appearing directly below and the marks for the various modes of transportation covered in this booklet. Finally, two additional levels of typographic coding based on size appear in white superimposed against the larger background elements to specify the precise content and applicable dates. The printed materials below (105) show comparable hierarchies based on contrasts in position and value.

Poster design has always been focused on the creation of effective information hierarchies. The most important elements must be large enough to draw the viewer in close, to a point where the specifics can be presented. This detail from a concert poster by Josef Müller-Brockmann (106–a) shows an elegant typographic hierarchy with three levels based on contrasts in size and position/alignment. These same typographic conventions can be adapted directly to the presentation of information hierarchies in user interfaces The standard labeling practice for property windows in the OPEN LOOK GUI (106–b), for example, is remarkably similar. Though the contrasts in typographic scale are less extreme, the global context is again established by the larger, darker label in the upper left of each region, while the shorter, right-aligned labels provide a local context for the denser, left-aligned information on the right.

106: An effective typographic information hierarchy based on size and position is apparent in this detail from a poster by Josef Müller-Brockmann (a). The same approach is used to visually encode the information hierarchy in the labeling standards for the OPEN LOOK property window (b).

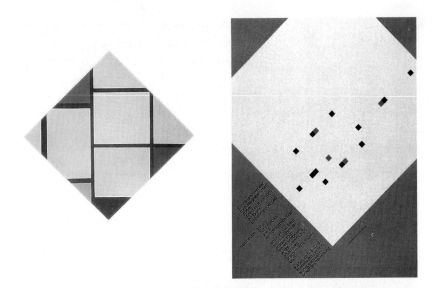

107: Structural relationships in, *Lozenge with Blue, Red, and Yellow,* by Piet Mondrian (a) are made explicit by the lines dividing the composition. © 1993 Estate of Piet Mondrian/E.M. Holtzman Irrevocable Trust. Though entirely implicit, relationships between elements are equally important in this concert poster from the Musica Viva series by Josef Müller-Brockmann (b). (See also color plate 6).

Relationship

Grouping and hierarchy are both supplemented and reinforced when elements are visually related to one another. Relations between elements can be based on any of the visual variables, but the dominance of position, size, and value provide the most effective visual cues. Of these variables, position in the two-dimensional plane is the most useful. The eye is very sensitive to alignment, as witnessed by the Gestalt phenomena of "good continuation" and "common fate" (97). Position can also be manipulated independently of each element's semantics, since other visual variables have a larger impact on the salience of the elements to which they are applied.

The De Stijl painter Piet Mondrian made visible all of the structure in his abstract compositions using explicit lines (107–a). The seemingly simple forms are in fact carefully related to one another in size, proportion, and position within the composition. The concert poster by Josef Müller-Brockmann (107–b) occupies the opposite extreme by implicitly suggesting strong relationships even across large amounts of space without the use of explicit internal structure. Subtle alignment of the poster's elements is enough to suggest the structured aspect of music without reducing the sense of freedom and energy. Even more complex internal structure is apparent in the poster

108: Relationships among elements in this poster by Piet Zwart create a captivating internal structure providing many pathways for the eye. © Piet Zwart/VAGA, New York 1993.

for a film festival by Piet Zwart (108). Every element is related to at least one other element, but the relationships are always implied, based on alignment along critical margins, rather than explicitly reinforced through the introduction of external elements.

Window layouts in graphical user interfaces can make use of the same principles of visual relationship based on alignment and similarity of form. While these effects are exploited automatically at the lowest levels (the items in a scrolling list, for example, are pre-aligned by the UI toolkit), developers must establish higher level relationships themselves. The spatial logic of a layout can help reveal the underlying semantic relationships of the individual components, but only if the visual relationships are carefully manipulated. When properly executed, the meaning of each element is implied by its location relative to its surrounding elements, and the need for explicit labeling is reduced.

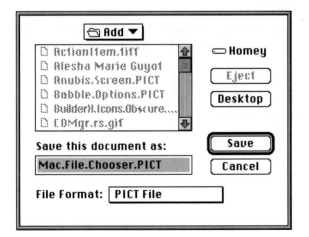

109: Poor use of *spatial logic* in the layout of components can obscure their semantic relationships. In the Windows file selector, the spatial ordering of filename, directory, and drive reverses the concepts' logical precedence.

In the Windows File selector (109), for example, the sequence of controls (reading from top to bottom) provides a poor spatial analog to the logical information hierarchy (volume, directory path, directory contents, and file-name). Its ordering of components is the reverse of the normal scanning order for the window, and additional, lateral motion is needed to take in the entire hierarchy. The Macintosh equivalent (110)uses a more compact, natural arrangement in which elements are scanned in an order corresponding to their position in the hierarchy. The perceptual salience of the pre-selected filename draws the eye "through" the hierarchy on its way to the textfield.

110: The Macintosh file selector places directory, contents, and filename in the correct spatial relationship. It also relates the Save command to its argument and the directory to its containing volume.

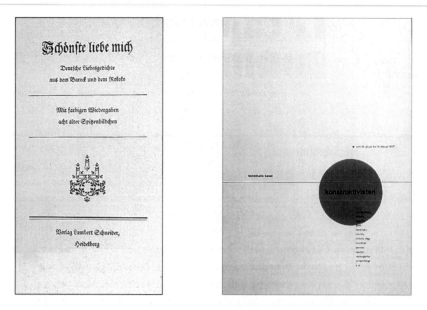

111: Balance in classical composition (a) is purely symmetrical, restful, and monumental. The *New Typography* of the 20th century (b) uses asymmetrical layouts to create more complex, task-oriented relationships among elements, but balance must still be maintained. Both designs by Jan Tschichold.

Balance

All of the previous goals must be accomplished while maintaining an harmonious global arrangement of the elements in the composition. The quality of *balance* ensures that the display remains stable in its position on the page or screen. Balance can be achieved using either symmetric or asymmetric layout, as demonstrated in these sharply contrasting yet equally striking designs by the great German typographer Jan Tschichold (111). Classic display typography (111–a), which evolved over centuries from conventions originating in monumental inscriptions and other forms of public proclamation, is simple, centered, and perfectly symmetrical. In the 20th Century,

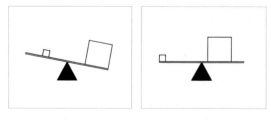

112: Balance in a composition is analogous to balance in physical quantities. Smaller elements can offset the "visual weight" of larger elements if placed higher in the picture plane and farther from the compositional center of balance.

typographic designers discovered the greater vitality and inherent visual interest provided by active, asymmetric layouts. The resulting "New Typography" introduced the revolutionary form language seen in Tschichold's poster for an exhibition on Constructivist art (111–b), which exploits a dynamic asymmetrical composition to create an appropriate (for the subject matter) tension without producing a sense of instability within the space it occupies. The *felt axis* of the composition is moved well to the right of center, but the horizontal rule and outlying element on the left provide the counterweights needed for a well-balanced display.

Balance in display design is analogous to balance in everyday physics. A composition is balanced when the visual weight of design elements on either side of the composition are approximately equal. The visual weight of the composition is distributed across the center of balance (the "fulcrum" in the physical analogy) like the weights on a scale (112). When the visual weight and distance from the center of elements on each side of this axis are physically equal, the impression of balance is guaranteed. Symmetrical layouts

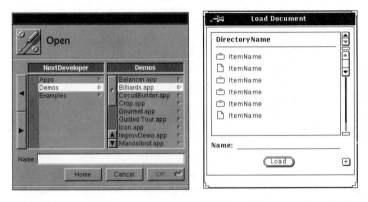

113: Axially symmetrical layouts ensure acceptable balance in these secondary window layouts from NeXTStep (a) and the OPEN LOOK GUI (b). The axis of symmetry can be vertical (b) or diagonal (a), so long as elements are balanced properly about it.

provide this visual equilibrium automatically. Asymmetrical layouts can achieve equilibrium as well, but their tenser, more dramatic form of balance, depends on careful manipulation to compensate visually for differences in the size, position, and value of major elements. As with a physical balance, lighter elements can balance heavier elements if their size or value (visual weight) is increased, or if they are moved farther from (or the heavier element moved closer to) the center of balance (112-b).

Window layout brings balance issues to the forefront of GUI design. Button placement policies, in particular, can affect the balance of the resulting displays. The large icon in the upper left-hand corner of the NeXTStep File selector (113-a) effectively balances the dialog's response buttons in the lower right-hand corner to produce a layout that is balanced along on a diagonal, rather than a vertical axis of symmetry. Other GUI standards such as OPEN LOOK (and particularly OSF/Motif) favor highly symmetrical window layouts by distributing response buttons in secondary windows and dialog boxes evenly across the bottom of the window (113–b). In practice, windows in most GUI applications are so over-crowded that balance is outweighed by more serious problems.

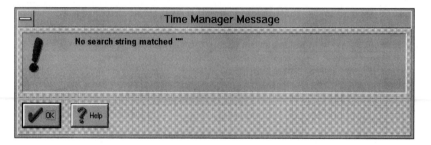

114: Using a "worst case" window size for all messages, as in this dialog from Time Manager for Windows, often leads to unbalanced layouts when messages are very short.

An exception is often seen when the amount of information presented in a window varies significantly from one presentation to the next. This problem is especially likely if the application employs a static window size designed to accommodate the worst case (i.e., the largest amount of information) presentation scenario (114). This dialog always places the response buttons and condition code on the left-hand side of the dialog. It leaves plenty of room for the text of the error message or warning. Unfortunately, this means that the window will go out of balance occasionally, particular when the message is as brief as the example shown here. Balance can be improved in these situations by *anticipating* the potential for empty space in the variable portion of the display and adjusting the fixed elements accordingly. Simply repositioning the response buttons in this dialog in the lower right-hand corner, while it would not address the problem of an overly lengthy default dialog size, would effectively balance the window even for messages as short as the one shown here.

Common Errors

Common shortcomings in organization and visual structure result from a failure to establish high-level regularities in the display by relating individual components. Some typical mistakes include:

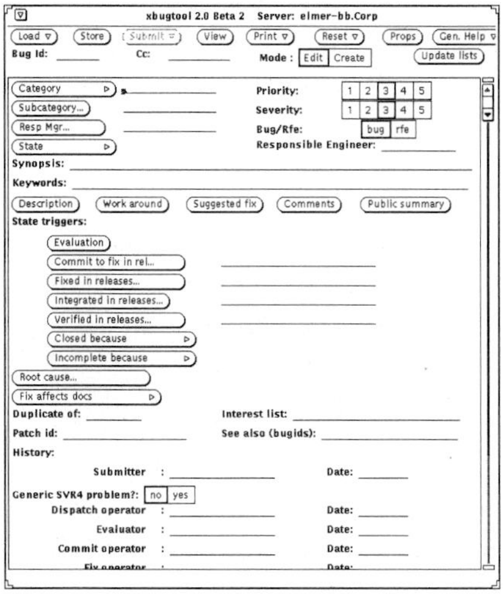

(a)

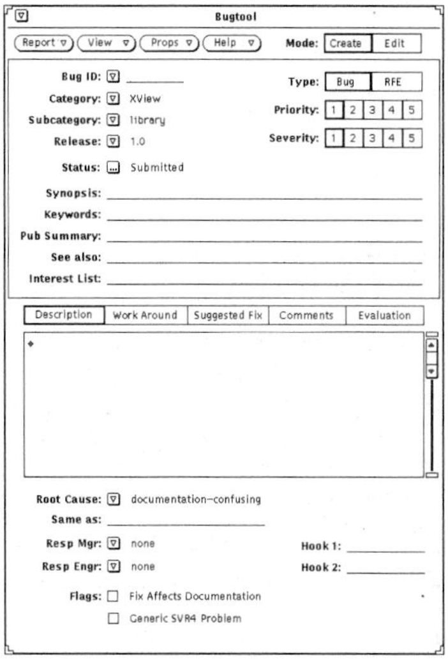

(b)

115: *Haphazard layout.* The most common problem of visual organization is without a doubt the failure to establish or reinforce logical relationships among components by establishing spatial relationships within the design. This original window layout (a) for an internal software defect tracking system (essentially the front-end to a highly structured database) suffers from a poorly organized structure in which weak relationships are established within the major component groups and practically none are established across groups. Note especially the distracting effect of the varying widths of the vertically stacked buttons. The existing design was improved considerably by reorganizing its contents and establishing stronger relations among the elements (b). Alignment was used to create a strong vertical axis along which the primary fields were positioned, as well as a subordinate axis on the right-hand side of the window for secondary controls.

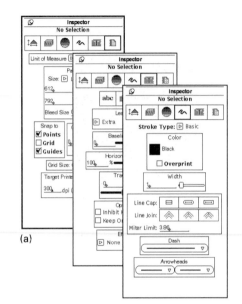

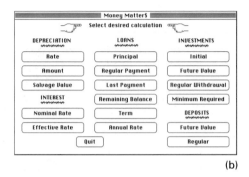

(a)

(b)

116: *Conflicting symmetries.* While symmetry can be useful as an organizing technique, it will not rescue a display from more serious internal problems. In both of these examples, the perceptual interaction between the information content and the closely spaced boundaries (button labels on the right and bounding boxes on the left) create a distracting "beat" that prevents the symmetry of the overall display from emerging. Unlike Tschichold's monumental frontispiece (111) the example on the left (a) features elements whose boundaries–but not their contents– are arranged symmetrically. In addition, the distraction produced by the unrelated widths of these hard-edged borders is heightened by their spatial proximity. The eye is drawn involuntarily to the mesmerizing outer contour of the centered bounding boxes, where sharp contrasts and intriguing spatial tensions have been unintentionally created. While the button labels on the right do not share a similarly noisy contour, they nevertheless how difficult scanning a column of vertically-centered labels becomes as soon as the labels are placed inside of buttons in multiple columns.

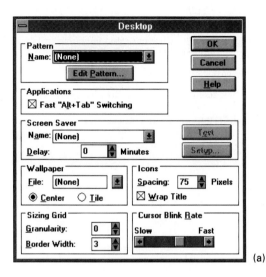

(a)

(b)

117: *Ambiguous internal relationships.* Both of these examples contain elements whose sizes and positions are similar, but not identical. The consistent placement of some internal margins only serves to increase the prominence of the many elements that are almost–but not quite–in alignment. In the Desktop Properties dialog (a), the careful alignment, both horizontally and vertically, of the bounding boxes is squandered in the completely haphazard arrangement of their contents. There is no apparent consistency in the size or placement of the individual controls, nor even in their spacing or separation from the enclosing border. In addition, the positions of many elements are similar enough to create the almost-alignment phenomenon.

Labels within each group, for example, are inset ever-so-slightly from the position of the group label appearing in the bounding box. The difference is not great enough to produce an effective perceptual distinction, but it is enough to be noticeable and distracting. The same is true of the two pushbutton groups and the prominent "column" of three-dimensional controls in the middle of the window. The almost-alignments are even more pronounced in the detail from Dashboard for Windows (b). While the vertical divisions are relatively uniform, the horizontal divisions on which elements in the three "rows" are positioned are essentially random.

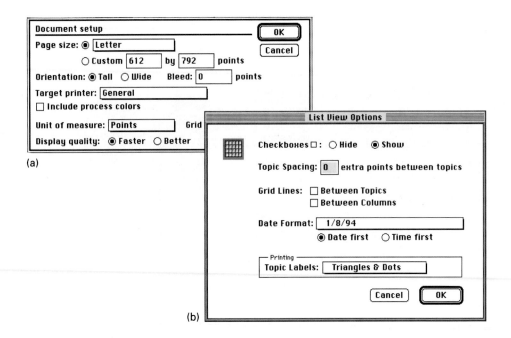

(a)

(b)

118: *Aligning labels but not controls.* Potentially useful internal structure is often squandered by failing to consider the natural margins within the layout. The controls in Aldus Freehand's Document Setup window (a) are dutifully aligned on the left (though note the intrusion of the check box) to make scanning for labels relatively straightforward. Unfortunately, the controls simply begin immediately after the label so that the controls themselves do not align with one another. This muddies the image of the dialog box and makes scanning for current values much more difficult than it needs to be. The List View Options window, from InControl (b) suffers from the same problem. In this case, however, the generous use of white space and otherwise sensible organization act to exacerbate the problem. Functionally, this arrangement is undoubtedly superior to the Document Setup example, but from an aesthetic standpoint, the general quality of the rest of the layout makes the failure to establish alignments even more prominent than it might otherwise have been.

```
┌─────────────────────────────────────────────────────────────┐
│ ┌─────────────────────────────────────────────────────────┐ │
│ │ AppleTalk ImageWriter LQ "ImageWriter"        7.0  ┌─────┐│ │
│ │                                                    │Print││ │
│ │ Quality:      ◉ Best       ○ Faster    ○ Draft     └─────┘│ │
│ │ Head Scan:    ○ Bidirectional ◉ Unidirectional    ┌──────┐│ │
│ │                                                   │Cancel││ │
│ │ Page Range:   ◉ All        ○ From: [    ] To: [  ]└──────┘│ │
│ │                                                  ┌───────┐│ │
│ │ Copies:       [ 1  ]                             │Options││ │
│ │                                                  └───────┘│ │
│ │ Output:       ◉ Normal   ○ Rough    □ Thumbnails         │ │
│ │               ◉ All Pages ○ Odd Pages ○ Even Pages       │ │
│ │               □ Back to Front □ Collate □ Spreads □ Blank Pages│ │
│ │               □ Registration Marks ○ Centered ○ Off Center│ │
│ │               OPI: [ ]              □ Calibrated Output   │ │
│ │ Tiling:       ◉ Off ○ Manual ○ Auto, overlap: [216 pt]   │ │
│ │ Color:        □ Make Separations  Plate: [All Plates]    │ │
│ │               □ Print Colors as Grays                    │ │
│ └─────────────────────────────────────────────────────────┘ │
└─────────────────────────────────────────────────────────────┘
```

119: *Alignment within but not across controls*. Even when strong margins are established for both labels and controls, problems can arise when potential margins within controls are ignored. The Apple Imagewriter LQ dialog shown here wastes the beginnings of a promising layout in the upper half of the window by permitting the internal control layouts to degenerate into total chaos in the lower half. Although the labels and controls have been neatly aligned at the highest level, the dialog is made unnecessarily difficult to scan by the density and lack of internal organization of the control groups themselves. Note too, the curious divergence from the standard Macintosh Print dialog ordering. Restoring the "Page Range" and "Copies" items to their standard positions on the first line would reclaim valuable space and allow the lower portion of the window to be structured more effectively.

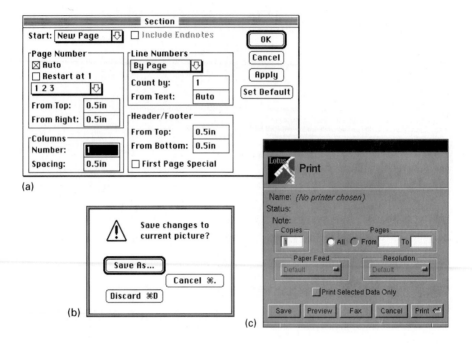

(a)

(b)

(c)

120: *False structure.* To relieve excessive display density (see facing page), many applications make heavy use of bounding boxes to more strongly group subsets of the window content. While the practice is encouraged by many environments, it should be used with restraint, since explicit structure is a very poor substitute for effective spatial segregation. This approach rarely rescues the layout and usually introduces new problems, such as the narrow gaps between the bottom of the textfields and the bounding boxes in the Section dialog from Microsoft Word (a). Under the influence of the black lines on either side, these 1-pixel gaps take on a gray tone and become emergent visual cues that compete for the user's attention as energetically as those denoting the relevant information. The bounding approach descends into absurdity when, as in the NeXTStep Print dialog (c), the boxes are used as grouping devices wherever an external label is required. Bounding boxes for single-item groups introduce more confusion than they alleviate. False structure can also arise from unintended configural effects, such as those seen in the strange confirmation dialog from DeBabelizer (b). While the layout succeeds in its main goal of being visually arresting, the highly unconventional button arrangement is exceedingly disruptive, since it breaks with both the visual language and the interaction pattern of the normal style.

bugtool properties

(Update tool) (Reset values in properties sheet)   (Update tool and .bugtraqrc file)

Configurable Fields   **Default Field Values**

Create Edit   Create Edit

☑ ☐ Keywords   ☐ ☑ Evaluation   (Category...)   deskset
  ☑ Responsible Manager   ☐ ☑ Commit to fix   (Subcategory...)   filemgr
☑ ☑ Responsible Engineer   ☐ ☑ Fixed in   (Release...)   3.0 ow_prefcs
☑ ☑ Work Around   ☐ ☑ Integrated in   (Hardware ...)   sun4c_75
☑ ☑ Suggested fix   ☐ ☐ Verified in   (OS version...)   4.1.1 revb
☑ ☑ Comments   ☑ ☑ Closed because
☑ ☑ See also   ☑ ☑ Incomplete because **Priority:**   [1][2][3][4][5]
☐ ☐ Hook 1   ☑ ☑ Submitter   **Severity:**   [1][2][3][4][5]
☐ ☐ Hook 2   ☑ ☑ Dispatch operator   **Bug/Rfe:**   [bug][rfe]
☐ ☑ Root Cause   ☐ ☐ Evaluator   **Responsible engineer:**
☐ ☑ Fix affects documentation   ☐ ☐ Commit operator   **Company:** Sun Microsystems, Inc.
☑ ☑ Interest list   ☐ ☐ Fix operator   **Employee:**
☐ ☐ Patch id   ☐ ☐ Integrating operator **Sun contact:**
☐ ☑ Company   ☐ ☐ Verify operator   **Cc:**
☐ ☑ Employee   ☐ ☐ Closeout operator   **Miscellane**
☐ ☑ OS version   ☐ ☐ Duplicate of   Number of r
☐ ☐ SO number   ☐ ☐ Old name   30   5
☐ ☐ Sun contact   ☐ ☐ Change log   (Text subw
                                                          (Auto upda
                                                          (View windo
                                                          (Start in mo
                                                          (BugTraq s
                                                          Server me

(a)

Bugtool: Properties

Category: [▽] Default Submission Info

Hardware Model: [▽] SPARCstation SLC

OS Version: [▽] SunOS 4.1

Window System: [▽] OW 3.0

Company: _____
Employee: _____
Sales Office: _____
Sun Contact: _____

(Apply) (Reset)

(b)

121: *Excessive display density.* Instead of increasing efficiency, forcing too much information into too little space typically results in a useless display. The large property window in the example above (a) originally filled an entire 19" workstation display. In an effort to circumvent this problem, the size for the controls and their label font was reduced to below normal so that the window consumed "only" 75% of the display. These changes, however, made the window harder to read and led to side effects in the alignment of elements in the right-hand column. The redesign (b) removed some functionality that had been rendered unnecessary by the restructuring of the primary window that was previously configured by these settings. The remainder of the information was reorganized into a single small window containing three separate "panes"– each containing a closely related subset of the information–between which the user can easily move using standard navigation techniques. (For views of the individual panes in the redesign, see Figure 175).

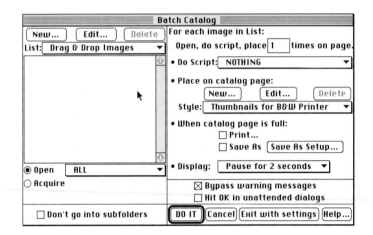

122: *All of the Above.* This amazingly unstructured layout violates nearly all of the principles we have described thus far. The exceedingly dense display has multiple areas of extreme spatial tension produced by elements that nearly touch the borders of one another or of their containing element. The radio buttons on the left, the pop-up menus on the right, and the buttons in every location, are all close enough to the adjacent visual elements to produce the kind of emergent perceptual effects seen in the Microsoft Word Section dialog (120-a). Dark patterns produced in the gaps between closely spaced elements begin to compete with the elements themselves for the viewer's attention. The presence of explicit structural elements (dividing lines) in the bottom portion of the display, far from clarifying the logical structure of the remaining elements, simply adds more spatial tension and nearly-aligned positioning to the confusion already rampant in the rest of the window.

Just as in nature systems of order govern the growth and structure of animate and inanimate matter, so human activity itself has, since the earliest times, been distinguished by the quest for order.

Josef Müller–Brockmann
Grid Systems in Graphic Design

Techniques

Organization and visual structure depend on careful planning and meticulous implementation. It is also assumed that prior analysis has revealed the conceptual structure of the information being presented. Without a clear understanding of the, effective organization is impossible. Given this information, however, four important techniques for structuring the display can be applied directly:

- Using Symmetry to Ensure Balance
- Using Alignment to Establish Visual Relationships
- Optical Adjustment for Human Vision
- Shaping the Display with Negative Space

Symmetry
Alignment
Optical Adjustment
Negative Space

It is virtually impossible to practice competent design without a command of these techniques. Fortunately, the methods are straightforward and mastery comes quickly with even a small amount of practice. Because of their near-universal applicability to interface design problems, these are among the most valuable tools at the designer's disposal.

123: In this poster by A.M. Cassandre, a strong axial symmetry balances the composition and emphasizes the ship's prow. © 1993 ARS, New York/ADAGP, Paris.

Using Symmetry to Ensure Balance

Symmetry – in all its forms – has a universal aesthetic appeal reflected in its most general connotation of *beauty as a result of balance or harmonious arrangement*. The ratio 1:1, which forms the basis of all symmetry, is easily recognized and inherently satisfying. Wherever a form is repeated, whether in translation (repetition), rotation, or reflection (mirror image), symmetry

124: The Chinese *yin-yang* symbol depends on *rotational symmetry* to evoke the impression of duality visible in its pair of opposing yet complementary forces.

acts to unify those parts of the configuration sharing similar formal characteristics. The rising popularity and effectiveness of asymmetrical layout in modern design reflects not a denial of the inherent qualities of symmetry, but rather, the need to present increasingly complex information in a task-oriented way. Symmetry remains a useful tool, particularly when the communication goal depends on balance, order, and simplicity.

Cassandre's travel poster *Normandie* (123) presents a powerful image based on its near-perfect symmetry about a central vertical axis. While effects this dramatic are rarely necessary in GUI design, the unifying qualities of the symmetrical composition are invaluable, particularly for lower-level components. In the realm of visual symbols, for example, the most powerful and memorable signs are always highly symmetrical. The Chinese *yin-yang* (124) is a familiar symbol employing rotational, rather than axial symmetry. Other

125: GUI standards, such as OSF/Motif (others include OPEN LOOK and PenPoint), rely on axial symmetry to ensure adequately balanced dialog layouts. When toolkit-level support is provided, effective design can be surprisingly automatic.

archetypal examples are seen in the star, the arrow, the cross, the swastika, the pentagram, the smiley face. In each case, axial or rotational symmetry binds the participating visual elements together to produce a single integrated form.

Symmetry provides an effective default strategy for organizing information in GUI applications. Some GUI standards such as OSF/Motif (125) strongly encourage symmetrical arrangement of windows and dialog boxes throughout the environment. The results are practically guaranteed to succeed on an aesthetic level. When the information content is not overwhelming, the sym-

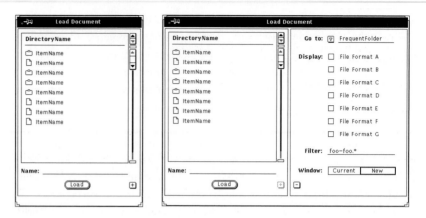

126: Symmetry about the axis of expansion enhances both the aesthetics and the understandability of multi-part windows. In the OPEN LOOK expandable window design, pressing the "+" button in the lower right(a) displays the secondary panel (b). When the widths of the panels are equalized, the axial balance of the window in its expanded state is virtually guaranteed. More importantly, the salience of the axis of symmetry enhances the division of space and accentuates the expansion and contraction buttons at the bottom-center of the window.

metrical layout provides a functionally appealing solution as well, since there is no need for emphasis or differentiation of subsets of the displayed information. Symmetrical layout simplifies the production process, whether manual or automated. For simple layout problems – such as the global organization of a dialog box – the approach is extremely effective.

For more complex layout problems, symmetry can encourage proper inter-pretation of the display at higher levels. The expandable pop-up window in Figure 126 divides its contents into basic (126-a) and advanced (126-b) functionality. By making the window layout symmetrical about the point of expansion, the functional division is reinforced as the visual division of the window into two equivalent spaces becomes more apparent. In addition, the symmetrical arrangement of the expansion and contraction (+/-) buttons across the axis at the bottom of the window makes their complementary role obvious without the need for intrusive verbal labels.

Symmetry ensures balance and clear organization, if sometimes at the expense of visual interest. Fortunately, the goal of effective interface design is not to entertain or excite, but to present information efficiently and non-intrusively, so the restful character of the symmetrical layout is often per-fectly appropriate. Given the ease with which it can be applied, the tech-nique is an invaluable starting point for effective design.

[Symmetry] is a useful and almost foolproof method for the solution of compositional problems for the inexperienced and unskilled visual message-maker. The rules to follow are as simple and clear as can be, and if they are followed rigidly, the results are predictably attractive. You just cannot go wrong.

Donis A. Dondis
A Primer of Visual Literacy

Because symmetry contributes to good design on several dimensions at once, its prominent historical role should not be surprising. In fact, asymmetrical design concepts are a very recent phenomenon that found widespread acceptance in print materials only in the 20th century. In contrast to the complexity of effective asymmetrical layout, maintaining symmetry is a relatively straightforward process that can be used to ensure adequate balance in almost any design:

Summary: Symmetry

1　Identify the axes along which symmetry will be established. In visual interface design this decision usually boils down to whether horizontal and/or vertical symmetry.

2　Symmetry about the vertical axis is more prevalent in human perception and is generally more useful in visual displays.

3　Center the information on the axis of symmetry by carefully balancing the amount of information on each side of the axis. The information need not form a literal mirror image provided the mass and extent are equalized.

4　Make sure the axis of symmetry is itself centered within the overall display context (i.e., the window or icon in question).

5　Use the squint test to verify the results.

Symmetry (at least in the axial sense) need not be present in every design. It is merely the simplest of several compositional techniques for ensuring good balance. Because of their inherent stability and restfulness, heavy use of symmetrical layouts can lead to "unexciting" displays. While this may be a drawback for a poster series or a retail packaging, it is perfectly appropriate for a user interface.

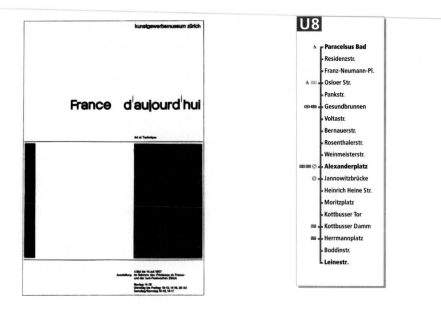

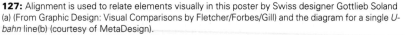

127: Alignment is used to relate elements visually in this poster by Swiss designer Gottlieb Soland (a) (From Graphic Design: Visual Comparisons by Fletcher/Forbes/Gill) and the diagram for a single *U-bahn* line(b) (courtesy of MetaDesign).

Using Alignment to Establish Visual Relationships

Effective design depends critically on meaningful global structure. Positional *alignment* of elements reduces the complexity of a display by making the global form cleaner and more understandable. By limiting exceptions to the positioning rules obeyed by elements within the composition, alignment makes intentional deviations more salient. Used in conjunction with negative space, alignment is an important tool for constructing visual hierarchies. The poster by Gottlieb Soland (127–a) uses one of the prominent internal margins in the French tricolor as a natural axis along which the bulk of the information in the poster is organized. The two pieces of text that hang to the left of this margin enjoy the highest degree of prominence available in the composition. Similarly, the route diagram for an U-bahn line on the BVG (127–b) uses vertical alignment to associate the station names to the right of the route line with the connection icons on the left.

Alignment is the most important means of establishing relationships among elements. In addition to providing the most general technique, it is among the most perceptually powerful and immediate. Objects in alignment create a strong attraction to one another even when separated by large distances. The eye exhibits a natural bias toward the perception of regular structure.

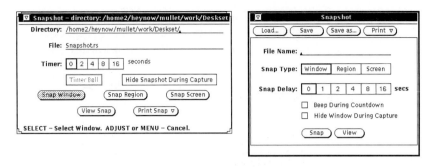

128: The redesigned layout (a) of an existing OpenWindows productivity application (b) shows the effectiveness of aligning elements to simplify the display. By re-factoring the haphazard group of five buttons at the bottom of the window (b) into two buttons and three settings–and by aligning the resulting groups–the functional organization of the tool is greatly clarified.

The viewer will try to make sense of an image by dividing it into regions along major structural axes. Careful alignment of elements in the display makes these axes crisp and clear. Noticeable tension results, however, when elements positioned near the axis don't quite align with it.

The additional "information" introduced by accidental and irrelevant variation in placement or sizing of interface elements is simply visual noise that inhibits communication. In the OpenWindows 2.0 Snapshot tool, for example (128-a), five buttons at the bottom of the window are positioned with no apparent spatial relation to the options and parameters appearing in the window above them. The redesigned layout created for OpenWindows Version 3 (128-b) shows the power of alignment in eliminating distracting irregularities and reinforcing meaningful relationships. In addition to replacing three of the buttons with the more appropriate exclusive settings, the design enhances the organization of the display by bringing all major commands, options, and parameters into alignment on the same vertical axis.

The tightly structured modular layout of the Workspace Manager in Hewlett-Packard's Visual User Environment (129) makes alignment almost automatic. With two minor exceptions in the lower corners, every major

129: A crisp module (see following chapter) ensures the clean alignment of elements in the *VUE Workspace Manager* from Hewlett-Packard. Compare the clear structure revealed here to the jostling confusion seen in the same company's *Dashboard for Windows* product seen in Figure 117 (b).

structural element aligns with at least one other in a simple, harmonious fashion. This crisply defined structure prevents the layout from becoming overly busy despite the fact that the Workspace Manager depends on component modules of four different sizes. The regularity produced by effective alignment makes the surface of the VUE "dashboard" far more transparent than its much busier counterpart in the Windows environment (see detail in Figure 117-b)

130: When alignments can be extended across windows in a multi-window application, the benefits of coherent visual organization accrue at a higher level.

Effective visual design establishes structural relationships wherever possible within an image or composition. When practical, structural relationships can even be extended across multiple windows in the application. The video conferencing application shown above is used to narrowcast live video over Sun's campus network. Because the individual windows are designed to relate to one another (and to the standard screen dimensions) at their default sizes, the application is far more unified, both functionally and aesthetically, than most multi-window applications. The control elements in the narrow windows on the left share a common width and internal subdivisions allowing vertical alignments to emerge naturally when the windows themselves are vertically aligned. The size and placement of the two upper windows relates them to the larger window (the main video screen) – with which they align horizontally – while helping to separate them from the transient lower window whose boundary falls on the same margin.

A regulating line is a safeguard against arbitrariness. It is a way of checking a work created in enthusiasm; it is the schoolboy's proof positive, the mathematician's QED.

Le Corbusier
L'Esprit Nouveau

The effect of alignment on a visual display is analogous to that of a conductor marking time for an orchestra. By coordinating the visual activity of many diverse elements, alignment works to ensure that all parts work together regardless of their individual roles. Alignment is a necessary (though not always sufficient) step toward a coherent display. This four-step technique is a good starting point:

**Summary:
Alignment**

1 Identify the major boundaries in the existing layout, and look for ways to enhance them by moving additional elements into alignment with them.

2 Look for elements and margins – both internal and external – that almost, but not quite, align with one another and bring them into alignment by altering the size or position of one or both elements.

3 Look for free-standing elements and make sure they are aligned with something else in the display – either a major margin or some other element to which they are related.

4 If an element cannot be related to anything else in the display, try to relate it to the proportions of the display itself by positioning the element to correspond to a regular division of the space.

You will be surprised at how quickly the establishment of proper alignment become second nature to you. Moreover, you will become increasingly aware of disorganized layouts and wonder why such simple goals receive such a pathetic level of support in most current-generation GUI toolkits. As exasperating as it may be, the extra development effort is almost always rewarded in the visual quality of the final product.

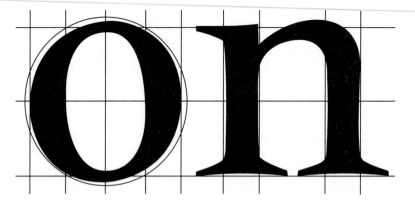

131: Proper alignment of curvilinear elements to the typographic baseline and the x-height of a font requires compensation for optical effects. Curves must extend slightly *beyond* the point of physical alignment to create the appearance of alignment. After Ruder (1981).

Optical Adjustment for Human Vision

Visual design is grounded in perceptual, rather than physical phenomena, so compensation for the peculiarities of human vision is often required. Proper visual alignment depends critically on careful *optical adjustment* to compensate for differences in shape and contour of the elements being aligned. In typography, for example, characters with curved bottoms must extend slightly below the baseline or to the left of the column margin (131) or the line will appear to undulate in waves across the page. Optical adjustment is a general phenomenon that applies not only to alignment, but to *scaling* and *spacing* as well. Curved elements in general must project slightly farther beyond the margin than linear elements, while more acute angles must project even further to achieve the same effect. The more acute the angle, more compensation is needed to maintain the proper alignment.

132: With *physically equivalent* scaling, rounded or acute forms appear too small relative to rectangular elements.

Typography   Typography

Typography   Typography

133: Optical spacing in typography depends not on equalizing the distance between characters (a), but on equalizing the area in the counterform between characters (b). Due to their larger counterforms, characters with curved edges must be spaced more tightly than those with straight edges.

In *optical spacing* (133), the rule of thumb is to equalize the area rather than the distance between elements. In typography, the tightest letterspacing is reserved for adjacent characters with curved edges or horizontally projecting strokes. The widest spacing is allotted to pairs with adjacent vertical stroke, with the remaining pairings falling somewhere in between. Although the phenomenon occurs most frequently in typography, the same set of issues arises whenever dissimilar forms must be evenly distributed across space.

To produce *optically* equivalent scaling (132, 134), circles must be slightly larger than squares and diamonds slightly larger than circles. The examples below show the physically equivalent (132) and optically adjusted (134) versions of these shapes. This phenomenon arises frequently in icon design,

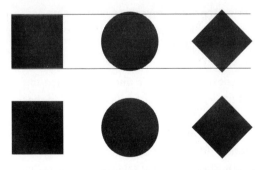

134: Extending rounded or acute elements slightly beyond the target dimension produces *optically equivalent* scaling.

where rounded or acute-edged images are combined with square images sharing the same maximum area (135). In order to match the scale of the rest of the program, square icons must be limited in size to substantially less than the maximum dimensions permitted by the icon format. The principle of acuteness applies here as well: the more acute the angle, the farther beyond the margin it must extend to be visually correct. Only icons with acute angles should be allowed to continue all the way to the limits of the image area.

Effective visual design accounts for the optical qualities of every design element and provides compensation where necessary. There is, unfortunately, no sure method for determining the necessary degree of adjustment mechanically. Careful observation and extended practice are the only routes to developing the necessary skills. Figure 135 shows examples of optical

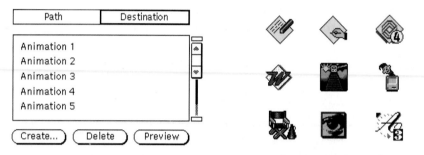

135: Optical alignment requires that open or round-ended controls extend slightly beyond margins established by rectangular elements (a). Optical scaling suggests that rectangular images be held to less than the maximum size to avoid dominating curved or angular images in the ensemble (b).

adjustment in GUI design. The most prominent parallel axis within the interface component should be used to establish the alignment relationship. Note that for this reason, non-critical elements such as scrollbars or auxiliary buttons may project beyond the margin of alignment in order to allow the stronger contour of the main control to create a more powerful visual impression. This is the GUI equivalent of "hanging" a quote – allowing the quotation mark to extend beyond the left margin of a block of text so that the first letter of the first line will align with those in subsequent lines. The goal of effective design is to create apparent visual relationships between conceptually related elements. Optical adjustment ensures that these relationships arise when, and only when, the conceptual relationship makes it appropriate.

Often inconspicuous, optical adjustment is the precise visual alignment of typographic elements in space... (that) is necessary for visual clarity.

Rob Carter, Ben Day, Phillip Meggs
Typographic Design: Form and Communication

As evidenced by these examples, optical effects are inherent in most visual design problems. Even the familiar vocabularies of geometrical and typographic form, which we have long taken for granted, depend critically on subtle phenomena that continue to elude the naive viewer precisely *because* they are normally corrected in advance by the design professional. With the current explosion of design activity in non-traditional settings (such as software development organizations), a widespread understanding of these effects is becoming increasingly important. Regardless of the particular application, optical adjustment is a three-step process:

Summary:
Optical Adjustment

1 Determine the *true* point of alignment, dimension of extent, or unit of spacing required. Translate this into the "normal" margin that would be occupied by a rectangular element in the same position.

2 Extend elements beyond the margin according to the sharpness of their adjacent angle. The greater the acuteness of the angle, the farther it will need to extend beyond the "normal" margin.

3 Use a "close-up" version of the squint test encompassing only the elements in question to verify alignment with the intended margin or visual equivalence of the relevant intervals.

As your experience with this technique increases, you will quickly become familiar with the situations where adjustment is usually necessary. In time, you will be able to approximate the required compensation even before you attempt the sort of fine-grained adjustment described here.

131: Proper alignment of curvilinear elements to the typographic baseline and the x-height of a font requires compensation for optical effects. Curves must extend slightly *beyond* the point of physical alignment to create the appearance of alignment. After Ruder (1981).

Shaping the Display with Negative Space

Designers in every arena are frequently pressured by their clients to include as much information as possible on every page or in every screen. Particularly in user interface design, there is a heavy emphasis on utilizing every pixel. But apparently empty regions are, in fact, being utilized in a well-organized display. They play the crucial role of directing the viewer's attention to the regions where important information is provided and allowing the global structure of the composition to assume a meaningful configuration. Without *negative space* – which is simply another way of describing the figural qualities of the ground on which the figure appears – there can be no meaningful global structure.

Negative space is often called "white space" in print design, where paper is the common, static background. Every competent designer knows that *white space is not wasted space* – it is a powerful tool that allows the designer to direct the viewer's attention to critical regions of the display. The "emptiness" of the left half of the poster by Josef Müller–Brockmann (136–a) focuses the viewer's attention almost involuntarily on a single line of text. Although the text is no larger or otherwise more prominent than the other information in the display its spatial isolation transforms it into the primary

```
┌─────────────────────────────────────────────────────────────┐
│ LaserWriter Page Setup                        5.2   ┌─────────┐│
│                                                     │   OK    ││
│ Paper: ⦿ US Letter  ○ A4 Letter   ○ Tabloid        └─────────┘│
│        ○ US Legal   ○ B5 Letter                    ┌─────────┐│
│                                                     │ Cancel  ││
│        Reduce or ┌────┐%    Printer Effects:       └─────────┘│
│        Enlarge:  │100 │     ☒ Font Substitution?   ┌─────────┐│
│                  └────┘                             │ Options ││
│        Orientation          ☒ Text Smoothing?      └─────────┘│
│                             ☒ Graphics Smoothing?  ┌─────────┐│
│         [↑👤] [↑👤]         ☒ Faster Bitmap Printing?│  Help  ││
│                                                     └─────────┘│
└─────────────────────────────────────────────────────────────┘
```

137: Three large areas of negative space in the Apple LaserWriter Page Setup dialog effectively segregate the three major control groups to produce meaningful global structure.

element (the title) of the entire composition. Herbert Bayer's cover design (136–b) uses negative space to create a strong vertical axis and to isolate and emphasize the title and the Bauhaus identity symbol at the bottom of the page. These powerful spatial effects can be achieved only when sufficient area remains as part of the ground from which the figure emerges.

Because screen space is always at a premium in GUI design, negative space must be employed judiciously. It's value is, if anything, greater than in print applications simply because of the dense displays. The use of negative space in the Macintosh Page Setup dialog box (137), while not as powerful as the examples on the facing page, is effective nonetheless. Here negative space is used to set off the response buttons, the printer effects options, and the criti-

```
┌═══════════════════════════════════════════════════════════┐
║                      Column Info                           ║
╠═══════════════════════════════════════════════════════════╣
│   ⓘ    Name: │Column                              │        │
│  INFO                                                       │
│         Type: │   Text      │   Left Aligned    │          │
│                                                             │
│  Data List: ┌──────────────────────────────────┐┌─┐        │
│             │                                   ││⇧│        │
│             │                                   │└─┘        │
│             │                                   │           │
│             │                                   │┌─┐        │
│             │                                   ││⇩│        │
│             └──────────────────────────────────┘└─┘        │
│             □ Sort & Match text using Data List order       │
│  Entry Helpers: │ None                        │             │
│  Auto-Enter:    │ Nothing                     │             │
│  Sort Order:    │ Normal     │      ┌────────┐ ┌──────┐     │
│                              │      │ Cancel │ │  OK  │     │
│                                     └────────┘ └──────┘     │
└─────────────────────────────────────────────────────────────┘
```

138: The excellent use of negative space and alignment on the left side of this dialog (from the InControl to-do list manager) is enough to overcome the unsystematic control extents on the right-hand margin.

cal scale and orientation parameters. A little more space above and below the scaling control would make this layout even more effective, but the existing design uses negative space more effectively than most window layouts. An even more clearly organized display appears in Figure 138. The Column Info dialog from InControl provides more than enough space to permit easy location and scanning of the labels in the left-hand column and the response buttons in the lower right.

139: The importance of negative space (and alignment) in making labels easy to scan is clear in these examples. When labels are placed above controls (a), the eye must skip over the intervening elements, which can be difficult even if the labels share a selective perceptual cue (such as a bold font). Scanning is simplified when the labels are separated by non-confusable white space (b).

The OPEN LOOK property windows in the Figure 139 compare the use of value and spatial isolation in separating groups of information – in this case, controls and their labels – for independent processing. OPEN LOOK is designed to make it easy to rapidly scan lists of labels to locate the desired control. This works well when the labels are physically separated from the controls. When labels are placed above the controls rather than to the left, (as is often done to preserve precious screen real-estate), the ease of scanning suffers tremendously. For the "labels above" approach to work effectively, additional visual information is needed to sharpen the distinction between labels and controls and produce the proper layering effect. Cleveland and McGill (1984, 1985) have shown position to be the most effective coding dimension in graphical displays. The use of negative space in display design is simply the most effective means of contrasting different categories of items on the basis of their spatial location.

Some space must be narrow so that other space may be wide,
and some space must be emptied so that other space may be filled.

Robert Bringhurst
The Elements of Typographic Style

White space is needed for proper figure-ground integration as well as for the effective manipulation of local compositional dynamics. The eye must be directed – both globally and at each major stopping point – toward the cues needed to locate the information of interest. Careful allocation of white space is the most effective technique for achieving this goal:

Summary:
Negative Space

1 Review the organization of the information into a prioritized set of chunks of manageable size. Note: the groups identified for techniques described previously serve this purpose as well.

2 Ensure spatial separation of independent units of information by adding extra white space between chunks. Extra space is needed even if explicit boundary delimiters are used!

3 Determine which elements – and these often include individual elements used as labels for larger, less important chunks – require additional visual emphasis.

4 Increase the white space surrounding critical elements by moving them into the margins, by moving other elements away from them.

5 Always remember that *white space is not wasted space!* Its role is to direct the viewer's attention to adjacent regions containing critical information.

Spatial segregation is the most powerful of the perceptual variables. It is also among the most costly, so its judicious use is essential. White space can be used to great effect in calling out the most important display elements when strong size or value contrasts are not available. When redundant coding is present, the need for spatial segregation decreases, though it rarely disappears entirely. The exact amount of space to allocate for display structuring is always a judgment call, but you will rarely go wrong by "calling out" the highest level of structure for which multiple tags exist within a given display.

Module and Program

5

Communication-oriented visual design is always concerned with the development of *programs*, or comprehensive systems of organization. Whether the designer's product spans multiple pages in a single printed piece or dozens of manufactured artifacts sharing a common design language, programmatic design is an essential facilitator. Programs are based on repeated sizes and proportions (module) or upon forms and ideas (theme) that bring regularity and structure to the user experience. The controlled variation seen in a well-designed program provides the flexibility needed for innovation while maintaining the integrity of a coherent aesthetic experience.

Aspects of program are applied throughout the spectrum of design activity. A corporate identity is not created by simply designing a mark. A printed book or brochure is not a singular entity; nor is it a collection of independent pages that can be designed in isolation. A GUI environment is not merely a random collection of programs that happen to operate on a bitmap display, nor is a GUI application a random assembly of "off-the-shelf" idioms and application-specific concepts. The designer must establish a program with sufficient flexibility to accommodate the demands of the each part while molding the components into an approachable, understandable system.

By establishing the rhythm and tone of the solution space, module and program orchestrate the synthesis of a complex solution for both designer and end-user. The benefits of a systematic approach include:

140: A standard design program ensures that informational brochures for the hundreds of sites administered by the U.S. National Park Service share the same high level of quality and consistency. Design by Vignelli Associates. (See also color plate 8).

Structure. Module is intimately related to structure. The module reflects and draws justification from structural requirements while the structure is revealed and reinforced through consistent application of the module. In most effective programs, the internal structure is drawn directly from the requirements of the communication problem. Highway signage, for example, has a clearly defined viewing distance, angle, and duration, all of which are used to determine the module upon which the program is based.

Predictability. Programmatic design simplifies the communication task by preparing the user to respond to a small number of familiar patterns in a predictable way. The critical nature of the information being conveyed means that traffic signage must be familiar enough to be processed accurately even in the absence of focused attention. The simplicity and regularity of the program make it easier to learn, easier to remember, and easier to apply correctly when a quick decision is required.

Efficiency. Modular design permits great economies of production once the general scheme has been extended to cover the entire problem space. The detailed plan that results allows large quantities of high-quality output to be produced in very little time while requiring minimal expertise. Because the program is clearly defined, highway signage can be assembled with remarkable quality and consistency by the maintenance arm of each local Department of Transportation instead of by a single central authority. This kind of efficiency is leveraged in exactly the same way by the corporate identity program, the weekly news magazine, and the GUI standard.

Grid-based design is essential to the development of effective large-scale information systems. The design program (the UniGrid) for informational brochures developed by Massimo Vignelli Associates for the U.S. National Park Service (140) imposes a coherent structure on the printed materials distributed at hundreds of Park Service locations. This beautifully designed system accommodates ten different page formats to address the needs of sites as diverse as the sprawling Yellowstone National Park and the urban Freedom Trail in Boston. Each brochure contains a map of the site, which determines the format and orientation of the brochure. The broad black banner and bold headline spanning the top of each sheet unify the formats and provide a visual anchor for the viewer. Standard column widths and typographic conventions (141) ensure quality, consistency, and economy across the full range of publications, freeing the Park Service design staff to focus on content development. The program based on the Unigrid retains its freshness and vitality even after nearly twenty years as the most successful design system in the American public sector.

Background:
Grid-Based Design

141: The flexible layout system used in the brochures for the U.S. National Park Service provides a paradigmatic example of programmatic design. The system is based on a single grid – the UniGrid – which is capable of supporting ten different publication formats. Because the same underlying grid governs the layout of each publication, even brochures that differ greatly in size share a unified typography, layout style, and folded size. Design by Vignelli Associates.

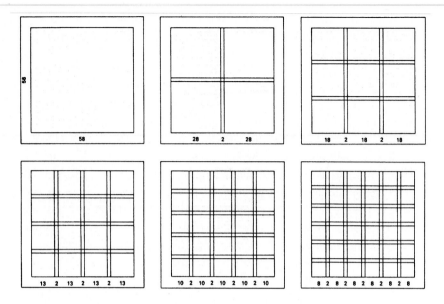

142: These typographic grids for book design subdivide the page uniformly into one to six columns. Grids for GUI design have important differences, but the goal of providing systematic structure is the same. From *Basic Typography: Design with Letters*, by Ruedi Rüegg, ABC-Verlag, Zurich, 1987.

The grid is the conceptual embodiment of the design program. It allows the static layout principles described in the previous chapter to be codified and propagated consistently across a series of displays, whether they are separate printed pieces, a series of pages in a book, or different screens in a graphical user interface. By structuring each presentation along similar lines, the grid ensures that users will benefit from experience with the system as they learn to predict where a particular piece of information will be found.

The grid is a tool that helps the designer maintain a coherent program that becomes apparent to users as their experience with the system grows. While the grid can greatly simplify and rationalize the design and production process, its use need not inhibit the development of novel solutions when unanticipated problems arise. When new, general problems are resolved in a systematic way, the grid can be modified to incorporate new techniques and exploited as a vehicle for propagating changes throughout the program.

Figures 142 and 143 show simple typographic grids for book design and some typical resulting layouts. Note the different formal qualities – particu-

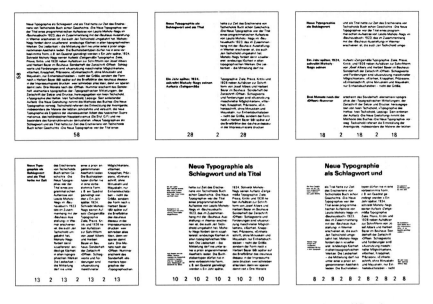

143: Each of the grids in Figure 142 leaves a distinct imprint on the resulting layout. When the *same* grid is used throughout a book – or GUI application – this imprint becomes a unifying element for the entire work. From *Basic Typography: Design with Letters*, by Ruedi Rüegg, ABC-Verlag, Zurich, 1987.

larly the density, rhythm, and opacity – of the layout programs dividing the space into one to six columns. A one-column grid (142 – a) provides almost no structure to guide the eye, and the page becomes impossibly dense (the layout is all too reminiscent of many overcrowded dialog box designs). As the number of columns increases, the flexibility of the program grows, since the designer can choose to respect individual columns or to aggregate them into larger units providing a pleasing contrast in the layout (143 – c, 143 – e, 143 – f). Images add an additional degree of freedom to the grid, but they are handled in the same way as text, with major grid divisions determining where important text and image boundaries should fall.

The grid divides the page rationally into a small number of primitive units along each dimension and permits important structural elements to be placed consistently across displays. Note that the grid specifies the widths of gutters (the spaces between columns) as well as columns and includes both horizontal and vertical divisions. Typographic grid systems are more than simple-minded graph paper. They are carefully structured programs designed to produce readily apparent global structure, harmonious proportions and aesthetically pleasing contrasts, and adequate readability given the

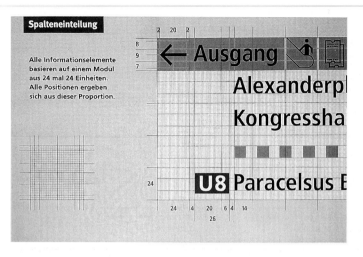

144: The grid's value extends well beyond page design. A modular approach is essential in large scale public information systems such as this signage program for the Berlin Transit Authority (BVG). Courtesy of MetaDesign.

chosen text and display fonts. Far from locking the designer into a rigid, overbearing regime, the grid frees the designer to worry about more central issues dealing with the content itself.

Grids have widespread applicability to all areas of two and three-dimensional design. Swiss designer Josef Müller-Brockmann uses grids extensively even for individual poster designs. The grid, however, truly comes into its own in the design of large information systems whose complexity would quickly become unmanageable otherwise. The signage program developed for the Berlin Transit Authority (BVG) by MetaDesign is a good example of the rational structure provided by a coherent system (144). The grid's basic

145: Grids can also be used to govern the internal structure of an image program. The familiar U.S. DOT pictograms are based on an underlying grid defining standard element positions and orientations that are applied throughout the image set.

unit is the square used to relate the size of the primary typography and the system's pictograms and directional arrows. The subdivisions of this basic unit and the offsets for various critical margin points are designed to ensure proper spacing between letters, words, and lines. By fully specifying the system in advance, the designers can turn control over to the client without foregoing the possibility of quality results.

Even image programs can benefit greatly from grid-based design, as evidenced by the familiar pictograms developed for mass transit signage by the U.S. DOT (145). In addition to establishing the overall size limit for each pictogram, the grid restricts positions and orientations of major design elements to ensure a strong family resemblance when the images are viewed as a set. Note how the major internal structural division in each pictogram falls on the grid's centerline. Note too how the restriction of angular elements to the 45-degree orientation, along with the repetition of basic forms across images, promotes consistency across the image set.

Principles

Design programs represent the pinnacle of achievement for systematic, communication-oriented visual design. The central element of any successful program is the grid, which provides a unifying framework for the diverse elements of the system. This framework must exhibit a focus that is natural for the information being conveyed while retaining the flexibility needed to deal with a variety of communication problems. The need to reinforce the program through consistent application of the framework must be balanced against the need to make conscious exceptions in dealing with unanticipated material.

Focus
Flexibility
Consistent Application

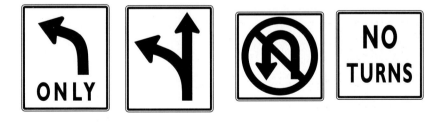

146: Traffic control signage employs a standard visual language combining textual and graphic notations. Because the signs are used fairly consistently throughout a nation's roadways, their meanings become clear "at a glance" to the experienced driver.

147: A crisp focus on the unit square is apparent in both positive and negative space in this concert poster by Josef Müller-Brockmann.

Focus

Any successful program should have a clear focus on one or a small number of modular units that reveal the underlying spatial logic of the program. In this exquisitely-structured concert poster by Josef Müller-Brockmann (147), the square embodies the basic unit of composition. Virtually every layout decision can be traced back to the size and position of the squares in the central vertical column. Major spatial divisions are multiples of one, one-half, or one-fourth of the unit embodied in the basic square. The resulting display ensures that each element is tightly integrated with the emergent whole while retaining the playful sense of randomness and freedom needed to characterize the music it promotes.

The same crisp focus on a central module is seen in the Japanese *tatami* (meaning, *"grid"*) mat system. The tatami system uses a dynamic symmetry based on the double square (148) to produce a space with clearly defined subdivisions upon which the traditional tea ceremony is based. The module used in the tatami system is based on an appropriately human-centered scale to bring important points on the "grid" within easy reach. By using the same grid to structure the dimensions of the tea room itself, the tatami system allows the common focus to unify the person, space, and actions.

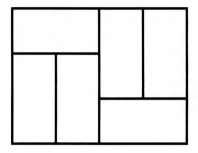

148: The human scale (3 x 6 ft.) of the *tatami* mat governs both the actions of participants and the subdivision of space in the Japanese tea ceremony.

A clear focus enhances the readability of a display by introducing a rhythm and regularity that makes make the structure predictable and explicit. These qualities simplify the movement of visual attention across the display by allowing the viewer to unconsciously estimate the distance between resting points and to skip over uninteresting portions when necessary. In this sense, the well-focused program functions very much like a spatial map of the information domain. Musical scores (149) provide one of the finest examples of this characteristic. Despite their flexibility and occasional complexity, they must communicate clearly and concisely to allow the musician to effectively divide attention between instrument and music.

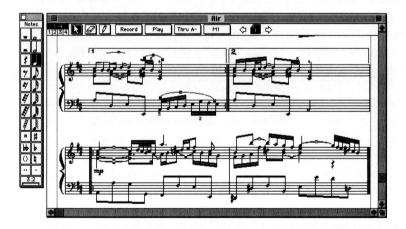

149: A clear focus on a well-chosen module produces a visual rhythm that pleases the eye with its patterning effect. A clear underlying unit also allows an image to be read as a spatial map in representing temporal or statistical phenomena.

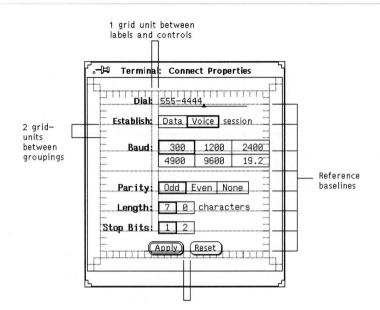

150: The focus on a key dimension in the design of a widget set allows a simple, parameterized layout system to be used throughout the OPEN LOOK GUI. Because each widget is structured in relation to the baseline of its typographic label, the widgets can be arbitrarily combined with uniform spacing on a standard grid.

A well-defined focus is essential in the graphical user interface as well. Individual applications and even layouts within an application will inevitably define their own higher-level structure, but important structuring devices are established most effectively at lower levels. A GUI standard, and ideally the user interface toolkits that support it, should provide mechanisms that make the systematic sizing and positioning of user interface elements the path of least resistance for the developer.

In the OPEN LOOK GUI, for example, elements are scaled and positioned according to a module based on one of four standard font sizes. Because the user interface elements are designed around an common module (the font size) and specify a common reference point (typographic baseline), a simple set of layout rules defining the canonical property window layout yields surprisingly credible results using only a single parameter. Designers position elements relative to the layout grid shown in Figure 150. Controls fill the window uniformly from top to bottom with the designer leaving one unit of space between controls, two units between groups of controls, and no extra space within controls spanning multiple rows.

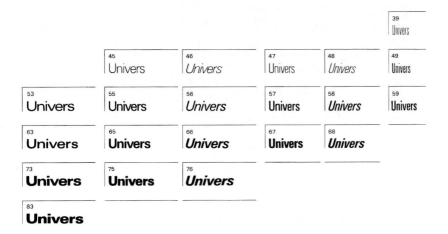

151: The incredible flexibility and dynamic range of Adrian Frutiger's Univers typographic program make it one of the most useful families ever created. The first digit in the numbering system indicates the weight of the face, while the second indicates both the set width and slant (even numbers denote italic faces; odd numbers denote increasingly narrow Roman faces), with "5" as the norm in either case. From *Typographic Design: Form and Communication*, Carter, Day, and Meggs (1985).

Flexibility

Flexibility in dealing with unanticipated situations is a hallmark of any successful design program. The best systems are consciously designed to encompass boundary conditions, since this is where breakdowns most often occur. Few systems provide a better example of this approach than Adrian Frutiger's Univers typographic family (151). The boldest and lightest faces push the limits of legibility, and the remainder of the program is designed to uniformly fill the space between these two extremes. The individual faces share ascender, descender, and character heights, allowing the varieties to be freely intermixed and the broad selection of available weights allows the family to represent almost any typographic contrast.

A similar flexibility is seen in the identity program created by Paul Rand for the design studios of IDEO (152). The individual elements can be presented in a wide range of permutations while still retaining the connectivity that

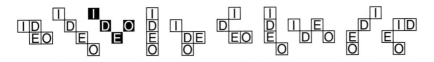

152: The flexible identity program created by Paul Rand for IDEO Product Associates reflects the creative, exploratory dynamic of the design process itself. In this program, the unifying element is not the order in which the elements appear, but rather, the rules that govern their connectivity.

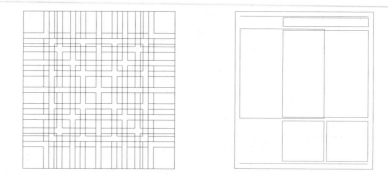

153: These unusual grid designs by Karl Gerstner (a) and Josef Müller-Brockmann (b) underscore the flexibility of grid-based design. The grid is a tool reflecting the overriding theme of the program, not a straightjacket into which each new design must be coerced. When the requirements of the program change, the grid must change as well.

defines the corporate identity. The flexible application is particularly appropriate in this program, since it emphasizes the wide range of capabilities and creative focus of the company. The importance of flexibility, it should be noted, does not eliminate the need for focus: in fact, flexibility makes focus even more important if the programmatic nature of the design is to be made apparent.

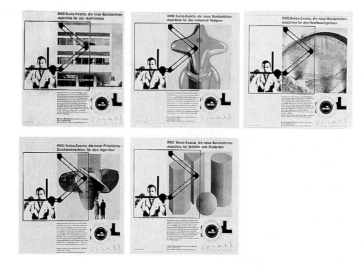

154: The series of advertisements based on the grid in Figure 153 (b) shows the integration of the internal structure of the photographic elements with the global structure laid down by the grid. Design by Josef Müller-Brockmann.

Layout grids can provide flexibility as well. Karl Gerstner's grid for the Swiss magazine Capital (153–a) is complex but recognizable as the internal structure is grasped. The grid provides for two, three, four, five, or six column layouts, each defined by a series of squares that grow smaller as the number of columns increases. The wide variety of layouts possible within such a flexible system contrast sharply with the closely synchronized advertisement series (154) designed by Josef Müller-Brockmann using a much more problem-specific grid (153–b). This example shows that grids need not be restricted to simple, regular constructions, and that they can be varied to suit the unique requirements of the composition or the task domain.

Layout programs developed for GUI applications demand an additional dimension of flexibility in supporting dynamic layout. Since windows can generally be resized by the user, they must be able to recompute their layout on demand. Most toolkits for the X window system, for example, support some kind of higher-level *geometry management* system based on constraints satisfied continuously as the window is resized (155). In this system, the grid is defined relative to the current size of the window (expressed as a percentage of its overall dimensions) rather than in absolute terms. While the designer may choose to enforce a minimum of maximum size for the window, users are otherwise free to tailor its dimensions to address the demands of the task.

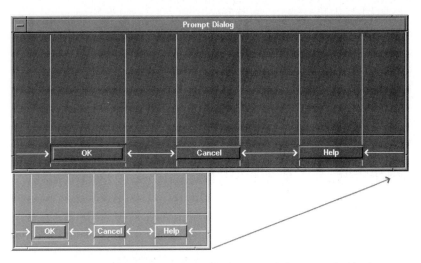

155: Constraint-based toolkits permitting "on-the-fly" layout as windows are resized by the user require grid systems with the flexibility to support dynamic re-configuration.

156: Consistent layout, typography, imagery, and color characterize the exquisite Dutch paper currency designed by R.D.E. Oxenaar. From the size and position of the denomination to the similarity of the portraits, these bills exemplify the *unity in diversity* that forms the core of every program. (See Color Plate 9, for additional examples). Photos courtesy of RC Publications, Inc., New York.

Consistent Application

For any design program to be effective it must be used consistently wherever it appears to ensure that its programmatic aspects will become visually apparent after even minimal exposure. The rich visual texture and extensive use of color and layering in the Dutch paper currency (156) are central aspects of the visual identity of this widely recognized program. The rich, colorful designs play a functional as well as an aesthetic role. The high end materials and processes needed to reproduce the delicate engravings and patterned overlays are intended to make counterfeiting difficult, if not impossible. In addition to its saturated colors and rich textures, the Dutch currency

157: A corporate identity becomes apparent only when the visual language seen in the identity mark and usage guidelines is applied consistently to the wide variety of products associated with the modern corporation. The program becomes the public image of the company.

employs a standard layout grid to produce a tight structural consistency across denominations. Note the consistent size and position of the portrait, denomination (both verbal and numeric), and texture band in each note. This visual consistency ties the bills together in a coherent system and is an essential aid to users who frequently need to thumb quickly through a wad of bills under poor viewing conditions.

Corporate identity programs depend heavily on the consistent use of color, imagery, and typography to establish a clear visual expression of the values, culture, and image of the ethereal corporate entity. These programs pose great challenges for consistent application because of the bewildering variety of objects that must receive the corporate mark (157-158). The program's elements must be applicable with minimal alteration to objects of vastly different scales, ranging from monumental architectural signage and vehicular graphics through product, packaging, and collateral, and on down to forms, stationery, and business cards. Successful identity programs may exploit nearly any visual characteristic, but the selected characteristic must hold up across the full range of applications and it must be applied consistently in each of these contexts.

Interface applications for programmatic design have requirements that are surprisingly similar to the corporate or product identity program. The familiar "look and feel" of standard GUI environments such as the Macintosh Desktop or Microsoft Windows helps users know what to expect when a new dialog box appears. The consistent appearance, placement, and meaning of important visual cues make it easier for users to interpret and respond to new situations as they arise. Like the harried consumer thumbing quickly

158: In addition to the products manufactured by the corporation, a corporate identity program must encompass the physical plant, equipment, printed collateral, and often a wide variety of novelties and collateral items, each with its own specific scale and material requirements.

```
┌─────────────────────────────────────────────────────────────────────┐
│ LaserWriter  "LaserWriter IINT"                    5.2    ┌─────────┐ │
│                                                          │   OK    │ │
│ Copies:█           Pages:◉ All  ○ From:       To:       └─────────┘ │
│                                                          ┌─────────┐ │
│ Cover Page:   ◉ No ○ First Page ○ Last Page             │ Cancel  │ │
│                                                          └─────────┘ │
│ Paper Source:◉ Paper Cassette  ○ Manual Feed            │  Help   │ │
│                                                          └─────────┘ │
└─────────────────────────────────────────────────────────────────────┘
```

159: The standard Print dialog is used consistently by virtually all Macintosh applications, creating a common point of reference even for relatively inexperienced users.

through a stack of bills, users often scan quickly through the dialog boxes in a GUI application, searching for a command or control whose location they have forgotten. Visual and structural consistency across windows, menus, and dialog boxes is as important in this context as in the paper currency described above.

A coherent layout program extending across applications (159, 160) permits the user to momentarily "ignore" familiar areas such as the response buttons and dialog title and concentrate on the areas containing the relevant information. When a portion of a dialog box's functionality is shared throughout the environment, its consistent presentation allows users to instantly recognize the common functionality and use it or ignore it as necessary. The template for the basic LaserWriter dialog (159), for example, is incorporated as a unit by most vendors, even when the vendor adds significant application-specific functionality of their own (160). The global consistency that results enhances the transfer or learning across applications and helps users work more efficiently.

```
┌─────────────────────────────────────────────────────────────────────┐
│ LaserWriter  "LaserWriter IINT"                    5.2    ┌─────────┐ │
│                                                          │   OK    │ │
│ Copies:█           Pages:◉ All  ○ From:       To:       └─────────┘ │
│                                                          ┌─────────┐ │
│ Cover Page:   ◉ No ○ First Page ○ Last Page             │ Cancel  │ │
│                                                          └─────────┘ │
│ Paper Source:◉ Paper Cassette  ○ Manual Feed            │  Help   │ │
│                                                          └─────────┘ │
│ ..................................................................... │
│ □ Print Selected Area Only        Encoding:                         │
│ □ Print Selected Channel Only       ○ ASCII                         │
│ □ Print Using Color PostScript      ◉ Binary                        │
│ □ Correct for Printing Colors                                       │
└─────────────────────────────────────────────────────────────────────┘
```

160: For application-specific extensions to the basic Print functionality, preserving the layout and functionality of the standard dialog can provide a familiar anchor for the new functionality.

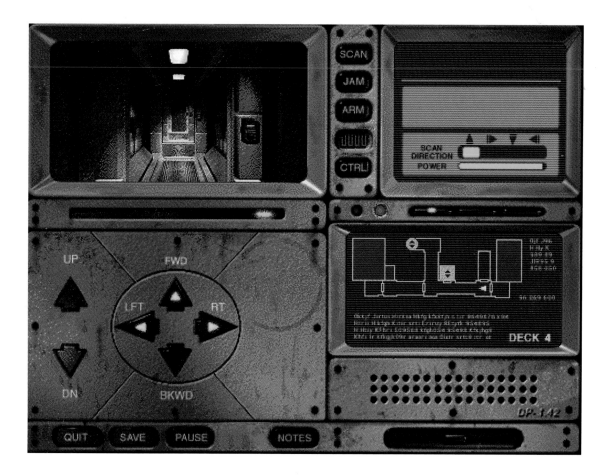

Plate 16: This screen from the multimedia adventure game *Iron Helix* typifies the movement away from GUI standards in "content" oriented entertainment and information products. The object of the game is to pilot a remote probe through a runaway space ship, seeking to gain control of the ship's computers while avoiding the ship's relentless (and deadly!) robotic defender. Because the design goal is to produce an immersive experience for the "user," it is perfectly appropriate that the control surface is a hyper-realistic (even to the point of damage and corrosion) and highly literal recreation of a plausible real-world console. While such imagery is highly engaging in this context, the same degree of realism might be distracting in a nonimmersive application.

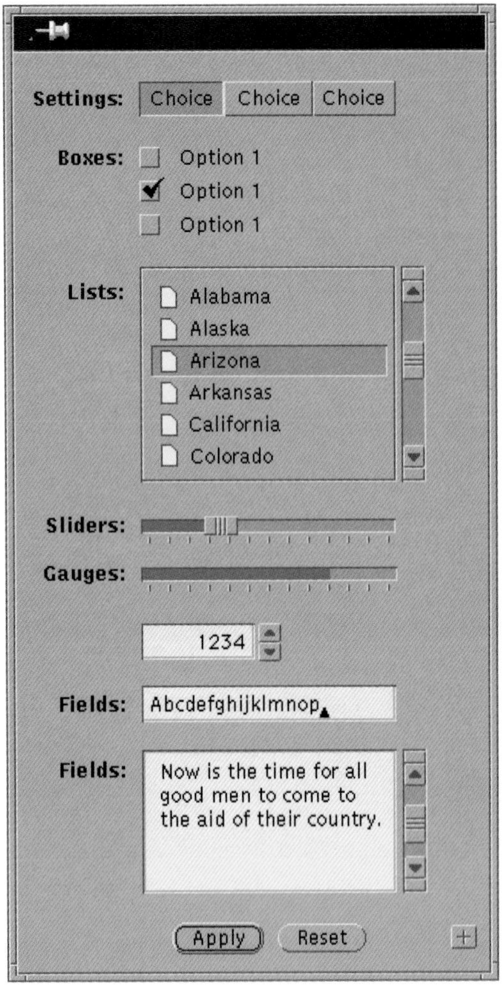

Settings: Choice Choice Choice

Boxes: ☐ Option 1
☑ Option 1
☐ Option 1

Lists:
📄 Alabama
📄 Alaska
📄 Arizona
📄 Arkansas
📄 California
📄 Colorado

Sliders:

Gauges:

1234

Fields: Abcdefghijklmnop▲

Fields:
Now is the time for all
good men to come to
the aid of their country.

(Apply) (Reset) +

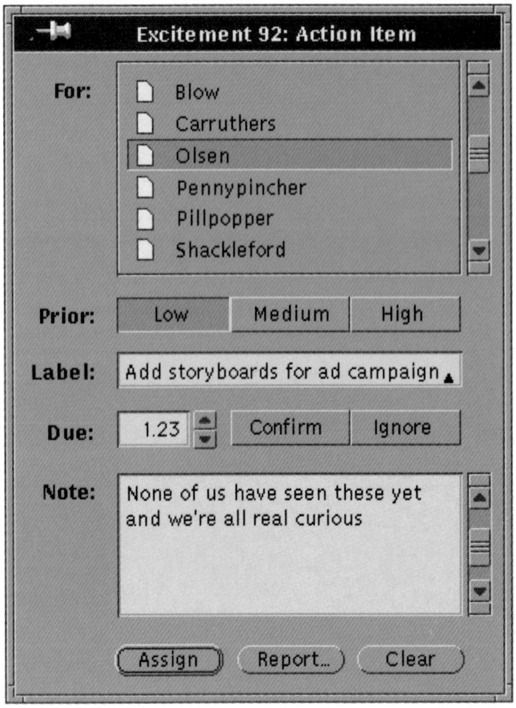

Excitement 92: Action Item

For:
📄 Blow
📄 Carruthers
📄 Olsen
📄 Pennypincher
📄 Pillpopper
📄 Shackleford

Prior: Low Medium High

Label: Add storyboards for ad campaign ▲

Due: 1.23 ⬍ Confirm Ignore

Note:
None of us have seen these yet
and we're all real curious

(Assign) (Report...) (Clear)

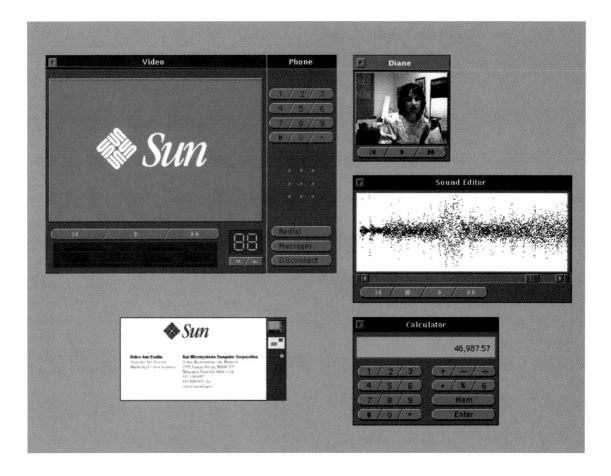

Plate 14: These concept studies investigating possible extensions to the OPEN LOOK GUI minimize the presentation of user interface elements while extending the existing widget designs in a visually and philosophically compatible direction. The introduction of diagonal divisions in buttons enabled the creation of menu and button "bars" while retaining the familiar round-ended form of OPEN LOOK command buttons.

Plate 15: (facing page) Two window designs showing the application of a modular widget set created as an extension to the OPEN LOOK GUI. *Compatible extensions* include 3D textfield and window borders, window focus feedback, and grooves indicating draggable elements.

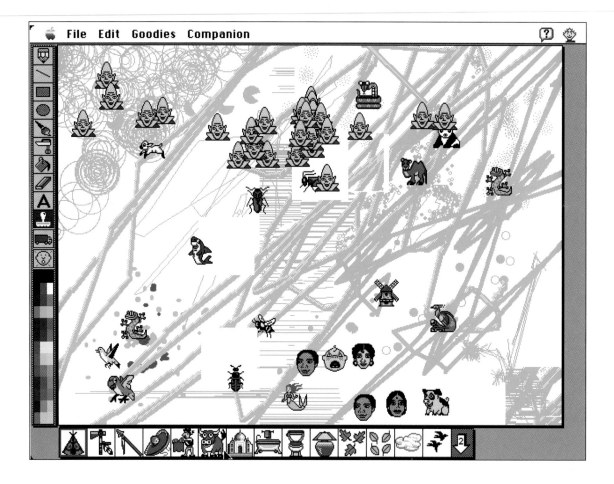

Plate 13: The stylistic approach seen in KidPix has much in common with that of the Swatch. Both products challenge the notion that tools must be serious artifacts oriented single-mindedly toward a purely functional goal, but they do so in a way that is *appropriate* for their target market and product concept. The bright colors, bold shapes, and large collection of predefined imagery (not to mention the ubiquitous sound effects) provided by the KidPix user interface are ideally suited to the product's young users—many of whom are experiencing a computer for the first time. Artwork provided by Alesha Marie Guyot, Sunnyvale, California.

Plate 12: The Swatch concept combines the product's low cost and large selection of designs to extend an unprecedented opportunity for personalization to the buyer. The product's exuberant graphic forms have made it an icon of popular cultural over the past decade. The success of the style has spawned a large number of imitators, but the Swatch remains a unique manifestation of the social movement it anticipated. The concept has been successfully extended to encompass new case designs and even new product categories (e.g., phone, pager, automobile). Photo courtesy of Swatch S.A. Swatch is a registered trademark of Swatch S.A., Switzerland.

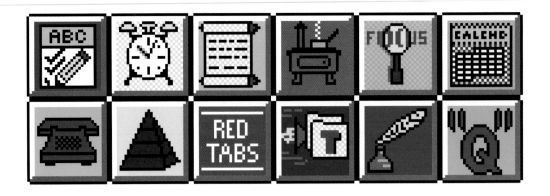

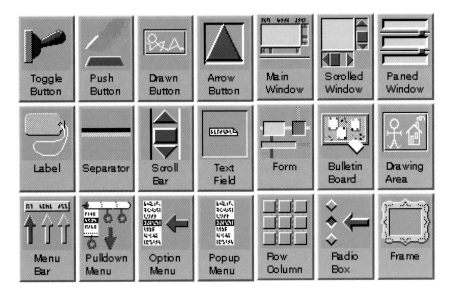

| Toggle Button | Push Button | Drawn Button | Arrow Button | Main Window | Scrolled Window | Paned Window |

| Label | Separator | Scroll Bar | Text Field | Form | Bulletin Board | Drawing Area |

| Menu Bar | Pulldown Menu | Option Menu | Popup Menu | Row Column | Radio Box | Frame |

Plate 10: These images for Nihon Sun exemplify the subtle application of color and detail in a coherent image program that is equally effective in both monochrome and color variations. A consistent level of *abstraction* and careful *coordination* of visual elements ensures that meaningful cues remain apparent in the ensemble.

Plate 11: (facing page) The imagery in each of these examples contrasts sharply to the subtle forms used in the Nihon Sun program. In each group, excessive (and usually irrelevant) variation in scale, color, form, and level of detail leads to an image set in which the individual elements compete with, rather than complement, one another.

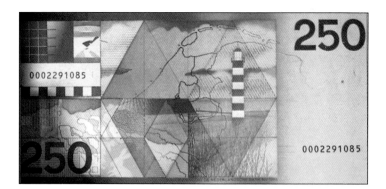

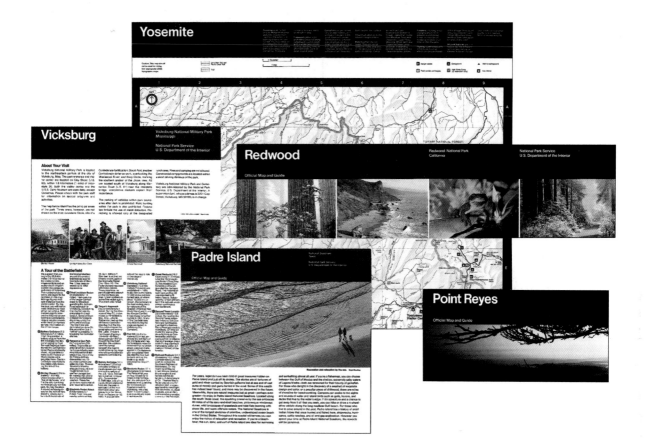

Plate 8: This flexible and comprehensive publication program, developed by Massimo Vignelli Associates for the US National Park Service, embodies the principles of systematic, communication-oriented design. The clear *repetition* of strong graphic elements in the header and the use of identical *modular* units to control text column placement and dimensions unifies the program while accommodating a wide variety of presentation formats.

Plate 9: (facing page) The colorful Dutch paper currency program, designed by R.D.E. Oxenaar, shows how *grid-based design* can be used to establish a coherent program. The underlying grid relates diverse visual elements while permitting significant local variation.

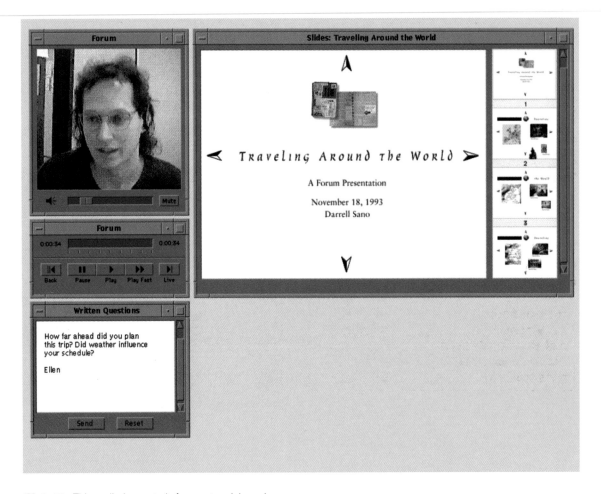

Plate 7: This preliminary study for a network-based video presentation system shows how the techniques of *alignment* and *modular construction* can be used to establish visual relationships even across windows in an application. Two strong vertical margins describe the extent of major control groups in each of the windows on the left. Note how the slider in the top window, the gauge and off-line playback controls of the middle window, and the response buttons of the bottom window all share the same external margins. Controls falling outside these margins in the first two windows are similarly aligned, and the windows themselves are sized to align with the main window in a typical display.

(a)

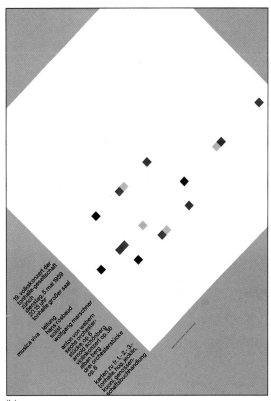

(b)

Plate 6: Each of these posters, designed by Josef Müller-Brockmann for the *Musica Viva* concert series, reveals a complex internal structure governed by a clear module. Both use the technique of *alignment* to produce emergent structure based on the implicit relationship of objects. In the first design (a), elements of the cross are aligned vertically with the margins of the headline and text blocks. The typographic elements are also related to one another on both vertical and horizontal dimensions. In the second design (b), the linear diagonals formed by the small squares align with the tops of the text blocks. The squares themselves align on the opposing diagonal to echo the text block– even down to the "hanging" text element defining the primary diagonal.

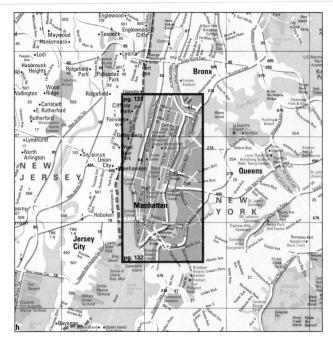

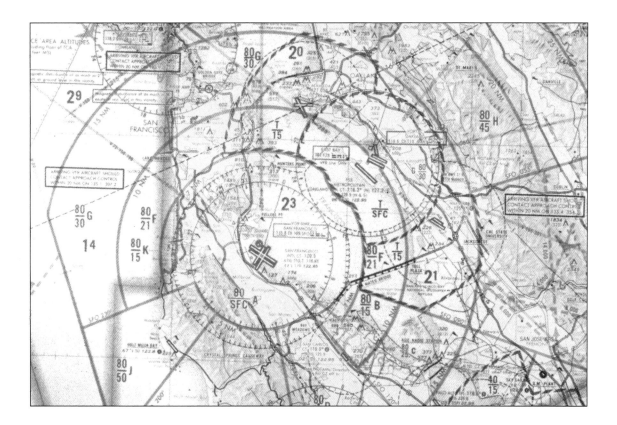

Plate 4: The US FAA Sectional Aeronautical chart uses subtle contrast in hue, value, texture, and orientation (curvature) to isolate each of several critical information categories within its perceptual *layer*. The subdued contrasts seen in each category prevent the layers from interfering with one another in dense displays for the metropolitan areas.

Plate 5: (facing page) These maps from USAtlas use similar *layering* techniques to isolate land masses, bodies of water, urban areas, and parks. The same restrained contrasts supplement the basic *reduction* techniques to ensure that major thoroughfares and important points of interest will emerge naturally from the display.

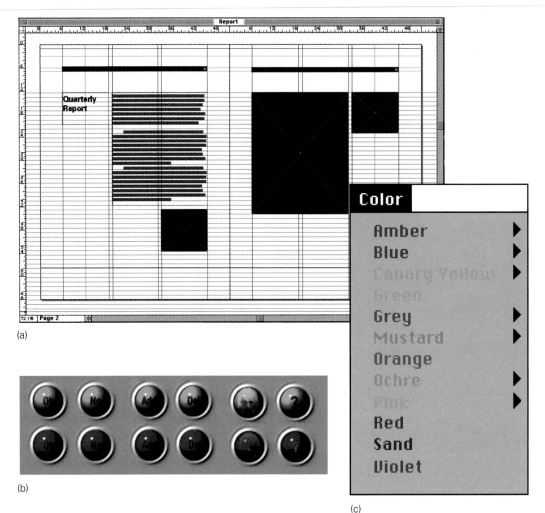

(a)

(b)

(c)

Plate 3: These examples illustrate the importance of *sharpening* as the key to establishing adequate contrast to ensure perceptual discriminability. The grid lines and alignment aides in QuarkXPress (a) use color effectively to help the eye effortlessly and naturally group individual lines according to their functional role. The color contrast works in this case because the number of levels is small and the background provides little interference. The same cannot be said of the buttons from Kai's Power Tools (b) and the menu showing color names in their actual colors (c). In each case the foreground and background elements are (at least sometimes) too close in color–and more important, in value –to provide adequate contrast and sufficient legibility.

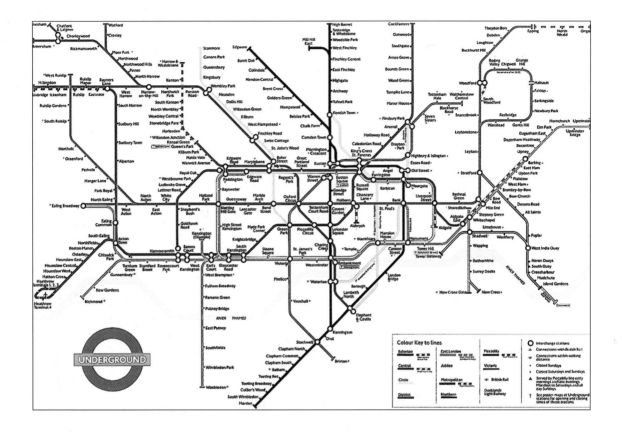

Plate 2: The famous route diagram for the London Underground system was the first representation of a complex transportation network in which complexity was reduced through a conscious decision to alter the geometry for simplified reading. So long as accurate connectivity information is retained, the user need not be concerned with minor geographical inaccuracies or the elimination of irrelevent surface detail. The use of *reduction* is especially effective. This technique allows suburban routes to be greatly compressed, since users are more interested in the sequence of stops than in the precise direction of travel or distance between stations. This highly successful approach has been followed by virtually all subsequent transit systems.

Plate 1: The EC 2 Phone by ECCO Design, Inc. illustrates the use of reduction, regularization, and leverage to produce a simple, elegant solution. Nonessential elements have been eliminated or moved to the phone's interior (an internal magnetic switch replaces the usual mechanical device to cut the connection automatically when the handset is placed on the phone base). The remaining elements, such as the buttons of the keypad, are regularized in their size, arrangement, and surface curvature. Finally, the common contour of the handset and base–in addition to holding the handset in place–produces a unity of form that leverages the angled surfaces to provide both an ergonomically oriented dialing surface and an effective shoulder cradle for hands-free operation.

Common Errors

Programmatic design applies within as well as across windows at both the application and system software levels. Failure to establish a coherent design statement at each of these levels is all too common.

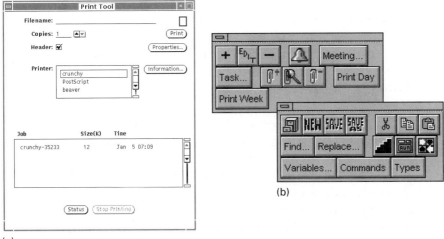

(a)

(b)

161: *Arbitrary component positions.* By far the most common shortcoming in the layout of existing GUI applications is the haphazard placement of controls and unsystematic variation in control sizes. The current generation of GUI toolkits is, again, at least partially responsible. Since the default button width in most toolkits is based directly on the length of the button label, the sizes of the buttons are often no more closely related than the lengths of their labels. The policy is especially disruptive when the buttons are stacked vertically, making the length disparity particularly apparent (a). While this approach may conserve a small amount of screen real estate (note the extension of the textfield into space "borrowed" from the Print button),

the savings are minor and hardly justify the disorganization that results. The misleading "information" provided by the variation in button lengths has no relation to the user's task. It is simply an artifact of the labels chosen. Similar distractions are created by components whose sizes are almost – but not quite – identical and which produce the sort of "near alignments" described in the preceding chapter (b). The tight spacing of the controls in these palettes makes the near total lack of alignment painfully obvious. Effective programmatic design establishes positions for each element, in addition to controlling the formal qualities of the elements themselves.

(a)

(b)

162: *Arbitrary component dimensions.* In the original Bugtool UI (a), the space conserved by shrinking button widths to match label lengths was immediately squandered on the seemingly arbitrary positioning of the buttons themselves and in the distractingly large and non-uniform gaps that separate the buttons in the top row. Even in the vertical button stack, the "reclaimed" space has not been re-used, since the fields are (as they should be) left aligned. Note the shortening of even the button whose label ("Resp.Mgr.") has been abbreviated. While other component groups are at times aligned internally, there are few if any relationships across groups throughout the window. Inconsistent sizing on the vertical dimension creates a similarly disquieting effect in this detail of dialog buttons from a disk cataloging utility (b). Note the use of four different button heights, each with no relation to the others. While undoubtedly based on defensible reasoning (the larger buttons' functions are presumably more important than those of the smaller buttons), this style is both globally inconsistent – when compared to dialogs in other Macintosh applications – and locally inconsistent – when considered in isolation. Users of this dialog are more likely to be distracted than enlightened by the unfamiliar code based on variation in button heights. With such a small set of visual elements, the use of the dominant perceptual cue is clearly overkill, particularly when each of the elements already has a "canonical" location in the standard layout paradigm.

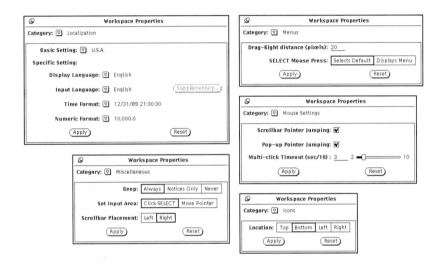

163: *Random window sizes and layouts.*
Programmatic design of secondary windows and dialog boxes is rarely seen in today's GUI applications. Because they tend to appear in isolation, dialog boxes are not usually viewed as part of a series by the developer. The user, however, encounters dozens if not hundreds of dialog boxes in a typical workday, and the lack of any real coordination has functional as well as aesthetic costs. Each of the five window layouts in this example displays a different subset of the functionality in the Workspace Properties dialog for OpenWindows 2. Each layout corresponds to a choice in the "Category" menu, which can be used to navigate directly to any other "page" within the same window. This high-frequency operation should be simple and

straightforward, but because the layout sizes are completely unrelated (note that no two dimensions match on any of the windows – not even positions of the critical Apply and Reset buttons), the process is slow, awkward, and disorienting. The window grows, shrinks, and changes its proportions so radically that the familiar impression of paging through a persistent window object is completely disrupted. When dealing with unconnected dialog boxes the effect is less pronounced, but still significant. Though some variation in size is inevitable, given varying levels of content, the dimensions and certainly the layouts can and should be more modular than this.

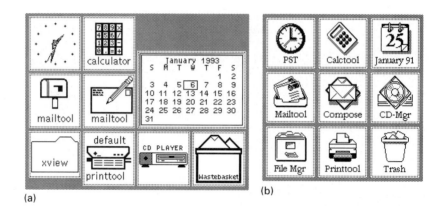

(a)

(b)

164: *Unrelated icon sizes and imagery.* Icons, like buttons, are typically presented in arrays and should therefore be sized consistently to avoid alignment problems of the kind seen in Figure 163 (b). These desktop icons from OpenWindows 2 (a) are consistent (with two notable exceptions) in their overall size, but vary greatly in their layout and typography, and in the scale, viewpoint, and density of the images themselves. Some images are so large that the label must be rendered within their boundaries, while others are so small (CD player) or light (folder) as to seem out of place when compared to the rest of the icons. Substantial variation in line thick–ness and level of detail can be seen across icons (CD player, calculator, wastebasket), and at least four different typefaces and three different capitalization policies are apparent in the labels. As might be expected, these inconsistencies arose largely because each icon was produced by the developers of the corresponding tool, with little or no coordination among development groups, with existing artwork (from multiple sources) being used wherever possible. Whenever the images in a set cannot all be produced by the same designer, the role of explicit, written standards is elevated from helpful design tool to essential coordination technology. The redesigned icon set for OpenWindows Version 3 (b) adopted a more consistent image size, orientation, and dimensionality across tools, resulting in a heightened image quality and a stronger product identity.

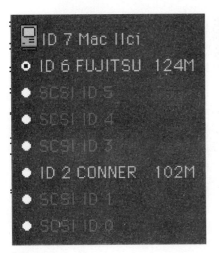

(a)

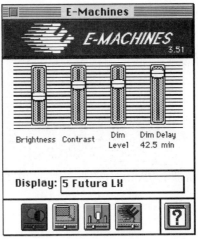

(b)

165: *Inconsistent control presentations.*
Faithful adherence to the conventions established by the target GUI environment appears to be one of the more difficult challenges facing the developer today. While the urge for creative expression is increasingly being suppressed in mainstream application development, it continues to thrive among developers of utilities and peripheral applications in nearly every environment. This detail from the Anubis SCSI Formatting Utility (a) shows one of the more energetic violations of the Macintosh conventions to date. The tri-colored radio buttons, in which the current choice is marked by a blue dot centered in concentric white and red circles, are reminiscent of the colorful roundels used as aircraft insignia. For added interest, the dark background is "marbled" with a random dot pattern. An even more unusual form of radio button is seen in the E-Machines monitor configuration panel (b). This window features a row of controls that *look* like command buttons (in a different GUI standard) but *act* like radio buttons, since they retain state (the button on the far left is selected, not disabled) and control the contents of the window. Still other visual inconsistencies must be attributed to shortcomings in the GUI standard itself. The unusual slider controls seen in this and many other Macintosh applications, for example, are a by-product of Apple's curious failure to specify the sort of generic slider visual defined by most other GUI environments.

(a)

(b)

166: *Inconsistent visual language.* When the visual language of a particular GUI standard is not used consistently throughout the user's environment, its ability to reinforce communication is greatly diminished. Radical departures from convention often produce adverse effects that extend well beyond the offending product. The DeskScan utility from Hewlett-Packard (a) uses non-standard "reverse video" window borders that disrupt the Macintosh active window feedback, since the dark gray title area is more prominent than the active window header even when DeskScan does not have the input focus. (It may also be the only Macintosh application ever with menus inside the main window.) In similar fashion, Apple's CD Remote desk accessory (b) shows that even utilities supplied by the vendors themselves don't necessarily respect the visual language conventions of that vendor's own environment. The window, which plays audio CD's on a CD-ROM reader, typically remains on the display after users return to their primary applications. There, its large black rectangle interferes visually with both selection and window focus feedback, since it is easily the most prominent object on the display. Non-standard applications like these always feel out of place in a standard GUI environment. Even when competently executed, the *overly* distinctive application eventually becomes an aesthetic irritant, if not an outright detriment to performance.

Techniques

Module and program are especially relevant to graphical user interfaces. Unlike a poster, letterhead, or logotype (any of which may involve only a single, static layout), a graphical user interface almost always includes many different displays – in the form of main windows, secondary windows, dialog boxes, and tool palettes. Three important techniques can be used to help the displays work together and bring a sense of regularity and predictability to the user's experience:

- Reinforcing Structure through Repetition
- Establishing Modular Units
- Creating Grid-Based Layout Programs

When creating design programs, the techniques of organization and visual structure for static displays must be extended to develop common local structures into themes that recur across displays. The rules of static layout still apply, but special attention must now be paid to the global ramifications of every local design decision.

Repetition
Modular Units
Grid-Based Design

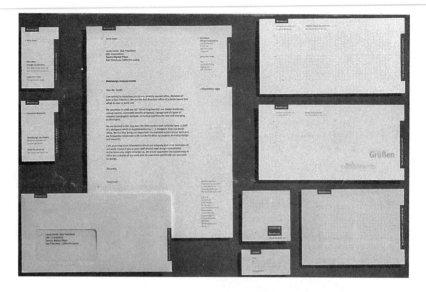

167: The use of repeated elements positioned consistently along the margins creates an emergent structure that binds together this stationery program by MetaDesign.

Reinforcing Structure through Repetition

A program's thematic character can be reinforced by repeating common elements throughout the individual participants. Simply repeating several elements in a standard location can hold a loosely defined program together. In the stationery system in Figure 167, the bright red bars and reversed typography at the top and right of each piece unify the diverse formats while keeping most of the "image area" free for content.

168: The repetition of dot elements in this identify program for Trevi faucets creates a patterned ground against which the figure of the "T" letterform can emerge. In addition to its inherent formal qualities, the dot pattern suggests the spray associated with the product. Design by Pentagram.

A similarly non-intrusive repetition can be seen in the "droplet" pattern used in the Trevi identify program (168). The repetition of circular elements throughout the program reinforces the nature of the product while enhancing the continuity of the system as a whole. In addition, the emergence of an intelligible foreground image from a regular background composed entirely of the same formal elements is inherently interesting – as witnessed by the near-universal fascination with repetitive pattern throughout human history.

Structural repetition is particularly important in user interfaces to online information systems where efficient navigation is of critical importance. The online catalog for Intellimation (169) exemplifies the orienting function pro-

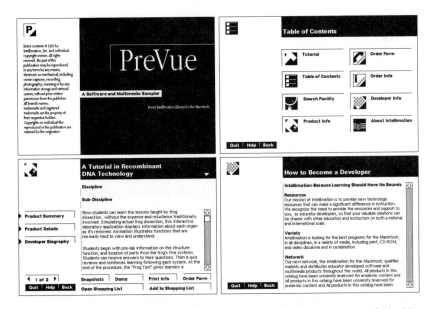

169: Structural elements that are repeated across screens (e.g., the icon in the upper left, the title bar, the buttons in the lower left, etc.) provide critical support for orientation and navigation in these screen designs from an online software catalog. Design by Aaron Marcus and Associates.

vided across screens by the careful repetition of structural elements. The continuity ensured by consistent placement of icon (upper left), title area (upper right), and navigation buttons (lower left) across the various screens is essential for efficient movement through the product space defined by the catalog. While every region contains standardized content, these critical areas exploit visually invariance – their size and color do not change from screen to screen – to maintain visual momentum across displays.

Thin lines – or rules – can also be used effectively as repeated structural elements. Rule reinforces implicit structure by making it tangible and visible. It provides natural lines of movement that lead the eye from one part of a composition to another and satisfies the human desire for order and structure in the visual field. The rather ordinary layout program in Figure 170 depends heavily on the rule linking dialog title with response buttons in each window. Rule is the most flexible element on which to base repetition, since it occupies practically no space and can be introduced to any region without significantly affecting the balance of the display as a whole.

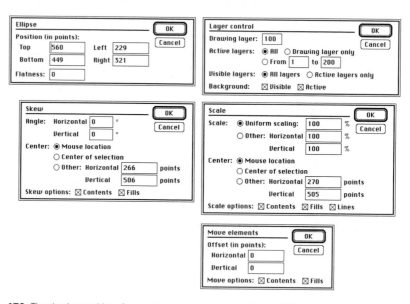

170: The simple repetition of a standard component group (the line linking title to default button) greatly enhances the apparent consistency of these dialogs from Aldus Freehand. Except for the low-level typographic conventions, however, the individual layouts have little else in common.

Rule is most effective in displays that are otherwise devoid of linear elements. The biggest source of interference for any rule is another rule competing for the viewers' attention and offering to lead them through the composition along its own route. Instead of beating the user over the head by explicitly delineating each contour, consider suggesting the visual organization implicitly using negative space and alignment of the elements themselves. The three lower components of the ubiquitous bounding box, for example, are usually redundant and merely add visual noise. A simpler system using only the topmost line is usually just as effective.

> Rule has the additional narcotic property of seeming to remedy weak design; it can balance a precarious layout just as a tightrope walker is preserved by his pole, it can be added as an afterthought to disguise the emptiness of a badly calculated page, or to create a semblance of unity running through unrelated spreads by its own reappearance in a standard position.
>
> **Douglas Martin**
> The Form of the Book

The programmatic effect of repetition can be based on content or visual characteristics and can be established using virtually any design element. The powerful human tendency to perceive regularity in the display leaves the designer with a wide latitude for choosing an element whose repetition facilitates communication while providing the comforting familiarity of a well-defined program. Effective use of this technique depends first on leveraging the inherent structure of the display, and only secondarily on the introduction of subsidiary structure:

Summary: Repetition

1 Start with rough sketches of the series of layouts to be produced.

2 Look for common margins or functional units that must be clearly perceived across displays. Individual displays should be adjusted to ensure consistent positioning of major structural elements.

3 Look for widely-spaced elements that should be visually related but which cannot be positioned next to one another.

4 Look for paths the user's eye needs to follow through the display. Repeated structural elements can serve as landmarks and guides that help users with the navigation task as they become familiar with the program.

5 Use standard locations and a consistent presentation style for rules, text, or images introduced to visually reinforce the naturally repeating elements of the design.

Failing other inspiration, the top and/or bottom of the layout can always be effectively emphasized using a light rule, since these normally appear in the same position in each layout. If both rules are used (an early warning sign of the addiction to the narcotic properties" described by Bringhurst), the lower rule should normally be of lighter weight to establish a contrast that helps lead the eye through the display.

171: Modular design provides the basis for the functional as well as the aesthetic excellence of the program in this stackable tableware system designed by Hans Roericht for Thomas/Rosenthal AG. From the permanent collection of the Museum of Modern Art, New York.

Establishing Modular Units

Proper choice of module is the key to any effective design program. The tableware in Figure 171 can be viewed as a system whose horizontal parameters are governed by the spatial layout of the place setting (which is in turn determined by human ergonomics) and whose vertical dimensions are governed by the volume requirements for each piece. Grid-based design generally requires the specification of both a vertical and a horizontal module. In a purely typographic grid, the vertical module is based on the point size and leading of the primary text font while the horizontal module is a function of both page size and optimum line length for the chosen font.

In the grid program developed by Vignelli Associates for the AIGA, a basic module is repeated to produce multi-column formats keyed to various standard paper sizes (172). The modular design allows the same typographic specifications to be used in each format. The imprint of the common module can be seen in designs using the grid as their foundation (173). Note that each major structural element begins on a grid boundary. Even the broad band at the top of the poster is part of the grid program as reflected in the top margin of the grid. Note too that, while the horizontal divisions are followed more closely than the vertical divisions, each is violated freely when dictated by the content.

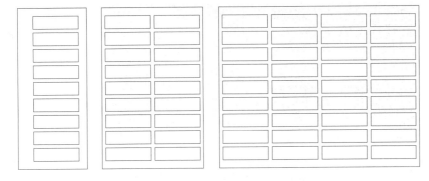

172: A standard column-width provides the module in this flexible grid program offered by the AIGA as a public service to non-profit organizations. Design by Vignelli Associates.

Layout grids for interface design differ from those for general purpose typography, but many of the same principles apply. Grids are based on the dimensions of the *controls* in the target GUI, which are in turn based on those of the primary display *font*. The internal structure of a well designed GUI is highly modular. With the parameters of the primary display font serving as a starting point, control sizes are adjusted to maximize the visual integration of label and control. As in the design of an alphabet, extensive sharing of formal elements allows a complete program to be derived from a small set of primitives. In the OPEN LOOK GUI (Sun Microsystems, 1989) as

173: This well-structured poster laid out on the same grid shows the value of even a very general design program. Each major element – the headline, the horizontal rules, the top of each column – begins on a horizontal grid boundary. Even where grid cells are locally ignored (e.g., within text columns) the vertical module ensures common baselines for all text. Design by Vignelli Associates.

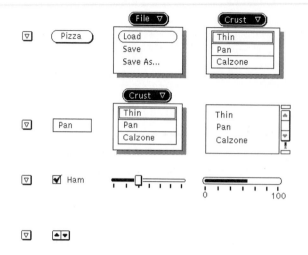

174: The modular design of the OPEN LOOK widget set attempts to ensure that critical *overall* dimensions (including necessary vertical spacing) are shared by analogous controls, making them interchangeable in various display contexts and simplifying automated layout.

few as 3-5 primitive measurements determine the dimensions of all major components (174). Control heights are based closely on the label dimensions. Control widths are variable, but are generally constrained to multiples of the basic grid unit. Spacing between controls is addressed by defining each control relative to a known reference point – typically the baseline of the primary label – that ensures the proper separation between controls under regular spacing. When combined with a simple layout system (see Figure 150) this modular widget set produces very effective layouts (175) through the almost mechanical application of a few governing rules.

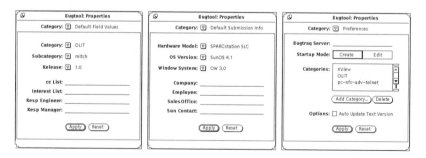

175: Effective window layouts can be achieved with a minimum of effort when the underlying widget set is designed to provide a modular architecture. The grid on which these windows are laid out is inherent in the internal dimensions and spacing rules of the OPEN LOOK widgets themselves.

Standardization demands that the number of units employed be as small as possible and that the units combine readily with each other.

Rudolf Arnheim
A Review of Proportion

If regularity and flexibility are the essence of modularity, then maintainability and extensibility are its inherent by-products. A small investment of design effort made at the beginning of a large project can pay huge dividends throughout the remainder of the product lifecycle. While the technique described here is superficially complete, its full appreciation will depend on experience with the actual application of the module to real layout problems and the difficulties and insights that result:

Summary:
Modular Units

1 Determine the vertical unit. In GUI design this means defining the standard control height and the spacing between controls. You will need to do this once for each GUI toolkit at each standard size you intend to support.

2 The vertical unit should allow any two controls to be placed next to one another, and should provide for proper spacing of multi-line controls, multi-control groups, and separations between groups. If labels are to be placed above rather than beside controls, the vertical unit must provide for correct positioning of labels as well.

3 Determine the horizontal unit. The unit should be large enough to accommodate most of the one-word labels in the design space and should be at least three times as wide as the vertical unit.

4 The optimum horizontal unit should provide 5-7 divisions of the typical display width and should be easy to factor evenly into partial or multiple units.

The temptation to locally employ a smaller-than-normal module to accommodate an especially dense display should be resisted at all costs. Any deviation from the focus on a single, central, module must be based on a clear communication goal and be applied consistently throughout the product or the benefits of the programmatic approach will be lost.

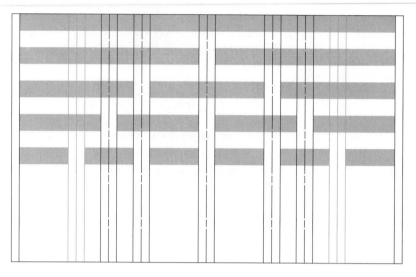

176: This *canonical grid* supports two-, three-, four-, and six-column layouts in any graphical user interface (the 1/6 and 5/6 divisions are implicit). The gray bars reflect the widths of components spanning (from top to bottom) 6, 3, 1.5, and 1 column-units, respectively, on the basic 6-column grid. The grid can be used with any vertical module, depending on the widget set and type size.

Creating Grid-Based LayoutPrograms

In this section we describe a general purpose layout system that can be used to solve almost any window layout problem. We call this the "canonical" grid for interface design, because it provides the flexibility needed to accommodate practically any combination of controls within a given window. Unlike a purely typographic grid, where the number of text columns is typically fixed by the page design, a layout grid for graphical user interfaces must be able to accommodate different numbers of divisions (i.e., "columns") on each line because individual widgets frequently have different numbers of internal components. Our canonical grid is designed to provide a fairly mechanical approach to achieving modularity and alignment in window layouts, and to that end it can be quite effective.

The canonical grid (176) is an abstract division of space that is scaled to the appropriate dimensions and superimposed on the empty window. The grid covers the entire area on which controls are to be arranged. The standard response buttons are not usually considered, since their positions are largely predetermined. The canonical grid may or may not be used to accommodate labels appearing to the left of the control layout. When the area reserved for labels is sized consistently across windows (this is usually a good idea), the canonical grid is simply scaled to fill the remainder of the window. We present examples of both approaches in the discussion below. The examples we present use an extended version of the OPEN LOOK GUI, but the same techniques can be applied to any GUI standard.

The canonical grid helps determine column positions and gutter widths for the most common layout formats. This basic version can directly accommodate 1, 2, 3, and 4-column layouts. Because any column can also be subdivided at the halfway point (faint guidelines are provided for assistance), extension to 6 and 8-column layouts within the same grid space is straightforward. The limiting factor is simply the visual noise that results when too many guidelines are incorporated into the grid. The vertical dimension is based on the proper inter-line spacing of components in the target GUI. For complex layout problems, a "custom" grid, developed along the same principles but omitting unnecessary margins, may indeed prove more useful.

To use the grid, simply match control widths to the appropriate column margins. In our first three examples, we start with a basic layout plan that

177: This two-column layout is based on the canonical grid (in our first three examples, the grid is not used for the labels in the left-hand column). To visualize this grid, ignore all but the middle three lines of Figure 176. The Name, Type, Vendor, and Note fields span both of the columns that remain, while the items in the Mode setting, Progress indicator, and Scope options span one column each.

includes the label column and use the canonical grid to lay out the remainder of the window. The basic 2-column example (177) shows a number of fields that run the full width of the window and two groups of check boxes, each of which spans the width of one column in the 2-column layout. Positioning the check boxes in the second group along a common margin improves the readability of the array and implicitly defines a key boundary. This same boundary is reflected in the division of the 2-item setting at the top of the window, and in the length of the progress indicator and positioning of its secondary label directly above the checkbox group.

The 1, 2, and 3-column textfields of our next example (178) demonstrate even more clearly how a multi-column layout accommodates elements spanning any number of columns up to and including the maximum. We begin with a good idea of the ordering of control elements and a goal of correspondence to the familiar envelope address format. To maximize alignment, items are always extended to the right margin of the corresponding row or column, even if less space would actually be required to accommodate the maximum-length entry. (We would not be using this space in any case, since

178: The imprint of the 3-column version of the canonical grid (ignore the middle and outermost gutters in Figure 176) is apparent in this layout. Note that separate elements fall on gutter margins, while abutting elements – such as the items in the Address setting – fall on the gutter centerline.

179: This layout follows the four-column version of the canonical grid (ignore the second and fourth gutters in Figure 176). Note the introduction of half-column elements (Size, Leading, and Kern). Any grid column can be subdivided about its midpoint (using the standard gutter width) if necessary.

doing so would reduce alignment and impede the visual processing of the rest of the display.) Thus the ZIP Code, State, and E-mail fields are lengthened to reach the next column margin. Fields should be extended if doing so helps unify the layout and clarify the relation between fields through their alignment. Extending the Name field in this case allows the short ZIP row to form a clear boundary between the physical and electronic addresses. By extending some fields (and shortening others) beyond their actual limits we can produce the best "silhouette" for the data in each layout.

Our next example (179) is dominated by two scrolling lists, each of which spans two columns on a 4-column grid. These elements, along with the 4-item setting at the top of the window, determine the choice of a four-column layout. The remaining controls fit neatly in the space below the scrolling lists. Note the shortening of the Size, Leading, and Kern fields to half the normal column width. Single-element controls should be extended to the right margin of the appropriate column whenever their "natural" width extends beyond the half-way point, but they can be held at the halfway point otherwise.

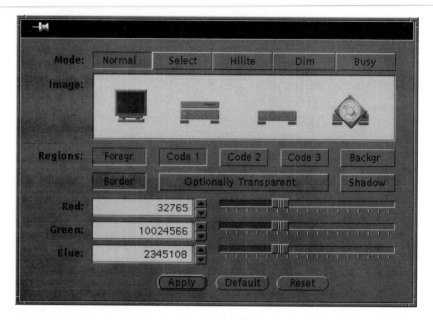

180: In this example, the full six-column grid is used to lay out the left-most label column as well as five columns of controls. Note the presence of controls spanning one, two, three, and five columns. Note too that elements of different widths can be placed in the same row without problems.

Our final example (180) employs a 6-column grid in which the first column is used for the labels on the left-hand side of the window (i.e., they are placed on the grid), with the rest of the 5-column display being reserved for controls. The margins of the 5-item setting at the top of the window are mirrored in the non-exclusive choices beneath the image pane. Note that an item in a component array can span more than the "normal" extent for other elements in the array if necessary to accommodate a long label. Good design is always flexible. If a component is too wide for the chosen column width, a higher-order grid may be needed for that row. Each row can use a different "version" of the canonical grid, but the layout will be most effective when the same column layouts recur across rows.

Besides governing layout, the grid can and should influence content decisions. When the grid suggests ways of re-structuring or re-ordering information to better fit the program, communication is often enhanced. While the designer must take care not to violate the semantics of the information being presented, "designing backward" may be the best route to clear communication.

The use of the grid system implies
the will to systematize, to clarify
the will to penetrate to the essentials, to concentrate
the will to cultivate objectivity instead of subjectivity
the will to rationalize the creative and technical production processes.

Josef Müller-Brockmann
Grid Systems in Graphic Design

Effective grid-based design requires both careful planning and a willingness to adjust the content itself when appropriate. Fitting the content to the grid should be viewed not as a concession to aesthetic indulgence, but as a way of regularizing the information and increasing its internal consistency in order to enhance communication (improved aesthetics are a welcome side effect). Except for the critical phase of determining the basic layout (and hence the proper grid structure), applying the canonical grid is largely mechanical:

**Summary:
Canonical Grid**

1 Determine any size restrictions on the area to be laid out.

2 Determine the basic vertical and horizontal modules. The vertical module is determined by the widget set, while the horizontal module is determined by the number of controls (and sometimes by the lengths of their labels). These parameters (row height, column width, and number of columns) define precisely the canonical grid that will be used for this layout problem.

3 Develop a rough layout sketch that approximates the sizes, positions, and orientations of the relevant control elements.

4 Use the canonical grid to adjust the sizes and positions of elements across rows. Short elements are extended to begin and end on grid boundaries, while long elements are allowed to span multiple grid units or are shortened to fit within the standard unit. In this way, the grid is merely being used to help establish consistent alignment relationships of the type described in the previous chapter. Symmetry-enhancing adjustments to control ordering and arrangement can also be introduced anywhere in the display.

5 For dynamic layouts, identifying the minimum size that can be accommodated by the layout is usually a better solution than trying to recompute the layout for arbitrarily small display sizes.

Applying the technique is much simpler than understanding (or writing!) this textual description. When the vertical unit is clearly established (as in GUI's that favor a standard "normal" size), the most difficult part of the problem is choosing a grid with the "right" number of columns. This will depend on the rough layout you've developed. If your "longest" control is a set of six radio buttons, you could use a 6-column layout (if the labels were very short), a 3-column layout (where the control would be split across two rows instead of one), or even a 1-column layout (with very long labels requiring six lines, in which case the grid would probably be determined by some other control with a larger number of divisions per line). Once the proper variant on the canonical grid has been chosen, placing the remaining controls should require only minor adjustments.

Image and Representation

6

Every blink of the eye brings a picture to
the human mind.

Adrian Frutiger
Signs and Symbols: Their Design and Meaning

Imagery is essential for communication throughout the product user interface. The "blink of the eye" is the span – the length of a single glance – over which the most powerful visual phenomena operate. Images are perceived as configurations that utilize many of the same the organization and grouping effects described previously. While effects such as the Gestalt phenomena operate across the entire visual field, their contribution to image recognition takes place primarily under focused attention. We find it difficult to recognize (beyond the vague sense that "something is out there") images appearing only in our peripheral vision or that are visible for very short periods of time. What the recognition process lacks in scope, however, it makes up in depth. Images we see can be recognized quickly and committed to memory with surprising persistence (many people "never forget a face").

Most of the factors considered previously – simplicity, structure, scale, contrast, program, etc. – are applicable to imagery as well. Images possess internal structure that must obey the same rules of organization considered previously for the display itself. Images appear, moreover, as part of a coordinated program when used in support of a graphical user interface. The effectiveness of the whole, is diminished by shortcomings in any of its parts. In this chapter, we add a discussion of the use of *representation* to introduce meaning to the visual display. Without effective visual representations, the graphical user interface is no more effective than a character-based interface using an unfamiliar script.

181: Contradiction between word and image is apparent in *La Trahison des Images, (The* Treachery of Images) by the surrealist painter Rene Magritte. The image predominates, and it is practically impossible to read the caption without first recognizing the pipe. © 1993 Herscovici/ARS, New York.

Few would argue that images are not among the most important elements in a visual computing environment. Their impact on the presentation of a conceptual model, the tightness of the feedback loop between person and machine, and the apparent tangibility of a synthetic virtual space is greater than any other aspect of the application. Images are particularly important in three areas:

Identification. When serving as representations of concrete, real-world objects, images make identification easy. We learn the names of things at an early age, but we must first learn to recognize the image of the named object. When word and image collide, as in Figure 181, the image dominates perception. The picture must be seen and recognized as a pipe *before* the logical conundrum (*"this is not a pipe"*) can be raised by the caption.

Expression. Imagery offers great latitude for expression and personalization in the designed artifact. Magritte could have chosen any of a variety of pipe forms and representation styles in *The Treachery of Images*. The sense of reality created by his selection of an ordinary pipe and realistic style of rendering simply underscore the contradiction being set up between word and image. The dominant position of imagery in human communication confers both the greatest opportunity for success and with the greatest risk of failure. When handled correctly, however, effective use of imagery can make your product more engaging and enjoyable.

Communication. Pictorial representations cross social and linguistic boundaries with ease when the objects being represented are relatively constant across cultures. Symbols can communicate with immediacy and impact, but they are dependent upon the culture in which their meaning is established. This dichotomy is clear in Figure 181. Magritte's painting can be recognized as a pipe by anyone (at least by those in Western cultures), but only Francophones will appreciate the full meaning of the work. Communication is always affected by the context in which it occurs. To place our discussion in context, we present a brief overview of the relevant aspects of *semiotics*.

Representation (literally, to *present again*) provides the basis for all communication. We can convey (and indeed, even consider) ideas about things that are not materially in our presence only by calling forth an appropriate mental representation. The manner in which such representations are interpreted by participants in a communication system to create shared meaning can be fully understood only within the interdisciplinary context of semiotics. Mihai Nadin (1989) defines semiotics as *"the general theory and practice of signs (whose scope includes) everything that is interpreted by human beings as a sign, and defines the circumstances under which interpreting something as a sign allows for its better understanding, or for an improved use of it."* The graphical user interface is a sign system, in which signs play the role of *intermediary* between user and program/programmer.

Background: Semiotics

A sign is defined by Charles S. Peirce (1931) as, *"something that stands for someone or something in some respect or capacity."* The sign itself is the product of a three-way *relation* between the *representamen* (that which represents), the sign's *object* (that which is represented), and its mental *interpretant* (the situated intelligence that performs the necessary substitution of signifier for signified). Nadin's (1989) diagrammatic representation (182-a) makes this triadic relationship apparent. Because each person is the product of a unique social, cultural, and experiential history, the manner in which the sign object is recalled by the representamen will be different (however slightly) for each *interpretant*. Clearly then, *"where we interpret a sign, we become part of it for the time of that interpretation* (Nadin, 1989)."

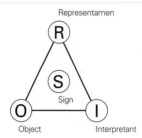

182: In Peirce's definition of the sign, the *Representamen* stands for some *Object* in the presence of a given *Interpretant.* (Nadin, 1989)

The triadic structure of the sign permits the sign process (*semiosis*) to be considered at three levels. *Syntactics* (183-a) addresses the internal structure of the representamen itself, particularly in terms of the relationships among its parts. *Semantics* (183-b) addresses the tacit relation between representamen and sign object (that is, the intended meaning of the sign). *Pragmatics* (183-c) considers the effect of the syntactic and semantic aspects in relation to a particular interpreter in their personal psychological context. Signs must be considered at all three levels to determine their appropriateness for a particular communication problem and to develop visual representations that can be expected to communicate effectively to a particular target audience.

The critical process of representation (the focus of analysis at the *semantic* level) depends on establishing a clear relationship between a representamen and its object. Peirce (1931) identifies three forms this relationship can take. An *icon* (184-a, 185-a) denotes its object by virtue of its own likeness to or

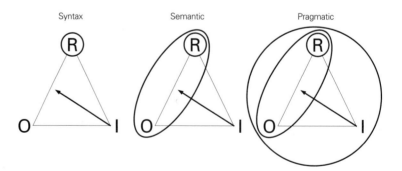

183: Sign processes can be analyzed at the level of *syntax* (a) – relations between elements of the representamen, *semantics* (b) – relations between representamen and sign object, or *pragmatics* (c) – the effectiveness of a given syntax/semantics for a particular interpretant. After Nadin (1989).

184: The concept of *Fire* can be represented visually as an *icon* (a) through visual resemblance to flames, as an *index* (b) through visual suggestion of smoke (sound, temperature, or smell would work as well, in this case), or as a *symbol* (c) such as the Medieval alchemists conventional notation.

resemblance of that object, on the basis of some quality or characteristic inherent in the icon itself. An *index* (184-b, 185-b), in contrast, refers to its object indirectly, by means of an association based on contiguity rather than on resemblance, and by virtue of its being actually affected or modified by the sign object. Either form may, over time, develop into a *symbol* (184-c, 185-c), which denotes its object by convention alone, and which thus depends on agreement between the parties in communication.

In common usage, the term, *icon*, has come to denote any small raster image appearing in a GUI display. This source of confusion has arisen because the imagery used in existing GUI's is predominantly (though by no means exclusively) iconic. We can say that the "desktop metaphor" seen in standard GUI environments such as the Macintosh Finder or Microsoft Windows, conveys the functionality of a suite of programs by analogy to the *semantics* of an office environment using an *iconic* form of representation.

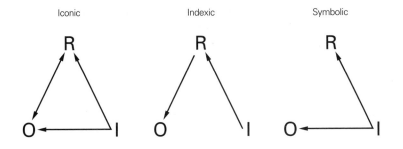

185: Representation can be grounded in an *iconic*, or resemblance-based (a), an *indexical*, or affect-based (b), or a *symbolic*, or convention-based (c) relationship between object and representamen. For best results, the same form should be used throughout an image set. After Nadin (1989).

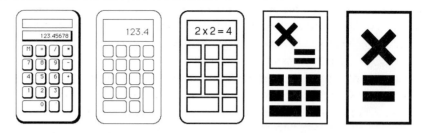

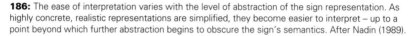

186: The ease of interpretation varies with the level of abstraction of the sign representation. As highly concrete, realistic representations are simplified, they become easier to interpret – up to a point beyond which further abstraction begins to obscure the sign's semantics. After Nadin (1989).

Finally, a given sign representation can be characterized by its degree of *abstraction* – the extent to which the *essential* qualities upon which the representation is based are isolated from the literal perceptual characteristics of the sign object. A photograph or realistic illustration provides a high degree of fidelity to a particular sign object (an instance of its class), and is usually easy to recognize as a result. More schematic representations, because they permit the selective omission of detail, are better able to represent a broader class of objects (as opposed to one of its instances) or to focus on some characteristic aspect of the object (rather than on the perceptual reality of a specific individual).

Interpretation is the process of reconstructing the meaning of a sign by identifying the sign object and grasping the significance of the connection between object and representamen. As shown in Figure 186, interpretation becomes easier (to a point) as the representation becomes more schematic. As the level of abstraction increases, the sign becomes progressively more generic, more canonical, and less complex. To complete the interpretation of a graphic sign in a GUI, the user must draw the connection between the iconic representamen and the corresponding system function. The problem is simplified when the sign object is concrete, but problems can arise if the representamen can be mistaken for the object. Understanding what a thing *represents* – as opposed to merely what it *depicts* – is a prerequisite for using the sign correctly, since the same physical representation can be used in many signs (See, for example, Figure 215 c, d). Users must recognize the icon on the display screen as a sign for the thing (e.g., an icon for a calculator program), rather than the thing itself (Nadin, 1989). Interpretation becomes more reliable when moving from left to right in Figure 188, since only the first two or (possibly) three signs could be mistaken for the object itself.

How can semiotics aid the practicing designer? First and foremost, an understanding of how signs are formed, transmitted, and interpreted can help the designer to systematically analyze a communication problem and provide the basis for the development of a coherent solution. To achieve this goal, the visual language used to represent the functionality of the system must itself be as coherent as possible, and it must be matched to the capabilities and limitations of the anticipated user. With an understanding of the user population, the designer can determine the form of representation (icon, index, or symbol) and degree of abstraction most appropriate for their existing background, skills, and tasks. Regardless of the decision taken, semiotics underscores the importance of, *"uniformly using whatever means of representation are considered adequate* (Nadin, 1989)." Because users learn the "rules" only through experience with the system, the visual language in which the rules are expressed must make them as clear as possible.

Principles

Imagery is at once the most obvious and least understood aspect of GUI design. It is rarely sufficient to simply "draw a good picture" of the thing being represented. Effective imagery must possess a perceptual immediacy that allows it to be recognized at a glance. For most images, this involves a process of careful abstraction in which all but the elements that most characterize the sign object are removed. When developing multiple images, care must be taken to maintain cohesion within the image set and to consider the physical, conceptual, and cultural context in which the images will ultimately be displayed. Mastery of these concepts is far more important than any innate "artistic" ability in developing an effective image program.

Immediacy
Generality
Cohesiveness
Characterization
Communicability

187: Many traffic signs communicate through an *iconic* resemblance to a given class of roadway feature. The high degree of *abstraction* is essential for both generality (the sign can refer to any similar curve) and recognizability.

188: Bold, simplified, symmetrical imagery ensure that the immediacy needed for an effective corporate identify program will be present in these familiar pictograms. Air Canada logo is a registered trademark of Air Canada.

Immediacy

Effective visual representations can be perceived effortlessly and involuntarily. Only under extremely poor viewing conditions – or during extremely short presentations – does the viewer "see" something they cannot recognize. This distinguishing characteristic of visual phenomena is apparent in the viewer's ability to holistically and automatically extract information from the "snapshot" of the overall display that can be perceived during the span of a single glance. The impact, or "graphical power" of effective visual signs springs directly from this quality of perceptual *immediacy*. Because we need not consciously analyze the pieces of a powerful image to understand the whole, we cannot avoid recognizing the image when it confronts us. Perceptual immediacy allows appropriately designed images to force their way into our awareness. By carefully manipulating the weight, balance, and sym-

189: The immediacy of this familiar symbol is enhanced by removing the verbal label.

190: These simple logograms, while more heavily dependent on a shared linguistic context than the pictographic imagery on the left, nevertheless possess a similar perceptual immediacy by virtue of their minimal form.

metry of the graphic sign, designers produce images with the impact and memorability required for effective trademarks, brand marks, corporate identities, and signage systems.

Signs to be "read" as images can be based on pictures (pictograms) or words (logograms). Each of the pictograms in Figure 188 and the logograms in Figure 190 presents a powerful graphic image because each has been reduced to the essence of the underlying sign through a process of simplification and abstraction. Note the solid forms, simplified contours, and complete absence of any internal detail. The fir tree of Boise-Cascade (188-a), the maple leaf of Air Canada (188-c), and the men of Henckels (188-f) are all highly stylized to emphasize their most important formal characteristics. The BMW mark (188-b) reduces the checkered standard of the Bavarian state to a single four-square motif, while the Westinghouse mark (188-e) recalls the image of a circuit board. The Mitsubishi ("Three Diamonds") mark produces a strong emergent form that evokes a subtle reference to the Mercedes mark (16).

Each of the pictograms is simple and direct, bold and clear, balanced – if not highly symmetrical, and well-integrated with its ground. The same is true of the logograms. Even when effectively designed, however, logograms – which are by definition purely conventional – are less universal than pictograms. Basing visual representation on the spelling (in one particular language) of a verbal label (190 a-d) is always a dangerous game to play. These signs may succeed in Western cultures, if only because common Latin roots have led to related spellings in many languages. For a more global pragmatics, however, this approach is an admission of failure and the practice should be avoided when possible. Note, however, that an effective graphical image *can* be constructed from an isolated verbal symbol when appropriate.

When stylized into simple geometric shapes or powerful graphic forms, pictographic images become symbols depending entirely on convention for their interpretation. While its original iconographic relation to the sign object may long since have disappeared, the symbol's ability to penetrate into the viewer's awareness – even in the midst of noise and distraction – is greatly enhanced. The quality of perceptual immediacy makes images ideally suited to public safety applications such as the labeling of hazardous materials, the signage needed for traffic control, or any other situation that demands a rapid, reliable response (189).

The graphical user interface includes many situations where the user's attention must be captured and a certain amount of context conveyed. The symbols appearing to indicate a particular class of dialog box or alert in most environments (191) are the GUI equivalent of the traffic sign. The immediacy of the image provides an important visual cue telling the user something about the nature and potential seriousness of the situation even before the detailed textual message has been read.

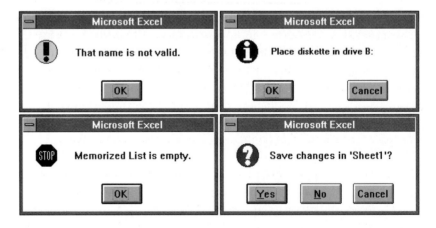

191: The immediacy of the supergraphic visual symbols (which arises from their size and color contrast with the contents of the rest of the dialog, as much as from the simplicity of the symbols themselves) provide important contextual information in these standard Windows dialog boxes.

192: Visual representations can be very abstract while still maintaining a high degree of iconicity. These icons are used to represent broad categories of goods and services in the SMART Yellow Pages™ telephone directory. Design by Richard Saul Wurman and The Understanding Business.

Generality

In GUI applications, imagery is normally used (there are exceptions) to represent a class of artifacts, rather than any particular instance of that class. *Generality* describes the ability of the individual sign to represent these higher-level groupings. Images with a high degree of abstraction (192) automatically provide a general representation of a class of similar objects by removing visual details specific to any one instance. The generality of these images, moreover, allows them to be interpreted as representative of a broader class (e.g., "painting supplies") than might be suggested by a photograph or detailed drawing of the same object (e.g., "No. 4 Paint Roller"). The images depend on highlight, shadow, and a consistent orientation of object and light source – rather than extensive detail or contour information – to convey the essential characteristics of the objects they represent.

A conscious retreat from photorealism need not result in a less recognizable image. In fact, the converse is often true. Generalization results in simpler forms that, because they contain less visual information, are easier to process, recognize, and react to. Generalization also allows elements of the original form to be selectively emphasized or de-emphasized to facilitate particular communication objectives as detail is removed from the image.

193: Two very different levels of abstraction are apparent in these icons. The realistic images on the left provide a representation that is more direct, but less general. Their accuracy strongly suggests that the icons in (a) represent *typical* individuals, rather than the more *general* populations seen in (b).

Generalization is essential when creating images of great perceptual immediacy and lasting graphical impact. The process of abstraction – upon which the generality of an image depends – leads to "better" forms that can be processed and assimilated more rapidly despite their reduced iconicity (193). It is no accident, for example, that the world's great mystical and religious symbols, as well as its alphabets, have evolved through a process of simplification and abstraction extending over many centuries. By removing details associated with the particular, the designer can use the general qualities that remain to establish a background, or context, against which the message can be delivered. The identity program for the Mandarin Oriental Hotel (194), for example, employs a greatly simplified paper fan motif throughout. The fan itself is stripped of all detail except that needed to identify it as a member of its most general class. The internal structural details, in particular, are merely suggested – not rendered – through judicious use of negative space.

194: Simplification of the iconic representation produces a more generalized interpretation of the paper fan in this identity. Design by Pentagram.

195: Simple, abstract representations such as these standard transport control symbols are generalizable not only across software applications, but across hardware platforms and product categories (e.g., consumer electronics) as well. They are widely understood when used consistently.

Generalized, conventional signs are seen throughout the human-computer interface, and indeed throughout product user interfaces in general. The familiar transport control symbols for sequential media (e.g., Play, Pause, Cue, Review, Stop, Record) have gained near universal acceptance in consumer electronics in recent years and are now used commonly in GUI applications (195) as well. Originally used in conjunction with textual labels identifying their function, these abstract symbols are now familiar enough to stand on their own. They provide an excellent example of a coherent visual language that can be adapted directly to the human-computer interface.

Many common GUI design problems, of course, have no corresponding real-world lexicon upon which to draw, so designers must invent their own visual language. The window management controls seen in most current-generation GUI's (196) are usually good examples of abstract imagery. Due to the severe space constraints, the number of pixels available is rarely sufficient for elaborate iconic representations. This turns out not to be a problem in this case. Since window management controls appear in nearly every window, they are learned through constant exposure when their meaning is not immediately obvious. Abstract, general imagery permits the designer to trade intuitiveness for efficiency of use in the resulting symbols.

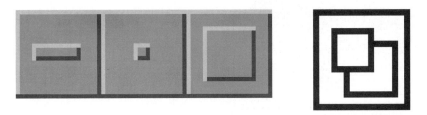

196: Generalized imagery is used throughout the GUI environment to represent standard control and feedback mechanisms. These examples from the OSF/Motif (a) and Macintosh (b) standards, are abstract symbols depending on constant exposure to ensure their understandability.

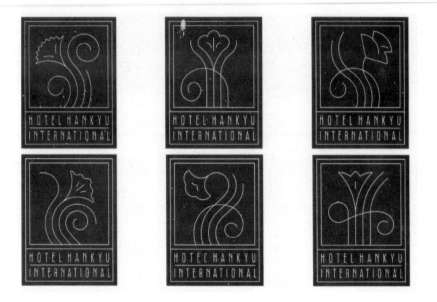

197: Cohesive image programs are created by employing the same visual primitives consistently in every image. In this identity and signage program for the Hotel Hankyu, the visual language is based on thin, organic linework, pronounced dark bias, and floral imagery. Design by Pentagram.

Cohesiveness

Images rarely appear in isolation. Particularly in user interface applications, each image generally forms part of a larger system in which many individual visual elements must work together effectively as a group. A cohesive system arises when shared formal qualities of the images themselves can be recognized effortlessly in early visual perception. Any of Bertin's visual variables can form the basis for the emergent properties of the group as a whole. The common visual characteristics that result allow each image to be perceived as part of the larger program even as it is distinguished from the other members of the ensemble.

Cohesive image programs can be based with equal effectiveness on bold or delicate imagery, so long as a consistent visual vocabulary is maintained throughout the program. The signage programs for the Hotel Hankyu (197) and the Mexico City Olympics of 1968 (198), for example, could hardly be more different at the syntactic level. Basic perceptual processes allow the viewer to recognize these differences effortlessly, and either system stands out in its environment due both to this contrast and to its internal consistency. Mixing and matching images from these two extremes would be confusing on both the functional and aesthetic levels.

198: A similar cohesiveness based on a very different set of visual primitives can be seen in these icons for the 1968 Mexico City Olympics. Bold forms, close cropping, and light/dark balance are used consistently throughout the set. Design by Lance Wyman, Eduardo Terrazas, and Manuel Villazon.

Note also the repetition of basic forms throughout both programs. The delicate forms, parallel lines and common curvatures of the floral imagery tie the Hotel Hankyu signs together as powerfully as the bold forms, undulating waves, isolated limbs, and close cropping unite the Olympics pictograms. Repetition of common forms throughout an image set helps users learn to "read" the resulting visual language and further enhance their processing of the information being presented. The waves in the Olympic pictograms, for example, make it easy to identify those icons representing water sports.

199: Coherent use of visual language is important wherever classification based on visual appearance is necessary. Their vertical orientation and turned down corner identify the objects on the right as documents, while systematic use of internal imagery identifies two levels of document category.

The consistent application of visual language in a coherent image program is essential to the success of a graphical user interface. The basic object categories (document, container, tool, etc.) need to be clearly and visually distinguished if a convincing artificial reality is to be created. The dog-eared document outline not only helps users distinguish the corresponding software object as a document, but also forms the basis for an extended visual ensemble of similar objects that can be recognized on the basis of their shared size, line thickness, and density (199).

Graphical applications can often benefit from coherent image-based representations as well. Figure 200 shows several excellent examples. The display selection icons for the DayMaker personal organizer (a) use a clear, concise notation to represent views of the current day, week, or month. The familiar spatial language of the calendar is leveraged by highlighting the corresponding range of cells in the icon. A similar spatial correspondence is exploited by the paragraph alignment commands seen in most word processors (b). The images use a consistent line weight and length to make the differences between the icons readily apparent. These icons contrast sharply with the equally common text style icons (e.g., Plain, Bold, Italic, Underline, etc.),

200: Cohesiveness in any image program depends on repeating elements and using common sizes, line weights, and densities. These buttons from various Windows applications use iconic imagery to represent day/week/month (a), and paragraph alignment (b), and symbols for logical inequalities (c). (Note how gratuitous dimensionality impairs the readability of the images in the left-hand column.)

with which it is practically impossible to create a coherent visual program if the intent is to encode the visual characteristics of the corresponding style attribute in the image itself. Even when the same font and size are used, the resulting images have little in common due to their variation in the basic perceptual variables (c).

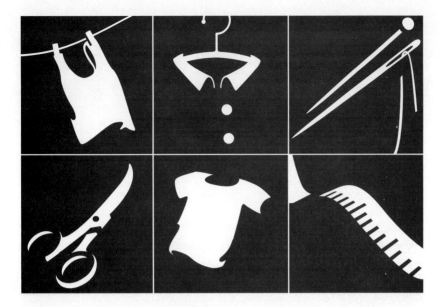

201: By focusing attention on a few essential aspects, visual representation can strongly characterize an object despite a relatively high level of abstraction. Design by The Understanding Business.

Iconic signs fulfill the representation function by calling to mind one or more essential characteristics of the sign object. Effective *characterization* requires a focus on these distinctive features. The images in Figure 201 emphasize the flexibility or rigidity of the material used in each object in the contours of each icon. The folds produce discontinuities that are accentuated by the removal of most other detail from the image and by the use of negative space to focus attention on important details. Contrasting material properties – such as the sharp, rigid needle and the limp, twisting thread or the regular unit markings and the undulating tape – enhance one another to help iden-

Characterization

202: These stamp designs by students of Armin Hofmann use visual cues such as narrow counter-forms and radial typography to emphasize curvatures that characterize their corresponding object.

203: Effective characterization depends critically on selecting a point of view from which the characteristics being represented are clearly visible. Design by Rudolf Modley.

tify the object in each case. Contrasts can often be used to underscore essential qualities in an image (202). The thin linear elements and radial typography in these stamp designs make the rounded forms at each stamp's focal point appear that much rounder. The curvature of the dove's head and outthrust breast of the pigeon evoke the birds' characteristic posture and appearance, while the spiraling curvature of the horn is similarly underscored by the thin slice of negative space delineating the bell.

Choosing the right point of view can be as important as determining which qualities to emphasize, since, from some vantage point, the parts that most effectively characterize the subject may be visible poorly or not at all. It would rarely be useful, for example, to depict a chair from above or a radio from behind. Similarly, the dress of each worker in Figure 203 would be unclear from any other perspective since the frontal view – which exposes seams, fasteners, pockets, etc. – carries most of the visual information. The

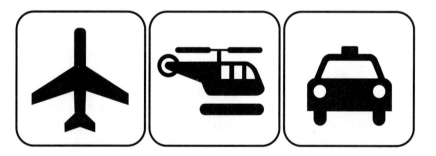

204: Effective characterization depends on choosing the right point of view, eliminating non-characteristic details, and exaggeration of defining features, as in these icons from the U.S. DOT's *Symbol Signs* program. Design by Cook & Shanosky Associates.

icons developed for the U.S. DOT (204) also show how choosing the right viewpoint can help distinguish objects. The most informative vantage point is usually the one with the most complex contour or the greatest amount of distinctive internal detail, but the viewer's experience can also influence the decision. The viewpoints chosen for the DOT icons, for example, are those from which these vehicles are seen most frequently in the viewer's everyday experience. This strategy allows the image set to exploit the viewer's familiarity with a particular characteristic viewpoint. As in the cartoonist's caricature, effective communication may demand exaggeration beyond purely physical accuracy to emphasize important components, such as the rotor blades of a helicopter or the sign on the roof of a taxicab.

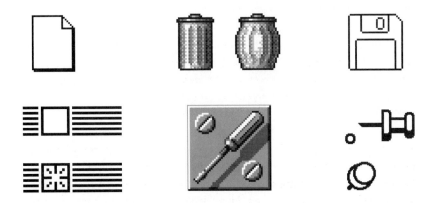

205: Expressive visual imagery from various GUI environments shows how characteristic features of the object (real or imagined) can be captured using contrast, viewpoint, and exaggeration. Changes in appearance in response to user actions add believability as well as useful feedback.

Visual representations that characterize their objects effectively can do much to add interest and vitality to the human-computer interface. Engaging visual details from real-world objects, such as the dog-eared corner on the "paper" document (205 – a) or the notch on the floppy diskette (205-c) are made more noticeable by their contrast with the rectangular contour of the rest of the icon. These enhanced representations – caricatures, if you will – do more than literal realism to create believable signs. They complement exaggerated animated representations such as the bulging Macintosh trash can (205–b) the playful "poof" of the Macintosh Close box (205–d) and the two-state setting of the OPEN LOOK Pushpin (205-e) in creating a convincing virtual world.

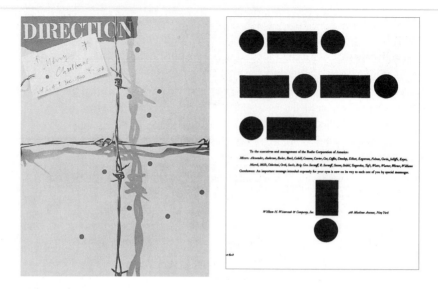

206: These designs by Paul Rand show the importance of shared context in communication. The cover on the left is an appropriate Christmas theme for a society engulfed in war, while the ad on the right is more than just a pleasing arrangement of dots and dashes to those who read Morse code.

Communicability

The *communicability* of any representation depends on a shared context between sender and receiver that allows signs to be interpreted within a pragmatics comparable to the one under which they were encoded. The experience of an image is affected not only by other images in the ensemble, but also by the physical, cultural, and conceptual environment in which it appears. Two extraordinary designs by Paul Rand (206) depend heavily on context for their appreciation. In the Christmas 1940 cover for Direction magazine (206–a), the use of a barbed wire cross as the ribbon on a gift wrapped package (note the Christmas tree shape of the perforations) provides a stark reminder of the war engulfing Europe. Whereas today, the semantic dimension is initially obscure, in 1940, the message was immediate. The adjacent newspaper advertisement (206–b) can be enjoyed purely as a visual analogy and a playful contrast between the dot-dash pattern at the

207: Cultural dependency is apparent in these icons representing mailboxes in the U.S.(a), Denmark (b), France (c), and Italy (d). Each could be interpreted as a control box or trash can by someone unfamiliar with the local convention. Line art is the property of Apple Computer, Inc.

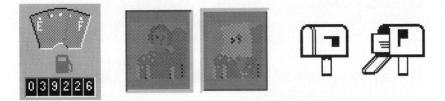

208: Each of these representations presents a poor analogy between sign object and system concept. The fuel gauge and odometer (a) are monotonic functions that have little in common with the actual pattern of memory or disk space usage. The "bag over the head" icon (b) means "suppress video preview," which would properly be represented as an invisible person. Finally, the ubiquitous American rural mailbox icon (c) is always used "incorrectly." The flag on a real mailbox is raised to tell the *mail carrier* that outgoing mail is present, not to tell the homeowner that incoming mail has arrived.

top and the exclamation mark at the bottom. The targeted audience, however, could grasp the design at a deeper level. Any one of them would immediately recognize the dots and dashes as the Morse code for their own company name (RCA). Context provides the key to correct interpretation.

Communicability demands that the pragmatics of a sign be considered very carefully. Precisely because we carry it about subconsciously in the form of our own life experience, the effect of context on our understanding of the world goes largely unnoticed. What is "obviously" a mailbox in one culture, for example, would be surprisingly unfamiliar to people from other cultures (207). Effective visual representations for international audiences should be based on aspects of the sign object that are truly universal within the target population (such as an envelope, in this example).

Visual metaphors can help users understand the working of their environment, but only to the extent that the mapping between image states and system states corresponds to the user's understanding of the real-world analog. In the rush to add familiar imagery to GUI environments, metaphors are

209: At the lowest level, communicability is affected by syntactic decisions. When the background color of an image is allowed to vary, the designer gives up any ability to ensure adequate contrast.

often stretched beyond recognition. The fuel gauge and odometer (208-a), for example, are supposed to represent the amount of free memory and disk space, though neither of these analogies is particularly relevant. The other examples (208-b,c) exhibit similar problems. Metaphorical signs involve a two stage interpretation between representamen and sign object, on the one hand, and between sign object and system function on the other. Only when the semantics of both relationships are clear will communication succeed.

Finally, the communicability of any visual sign depends on its physical display context. Employing narrow, colored figural elements on a ground whose color can be customized by the user, for example, will inevitably lead to situations where the icon is illegible (209). The need for adequate contrast between figure and ground is so critical to image recognition that an icon

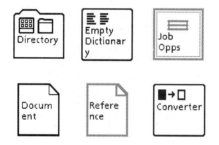

210: Competition between visual and verbal elements at the syntactic level will subvert communication regardless of a sign's appropri–ateness at the semantic or pragmatic level.

should never relinquish control of that portion of the background that falls within the boundaries of the image itself. For similar reasons, images rarely provide an effective display context for textual labels. In GUI applications, the addition of an internal label places additional formal constraints on a visual representation, which must depend largely or exclusively on contour information to ensure proper interpretation. The "natural" size of an image in the target environment, moreover, restricts the length of the label as well. The curious decision to place labels within icons in the Xerox Star and Viewpoint environments produces a number of bizarre line breaks (210). While the labels can be read, they are distracting enough to divert the attention from the visual qualities of the image itself. A more effective syntax would ensure that word and image complement – rather than compete with – one another in supporting the sign's interpretation.

Common Errors

The advantages of imagery are realized only when the image is appropriately designed and carefully produced. Problems can arise at the level of *syntax*, which governs relationships between elements within the sign; *semantics*, or the meaning of the sign elements; and *pragmatics*, or the suitability of the image for a particular physical display and set of interpreters.

211: *Misleading syntax.* The elements of any visual representation must combine properly to form a coherent sign. Every apparent logical relationship between elements in the image should reflect an analogous relationship between the corresponding sign objects. These images from an air terminal signage program are extremely confusing because the logical relation of the aircraft to the arrow is unclear. Because the viewer assumes that all elements of the image exist within the same coordinate system, the arrows appear to be "pushing" the tail of the plane to the left in each image. The intended meanings – Take Offs and Landings– can be understood only when the viewer realizes that

while the *aircraft* is being viewed from above, the *arrow* is being viewed from the side. While the selected viewpoint makes the aircraft easily recognizable, it is a highly unfamiliar vantage point for take-offs and landings. A more natural perspective presenting the aircraft in a side view – with the nose pointed up or down, for takeoff and landing – would communicate more effectively. This representation would place the aircraft in the appropriate attitude and bring the elements of the sign into a more compatible spatial relationship.

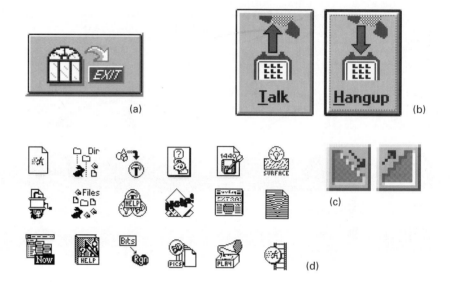

(a)

(b)

(c)

(d)

212: *Poorly integrated structure.* High quality images exhibit a spatial unity that ensures the parts work together to strengthen the whole instead of competing for the viewer's attention as independent elements. A well designed image never needs to be disassembled to be understood. When the parts of an image must be individually analyzed and then put back together to reach the proper interpretation, the perceptual immediacy of the image disappears completely. The "Exit" icon above (a) not only forces a serial reading, but even worse, it is ambiguous once the parts have been reassembled (does the icon mean "Exit to Windows" or "Exit Windows"?). When the visual variables needed for discrimination – primarily orientation – are identical in two signs ambiguity at the syntactic level can produce the wrong response even when the semantics and pragmatics are clear. Discriminating between two images that differ only in the pointing direction of an arrow (c, d), for example, is slow and error-prone even though the correct interpretation is clear following the proper reading. The same problem arises when an image is overly detailed, or when its individual elements are so small that they become difficult to recognize on their own merits or even to group together into the same perceptual unit. In all of the monochrome examples above (c), the sensation is more like reading a newspaper than looking at a picture.

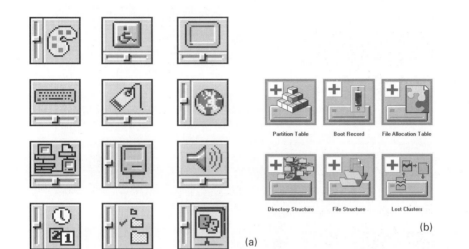

Partition Table Boot Record File Allocation Table

Directory Structure File Structure Lost Clusters

(a)

(b)

213: *Dominant secondary elements.* Creating composite imagery is always fraught with syntactic problems. When secondary elements are balanced correctly, they can provide valuable context without unduly interfering with the image as a whole. Unfortunately, this is easier said than done. When individual elements are too weak, the problems seen in Figure 212 quickly arise. At the opposite extreme, when secondary elements are too strong, they can so dominate perception that the rest of the information in the image can be extracted only with difficulty. Dominant program characteristics are apparent in the standard control panel icons from the Macintosh System 7 (a). The heavy, 3Dslider control draws the viewer's attention from the primary image (telling them which parameters the icon controls) even as it identifies the icon as Macintosh control panel. (Note that the distracting effect of the slider is heightened considerably by its frequent alternation between horizontal and vertical orientations.) The gray pseudo-dimensionality intensifies this masking effect by lowering the contrast and making individual icons harder to recognize in the first place. The same problems are produced by the red cross and disk drive elements in the disk utility icons above (b). Together, these elements are so much more prominent than anything else in the images that it becomes difficult to ignore them and focus on the distinguishing elements of the individual icons.

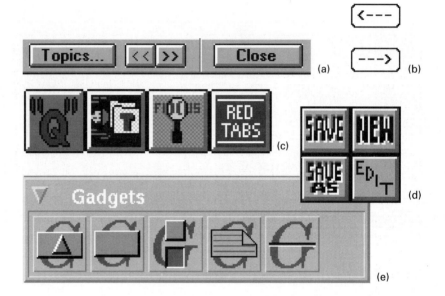

(a)

(b)

(c)

(d)

(e)

214: *Using type as image.* Effective visual representation depends heavily on the use of high quality images. Using poorly rendered or poorly integrated textual elements as graphical devices in a pseudo-pictorial representation is even less effective than using a poorly rendered image. Even "graphical" characters from a standard font, such as "<"and ">," (or worse, the strings "<--" and "-->") are not strong enough to serve as stand-alone graphical elements (a, b). Every GUI toolkit supports graphical as well as textual button labels, and bold, clear arrow symbols are trivial to produce. Similarly, the use of *verbal* phrases (e.g., "Red Tabs") as *visual* signs (c) ensures that any advantage of pictorial representation will be lost. Forcing these verbal symbols into a small raster image format provides virtually no benefit from a communication standpoint – it simply makes them harder to read. Even when supported by graphical stunts such as the ubiquitous magnifying glass, the verbal label produces a weak visual sign. The idea that grotesquely distorted words serving as toolbar images (d) add any value beyond their textual menu equivalents is self-evidently absurd. A more common crutch is the use of a single character to suggest some aspect of a sign that is difficult to represent graphically (e). When the verbal element dominates, its abstract nature ensures that unintended associations will arise in addition to – or instead of – the one intended. When the pictorial element dominates, the "background" character simply adds visual noise.

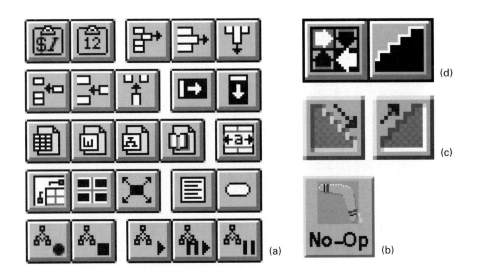

(d)

(c)

No-Op

(a)

(b)

215: *Using images for abstract concepts.* Images of familiar, concrete objects are easy to interpret correctly. Iconic representations excel at the identification function precisely because of the directness of the relationship (resemblance) on which the sign is based. Abstract concepts, processes, or situations, because they are less tangible, depend on less direct forms of representation in which even a well-designed image may be difficult to interpret correctly. Even when the sign's syntax is clear, its semantics can be obscured by the weak, largely conventional association between the visual elements of the sign and the abstract or temporal aspects of the signified. The example above (a) shows just a few of the dozens of icons that can be added to the toolbar of a lead-ing spreadsheet application. (How many you can identify?) Many of these examples are almost diagrammatic, yet their meanings remain unclear. Perhaps the ultimate example of a concept that is impossible to convey graphically is the *NoOp* ("does nothing") function. The boomerang analogy (b) is very weak (it would be more appropriate for *Undo*), and the visual sign would fail completely without the accompanying text. When meaning is conventional, the same image can be used in different signs. The stepped images (c, d) can be readily identified as stairs, but this does not reveal their full meaning ("sort by increasing or decreasing order" and, "step through a macro," respectively). In all of these examples, verbal representations would have many advantages.

(c)

(a)

(b)

216: *Images based on obscure allusions.* When portraying abstract concepts, the designer often has no choice but to substitute an evocative concrete object. The semantic relation, however, is rarely a strong one, even with a well chosen metaphorical reference. When the allusion is strained or obscure, the meaning is never apparent. One of the better examples of this phenomenon is the "stove" icon above (a). This icon represents a Master Task List of things you'd "like to do someday but don't want to schedule for a particular day." The viewer is supposed to notice that the pot of boiling water – like an item on the Master Task List – is on the "back burner" of the stove, and thus make the leap to enlightenment. Few examples are this obscure, but many have similar problems.

The tool palette on the right (b) relies heavily on literal, concrete metaphors to suggest the corresponding functions. The magnet tool lets you move an entry from one page to another in an appointment book. The axe tool is used to break the links established by the anchor tool, and the footprints represent the Backtrack function...a navigational aid allowing you to retrace your steps. Even when a visual reference is fairly direct, unnecessary embellishment of the image (c) can distract if it evokes additional, undesired associations. The Label icon above, for example, seems more like a price tag, or ticket, while the Scrolled Text icon, thanks to its dog-eared paper element, misleadingly suggests a file- or document-level operation.

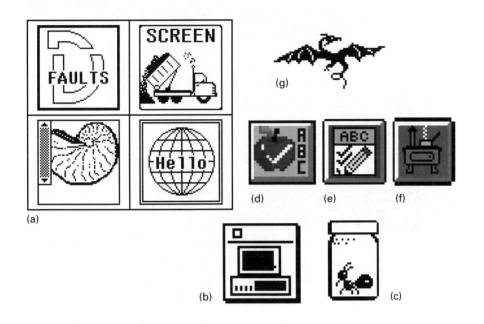

(g)

(a)

(d)   (e)   (f)

(b)   (c)

217: *Culture or language dependencies.* The pragmatic aspect of an image describes assumptions about the viewer and the viewing environment that are implicit in any visual representation. An image may "work" for some viewers, but not for others. If the image relies on inside jokes, figures of speech, slang, or other terminology that is well-known only within a particular subculture, than it will be intelligible only to members of that group. The icons for *Hello World*, *Screen Dump*, *Defaults Edit*, and *c-shell* (a), for example, use visual and verbal puns that are recognizable only to those for whom the concepts are already familiar. Other images depend on historical knowledge of an industry or product. The "DOS" icon (b) is a very literal representation of the original IBM-PC, which bears little resemblance to the "DOS" PC's of today. Unless the viewer knows what PC's *used to* look like, communication is likely to break down. Similarly, the origins of the term, "debugger" (c) are familiar to most developers, but not to many end-users, while the reference to the "apple for the teacher" tradition in American schools (d) would have little meaning in cultures without this custom. Linguistic dependencies operate on many levels. Users in non-Western cultures, for example, would have trouble making the connection between, "ABC" and "spelling" (d,e). Familiarity with the figure of speech equating "back burner" with low priority is a precondition for understanding the stove image (f), while simple phonetics are sufficient for the "drag-on" target (g).

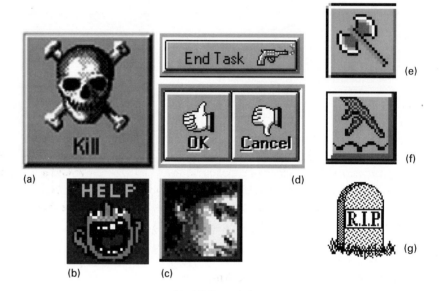

218: *Offensive or suggestive imagery.* Imagery that some users may find personally or culturally offensive should always be avoided in commercial products. While examples as extreme as the *Kill* icon from NeXTStep (a) are rare, it is not hard to find images that would be considered at least mildly upsetting in some cultures or to some users. Even otherwise benign icons may be offensive if they are overly intrusive (b) or even suggestive (c). Gestures too have different meanings in different cultures – the "thumbs up" sign (d) does not mean "OK" in the Middle East, for example! – and even the depiction of "disembodied" limbs (f) is considered taboo in many parts of the world. Images related to death, injury, or violence, in particular, are almost never appropriate in an office environment. The typical user is not even aware of the "dead" software entities to which the tombstone (g) and pistol (d) icons refer, and the grisly connotations of the battle axe (e) have little to offer an office automation task. All of these images add unnecessary fear and confusion to the typical user's experience. Today's hardware and software environments are already intimidating for most non-technical users. Adding stress-inducing imagery can only compound the problem.

One does not put signs along a railroad track saying, "Please come to a stop." Instead, we have very sensibly devised colored signals, which are kinds of ideograms and are infinitely more expressive and more readily understood than verbal messages. Obliged to get its message across rapidly, the poster uses the same language—the image, the true vehicle of thought.

A.M. Cassandre

Techniques

Sound draftsmanship is a skill that develops only after years of practice, but electronic media are continually decreasing the importance of manual techniques. Far more important than a skilled hand are a sensitive eye and a knowledge of how to use visual representations correctly. These can be acquired more easily than a general proficiency in illustration. Three simple techniques can help improve the quality of your images:

Selection
Refinement
Coordination

- Selecting the Right Vehicle
- Refinement through Progressive Abstraction
- Coordination to Ensure Visual Consistency

Effective visual imagery can be produced (or at least art directed) even by those without a lot of natural "artistic" talent. The only real requirement is an appreciation for the role of imagery and a basic understanding of visual language (Dondis, 1984, Bertin, 1985, and Tufte, 1989, are especially enlightening to this end).

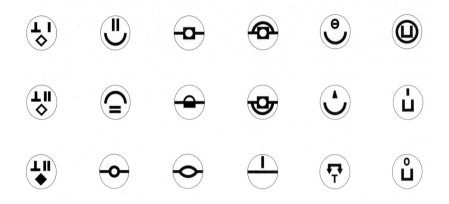

219: Even well-designed images are poorly suited to the problem of representing abstract concepts and complex processes. These elegant symbols representing common data processing operations never gained popularity or widespread use. Design by Tomas Maldonado. © Olivetti S.p.A.

Selecting the Right Vehicle

Designers choose between verbal and pictorial representations every day. As the world moves to graphical user interfaces, there is a growing prejudice favoring the use of images. In many cases this represents nothing more than a naive technological determinism demanding that the graphical display be exploited to its "fullest" irrespective of task demands or user needs. It is also widely assumed, however, that images are, on their own merits, more useful, interesting, and (of course) more "fun" than verbal representations. Today's proliferating toolbars often attempt to provide an icon for every function in the application. While they may be popular for other reasons, we have yet to hear someone claim that toolbars are helpful *because* their icons are easy to understand.

Pictorial images can be very effective in representing familiar concrete objects from the user's everyday experience. Pictorial signs have also been shown to be far superior to verbal signs for representing inherently spatial concepts (e.g., traffic directions) under brief presentations and poor viewing conditions (Carr, 1973). Images are much less useful, however, in representing abstract concepts or operations without a familiar experiential reality. Particularly when the connection to the sign object is narrow or tenuous, based on obscure language- or culture-specific allusion, failure of interpretation can be expected. Even when carefully designed as part of an elaborate symbol system, images for abstract processes or conditions (219) are purely conventional – they must be learned before they can become useful.

Effective design respects the capabilities and limitations of the material or medium. This principle extends to choice of representation as well. Words convey nuance far more effectively than pictures. The four iconic signs on the left in Figure 220 are more ambiguous than the corresponding verbal labels on the right. The useful semantic distinctions between bar, snack shop, cafeteria, and restaurant are difficult to express visually because the tangible elements with which the viewer is already familiar – the tableware, the eating utensils, even the food – are roughly comparable in all four settings. These well designed images make the distinctions recognizable with just a little practice, but only when viewed as a set. In isolation, the individual images again seem to be applicable to more than one alternative. The verbal labels, in contrast, are immediately understood along with all their subtle connotations.

Visual interface designers face these problems on a daily basis. Even an appropriate conceptual model will fail if the user is unable to correctly evaluate and interpret the underlying system states based on the visual feedback presented (Norman, 1988). The difficulty of developing visual representations that effectively distinguish between *Save* and *Save as*, between *Cut*, *Delete*, and *Clear*, or between controls with similar or identical appearance but different behaviors, should not be underestimated. The problem is especially common in "toolbars" which, for all their popularity in the Windows environment, exhibit very little similarity across applications in the graphical devices they use to represent the same set of abstract operations (221–a). Those toolbar icons reported to be most useful typically correspond to concrete attributes of visible objects, such as font attributes, paragraph alignment, linespacing, or to concrete system objects such as printers and folders.

  Bar

Snack

 Selfservice

Restaurant

220: Words are usually more effective than images for conveying subtle distinctions or shades of meaning, even when the concept being represented is fairly concrete. After Frutiger (1981).

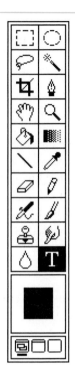

221: Toolbars in Windows productivity applications contain abstract commands (which are also presented as verbal menu items) that are difficult to represent clearly using images. Tool palettes in graphics applications, in contrast, represent persistent modes providing concrete visual feedback.

The visual confusion of most Windows toolbars contrasts sharply with the success of tool palettes in various graphics editing applications (221–b). Tool *palettes* differ from "toolbars" in that most of the icons they contain represent actual application modes (i.e., the "tool" you have picked up) that maintain a tangible existence of their own by virtue of their persistence and visual feedback. The changing shape of the mouse pointer, for example, is usually related to the icon (tool) corresponding to that mode. Because a tool providing proper feedback is more concrete than an abstract verbal command (which becomes visible only indirectly, by virtue of its effect on its target object), the tool palette is both more natural and more effective than the icon bar. A well-organized GUI application should place commands in menus, where the more descriptive verbal representation can be used (along with a suitably mnemonic accelerator), and reserve the visible portion of the display for important tools and direct access to properties with an inherently spatial character.

An essential aspect of visual imagery is the speed and directness with which recognition and identification take place. This critical advantage, however, is heavily dependent on the quality and familiarity of the image, as well as its appropriateness for the concept being represented. Choosing and using the right medium for a particular communication task is more a discipline than a technique. Four simple rules should nevertheless be kept in mind when considering these problems:

Summary: Selection

1 If the concept to be communicated is a concrete, familiar object or a tangible, externally obvious state, use an iconic sign.

2 If the concept to be communicated will be used repeatedly throughout an application or environment, consider establishing a conventional symbolic or indexical sign, especially if an existing sign can be borrowed from the "real" world.

3 In most other cases – and particularly when the concept to be communicated is an abstract process or a subtle transition between states – a textual label should be used.

4 Avoid, as much as possible, the mixing of purely textual, iconic and indexical or symbolic signs within a single image set.

Historical debate over the relative strengths and weaknesses of visual and verbal representations has focused on which vehicle is *inherently* superior. Interface designers follow this misguided path by trying to do everything *either* textually *or* graphically. The optimal representation varies with the communication problem. Fortunately, the recognizability and understandability of visual representations can be easily and economically subjected to early usability testing (cf., Nielsen, 1993, 37–40). You don't even need a functioning product – a simple list of visual (and verbal) signs can be used to gain a useful assessment.

222: A gradual process of simplification and refinement can be seen in the evolution of the Pepsi Cola identity and trademark. The familiar waveform motif has evolved from a calligraphic flourish through the bottlecap application to its use as an abstract symbol. Used by permission of Pepsico.

**Refinement
Through Progressive
Abstraction**

Abstraction is the process by which the essential qualities of the thing being represented are separated from the actual physical object or event. By removing superficial or idiosyncratic details, the designer helps the viewer see the formal qualities that tie the representamen to its object. Good imaging, like good writing, is always the result of a careful process of revision and refinement. In visual, as in verbal communication, the objective is to distill the message to its essence. Only a crisp message will be processed efficiently and interpreted correctly. Image *refinement* depends on a continuous process of simplification, removal of extraneous detail, and regularization of irregular elements. Developing the "correct" form for a given subject and communication objective may require that you start over several times, using the most promising results of previous explorations as a starting point.

223: Typographic forms such as the question mark symbol from the U.S. DOT series (a) must be carefully adjusted when they are to be read as images. The other examples (b) are all from classic typefaces, but none have the graphical integrity to stand on their own.

224: These pictograms for the 1964 Tokyo Olympic Games convey a simple elegance through effective use of negative space. By using the background as part of the image, these icons reach a higher level of abstraction and engagement. Design directed by Masaru Katzumie.

The visual history of a trademarks or product identity reflects the same process of refinement – albeit one stretched out over many years – seen in the movement from concept to finished design for a single product. The Pepsi Cola identity (222) has evolved over nearly a century from the ornate, decorative logotype on the left, to the increasingly stylized and graphically powerful mark on the right. Note how each revision has incorporated the flourishing forms seen in the original logotype. At each revision, however, the flourishes have become increasingly independent of the lettering style as the style has grown bolder and more modernized. The most recent design increases the focus on the flourish and circle (i.e., bottlecap) motif that forms the core of the product identity.

As visual forms are refined, they become simpler, bolder, more direct. Comparing the question mark seen in the U.S. DOT symbol (223-a) set to the unaltered examples on the right (223-b) shows the degree of refinement needed to produce the *Information* symbol. Each of the smaller question marks is part of a beautiful, classic font, yet none have the proportion, balance, or graphical power, to stand alone effectively as an independent visual symbol. The individual characters in a text font are always subservient to the whole, since letters must be designed to work well together rather than as individual elements. (This is why text characters make poor substitutes for graphical elements in a GUI.) The U.S. DOT question mark, for example, cannot be found in any existing text or display font because it has-been hand tuned to meet the special requirements of a large display graphic.

Highly refined images operate on many levels. Most importantly, they work effectively at the lowest levels of perceptual processing, where their simplicity enhances the perceptual immediacy of the image. One refinement technique exploits the figure-ground reversal phenomenon that so interested the Gestalt psychologists (Wertheimer, 1958). Figure-ground relationships can be consciously manipulated, as in the pictograms for the 1964 Tokyo Olympics (224). By making the areas of positive and negative space approximately equal, and using both to represent essential elements of the figure (or better yet, separate, but complementary figures), the image can be made to exhibit a playful instability between the alternate interpretations. Using "negative space" (defined by the absence of ink) effectively can create visual interest even as it simplifies the resulting image. The eye delights in completing the image by filling in the "missing" contours.

225: These icons for localized desktop utilities from Nihon Sun depend on careful refinement to convey subtle distinctions within categories. The icons in the second column, for example, represent font editors for Chinese, Japanese, and Korean, respectively. The subtle application of color and texture provides visual cues that help establish category membership. (See also Color Plate 10).

Careful refinement allows subtle relationships to be established between elements in an image set. Many successful monochromatic icon series fail when color is applied because the colors either work poorly together or break up the internal structure of the icon set. The detailed icon set in Figure 225 shows how the careful application of a few colors, used meticulously and purposefully, can produce the minimum adequate contrast in the background elements while permitting the foreground elements to be sharply distinguished.

A good map tells a multitude of little white lies; it suppresses truth to help the user see what needs to be seen.... the value of a map depends on how well its generalized geometry and generalized content reflect a chosen aspect of reality.

Mark Monomier
How to Lie With Maps

Abstraction begins with a literal representation and works backward to extract the essence of the target object. Beginning with an accurate representation eliminates subtle errors in scale or proportion that can undermine the effectiveness of the final image. Don't assume you "know" what something looks like: always find a high-fidelity original upon which to base your work. When the right original has been found, the process can proceed:

Summary: Refinement

1 Determine the appropriate level of abstraction for your image set, based on the subject matter, audience, and display resolution.

2 Begin with an image seen from the viewpoint including the most characteristic contours. The source can be a photo-graph, drawing, or sketch of the object from the desired point of view.

3 Use the *trace overlay technique* to rapidly develop a series of drawings derived from the initial image. Omit details until only the most essential or characteristic elements remain. Experiment with different combinations of elements to identify those that best characterize the object.

4 Simplify complex shapes into regular geometrical forms where possible. Repeatedly tracing the outline of the shape through multiple layers will itself tend to regularize the image.

5 Eliminate contour information that is not required for recognition of the object. Experiment with negative space to suggest contours.

Image development is visual design in a microcosm and many of the techniques discussed previously are relevant here as well. Note, for example, the direct incorporation in the last three steps of the simplification techniques of Reduction, Regularization, and Combination. Scale, contrast, and proportion are important as well, and must be manipulated carefully and consistently both within and across images.

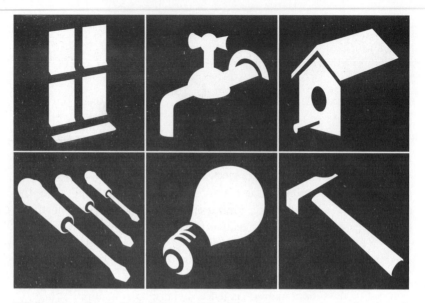

226: These icons from the Pacific Bell SMART® Yellow Pages share a common image orientation and viewpoint, as well as a similar level of abstraction. Awareness of the program can aid in the interpretation of images that might otherwise be obscure. Design by The Understanding Business.

Coordination to Ensure Visual Consistency

For a set of images to work together effectively, they must share a coherent language of form that makes the interrelatedness of every image in the group immediately apparent. This level of integration can be achieved only by consistently manipulating the perceptual characteristics of each image to balance similarity and differentiation across the ensemble. The most important parameters to standardize are the dominant visual variables of size and value (often described as the "visual weight" of the image). Consistent application of the rest of Bertin's (1985) visual variables is almost as important, as are the use of a consistent point of view and level of abstraction.

Most images in GUI applications are roughly consistent in size, if for no other reason than that UI toolkits prefer to deal with bitmaps in digitally "natural" sizes. While care should still be taken to ensure that image scales are optically – as well as physically – equated, real problems are seen more frequently in the visual weight and level of abstraction of the images. These qualities often vary wildly within an icon set, and they almost always vary substantially across icon sets in the same environment. While some lack of cross-application coordination is unavoidable, the use of style rules and platform standard imagery can help to define a coherent direction.

227: In this final example from the SMART® Yellow Pages series, the formal choices differ substantially (e.g., orthographic vs. perspective views, extreme vs. moderate abstraction) from those in Figure 226, yet the same *internal* consistency is apparent. Design by The Understanding Business.

The imagery in Figures 226 and 227 (see also 192 and 201) shows the level of integration that can be achieved within an image set by combining elements of the same formal vocabulary. In the first set, where each object is represented by a few planes or surfaces with simplified exterior contours and virtually no interior detail, the unifying factors are the level of abstraction, oblique orientation, and perspective view. Note how the consistently positioned light source underscores both the common orientation and point of view. The second set relies on an absolute uniformity of line weights and a consistent, linear drawing style. These images too show a minimum of inter-

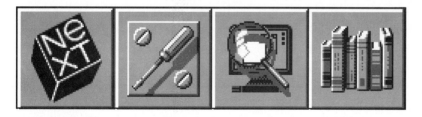

228: Perhaps in hope of compensating for the lack of color in the display, images from the initial NeXTStep release were strongly biased toward maximum concreteness. The detailed iconic representations make the cube symbol of the corporate identity appear somewhat out of place.

229: These icons from OpenWindows 3 use orientation as part of a visual language. Oblique images of documents and media designate tools or devices rather than the documents or media themselves.

nal detail and are likewise consistent in both their orientation (45 or 90 degrees) and their flat orthographic presentation. Icons in existing GUI applications have rarely used abstraction as effectively as in these image sets. The original NeXTStep icons (228) provide a good example of the opposite, representational extreme. The NeXTStep environment began with a highly-illustrative, sharply dimensional style that maximized the impact of their high-resolution grayscale display. Because only four colors were available, the resulting images are more effective than many current GUI icon sets that use color with far less restraint.

230: This monochromatic version of the Nihon Sun icon set (225) shows the concern for visual compatibility with existing OpenWindows icons (229, see also 204). Orientation cues are used in the same way, and existing formal elements such as books and brushes are incorporated or adapted.

The multi-colored Nihon Sun desktop icons (225) were designed to use color effectively in an 8-bit environment. To integrate cleanly with an existing set of monochromatic icons (229), a monochromatic version (230) was created simultaneously. This set was required to work consistently with the visible language of the existing monochromatic icon set. The new icons were also required to be compatible with the new color imagery. The new, slightly more illustrative image program as successfully integrated with the existing icon set by adopting similar size, orientation, line thickness, and point of view.

> [In designing image sets, the designer] is looking for the most characteristic visual quality of the object being represented in each case together with the maximum consistency of treatment.
>
> **Peter Wilbur**
> Information Design

Consistency is particularly important in an image set. Because they are such powerful attractors to begin with, images can totally dominate the display if allowed to flower in all its glorious variety. It is better to relate the images visually so that they form a perceptual layer of their own. Users can then attend to the images when necessary and ignore them when appropriate. Achieving consistency in an image set is simply a matter of equating as many of the images' visual qualities as possible:

Summary: Coordination

1 Begin with sketches of a full set of images that have been sufficiently developed to establish the visual characteristics of each image.

2 Use a similar or identical point of view and type of perspective for each image. Determine the predominant viewpoint and redraw any divergent images from the new perspective.

3 Use a similar form of representation and level of abstraction (i.e., don't combine icons with symbols).

4 Use a consistent size, orientation, layout, color, and overall visual weight for each image. Use a layout grid to help ensure consistent internal structure across images.

5 Wherever possible, use the *same* elements – including line weights, curvatures, textures, and forms – throughout the image set. In fact, it is not difficult to completely redraw the entire image set using standard components once a formal vocabulary has been defined.

This technique will help you produce image sets that are functional as well as aesthetically pleasing. Regularity within the image set helps distinguish its members from images outside the set. Regularity also makes the individual members more identifiable, since their distinguishing characteristics stand out more strongly as local inconsistencies. Extending the set by adding new images is simplified as well since the design constraints are clear.

So What About Style?

7

Style is the visual synthesis of the elements, techniques, syntax, inspiration, expression, and basic purpose.

Donis A. Dondis
A Primer of Visual Literacy

Style encompasses all those characteristics of a particular *approach* to problem solving that distinguish one design from other solutions to the same problem. In addition to the apparent *formal* characteristics of the design, a style describes the *means* by which aesthetic ends are achieved, the *values* reflected in those ends, and the *culture* within which those values prevail. The same information can be presented in many different graphic styles, just as the same application program can be realized in different GUI environments or the same algorithm implemented in different high-level programming languages. The choice of style, however, does *affect* the choice of material and – more importantly – the emphasis placed on its different aspects as a means of communication with the intended audience.

In visual design, a legitimate style produces a unique *visual language* reflecting the moral and aesthetic values of the culture within which it arises. All styles build upon (or react against) the forms embodied in their predecessors, but significant stylistic movements are never based on superficial embellishment, eclectic imitation, or self-conscious ornamentation. A style that panders to the fashion of the day will be short-lived and soon forgotten. Such is the fate of style for the sake of style, or originality for the sake of originality. Fashion is driven by the need (psychological, social, commercial) for constant change and variety. While a style may become apparent only in retrospect (Gombrich, 1984), its broader scope and greater endurance reflect its deeper connection to the intellectual fabric of its time.

231: The unabashedly synthetic materials, exotic patterns, and colorful, decorative intent of the Swatch® – along with considerable marketing savvy – have shattered the image of the stately timepiece throughout Western culture. Swatch is a registered trademark of Swatch S.A., Switzerland.

While largely independent of content, the chosen style is itself *part of the message.* Its pragmatic implications must always be addressed in effective communication-oriented design. Because it governs formal decisions, style is the first thing people notice in a design. It tells the viewer how to interpret the design by providing clues to the cultural context within which it was created and the audience for whom it is intended. Perhaps most importantly, style provides a means of connecting with an audience at a very primitive level. This *expressive directness* makes style a central component of the aesthetic experience. When used with honesty and integrity, style provides several key benefits:

Emotion. Style provides great latitude for expression. Because they are largely independent of content, stylistic decisions place few restrictions on the designer's imagination and creativity. The familiar style of the Swatch consortium (231) expresses a personal, playful attitude that shatters the image of the stately timepiece as family heirloom. The wristwatch becomes a fashion accessory – and an expression of the wearer's personality – with different designs for different occasions.

Connection. Because style emerges from a shared cultural experience, it produces a direct sense of identification in those who are part of that culture. For those on the outside, style can also provide a basis for understanding, if not appreciating the culture, through the designed artifact. Individual Swatch designs reflect a frame of mind and an attitude (not always the same one!) toward precision, accuracy, seriousness. The large collections introduced twice yearly provide a variety that offers personalization.

Context. A recognizable style provides a historical, cultural, and artistic context that – to the extent it is familiar – makes the message and function of the designed artifact immediately apparent. The success of the Swatch has spawned many imitators, but the original retains a continuity of form, content, and expression that continues to set it apart. The Swatch product line has evolved and expanded to include new mechanisms, and new physical packages (even telephones and soon, an automobile!). It succeeds because it continues to evolve with the underlying social context, while the competition just tries to *look like* a Swatch.

Principles

The effectiveness of a graphic style depends more on the selection and combination of formal elements rather than on the particular forms themselves. Effective styles must be *distinctive* enough to be readily identifiable. They must possess an *integrity* that reflects the central ideas of the worldview they represent, and be *comprehensive* enough to generalize across a range of design problems. Finally, and most importantly, they must be *appropriate* for the problem, the designer and the targeted consumers. Styles that meet these criteria rarely disappear completely. Instead, they inform the development of new styles and frequently experience revival and rebirth.

Distinctiveness
Integrity
Comprehensiveness
Appropriateness

232: Highway route markers exhibit considerable stylistic variation from state to state (a,c) and between state and federal (b) levels. By contributing to the navigational context, each distinctive approach can become a meaningful sign in its own right.

233: The distinctive forms and unprecedented (in the computer industry, at least) black surfaces of the original NeXT hardware created an immediate sensation. This visual language evokes images not of computation, but of sophisticated personal electronics. Courtesy of frogdesign.

Distinctiveness

To maintain its visual and conceptual identity, a style must be easily distinguishable. Though it may be influenced by its predecessors, a successful style must always add something new and uniquely relevant to the cultural context in which it appears. The visual impact of the original NeXT cube (233) was heightened by the sharp visual contrast of its black magnesium housing with the putty-colored uniformity seen in all other systems at the time. The dark sheen, exposed louvres, and stark geometric forms is evocative of both personal electronics and sophisticated technology. The exotic forms were well-matched to NeXT's original target market, but they undoubtedly hindered its later acceptance in the corporate world.

234: These promotional spots illustrate just two of the countless variations on the MTV logo that appear regularly on the original music video channel. The MTV Logo appears courtesy of MTV Networks, a division of Viacom International Inc. © 1993 MTV Networks. All Rights Reserved.

The dynamic visual identity and thematic signature of the MTV network (234) stands in sharp contrast to the cool, restrained design language of the NeXT hardware and display. The style established by the original music video channel on American cable-television reflects the nature of the channel's content. Like the music video, MTV's promotional spots are humorous and ironic, with quick cuts and visually stimulating colors, textures, and patterns changing in tight synchronization with a musical theme. The wide variety of media range from hand-drawn illustrations to 3D computer graphics to photomontage. In this case, as with the Swatch, the unifying elements of the style have more to do with dynamics and point of view than with any particular characteristic of the diverse visual forms.

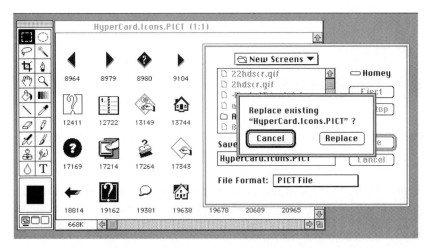

235: The success of the Macintosh created a vocal community of users who insisted on "Mac-like" behavior in every application. Simply using the right toolkit was no longer enough. Applications had to follow the expected style of interaction in critical situations or risk rejection by the marketplace.

In similar fashion, the style of a successful GUI standard depends greatly on its *feel* as well as its *look*. The Macintosh interface includes conventions that encompass more than just the on-screen appearance of the application. Macintosh users came to recognize – and *demand* – applications that were fully "Mac-like" in their organization, appearance, *and* interaction (Tognazzini, 1989). The expectations reflected in these demands rely upon the visual language of the display to *provide a perceptual connection* to the underlying behavioral model (235). Users are at best, uncomfortable, and at worst, confused and disoriented when the familiar visual cues, affordances, and feedback are not present.

236: The same form language and impression of infinite space is present in the book cover by Piet Mondrian (a) (© Estate of Piet Mondrian/E.M. Holtzman Irrevocable Trust), and the *Red-Blue chair* (b) by Gerritt Reitveld (© Estate of Gerrit Reitveld/VAGA, New York 1993).

Integrity

To remain coherent, a style must be internally consistent. The integrity of the formal style reflects the underlying philosophy on which the form is based. The utopian De Stijl (literally, "the style") movement that flourished in the Netherlands throughout the 1920's represented one of the first systematic attempts to break with traditional conventions of representation and design. The goal of its practitioners was to create a new visual language that was at once, *"so coherent, so intelligible, and so complete that the distinctions between art and life would eventually be erased, when everything produced by human agencies, from tea cups to town plans, would participate in a universal, visual, and intellectual harmony"* (Hamilton, 1967). De Stijl's unprecedented focus on simple geometrical shapes and pure primary colors reflected the emerging philosophy of Modernism and provided the movement with the most recognizable formal vocabulary in modern design.

De Stijl's focus on basic forms is seen clearly in the Red/Blue Chair, by Gerrit Reitveld (236-b), and in the cover design by Piet Mondrian (236-a). The construction of the Red/Blue chair shows Reitveld's concern for structural integrity, economy of production, and visual simplicity. The absence of flush joints suggests a space without fully or explicitly defining it. Similarly, the negative space in Mondrian's cover design can be read alternately as figure or as ground, creating a playful spatial tension. As in Mondrian's abstract paintings, the structure of both designs produces a delicate balance between the opposing forces of linear and planar elements. In keeping with the idealism of the De Stijl movement, each of these examples can be enjoyed purely as an expression of the universality of space that exhibits intrinsic aesthetic merit without compromising its functional role [the Red/Blue chair was produced as a monochromatic furniture piece, and was quite comfortable (Friedman, 1982)].

While perhaps not as visually arresting as the language of De Stijl, the extensive cartographic generalization and consistent formal vocabulary of the maps created for USAtlas by The Understanding Business (237, see also 36) produces a similar perceptual unity that makes these images immediately recognizable as part of the same series. The muted colors, minimal detail and superimposition of main arteries represents a radical departure from the forms used in conventional road map design. This new visual language for map design not only permits the graphical treatment to be very consistent, but also makes the maps easier to use (for the intended audience) than conventional designs. Even the "drop shadows" provide an essential cue that makes freeways (the most desirable routes for the intended user) *emerge* to form their own perceptual layer "above" the rest of the map.

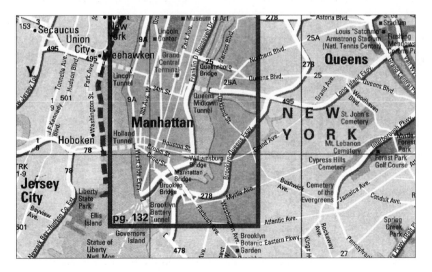

237: The visual integrity of the maps produced by The Understanding Business derives from a relentless focus on the needs of the reader. The maps are used in a wide variety of applications, including the ACCESS® travel guides, US Atlas, and the Pacific Bell SMART® Yellow pages.

Because GUI environments are social constructions produced by dozens or even hundreds of independent development organizations, a comparable integrity of style is not easily achieved. The highest level of integration is seen when a completely new environment is first introduced. Apple's Newton Toolkit (238) is a leading current example that is similar in its visual and conceptual integrity to thoughtfully designed predecessors such as the Macintosh and PenPoint interfaces. Most components in the Newton user interface are simplified versions of the canonical widget types. While the visual language itself has many ragged edges, the net effect of even loosely coordinated elements is nevertheless a unified visual experience.

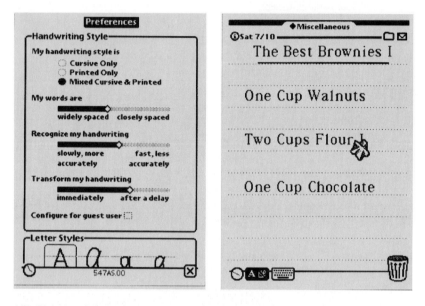

238: Reduction of detail complements frequent allusions to hand-drawn gestures and paper forms in the Newton toolkit. The simplified representations needed to efficiently utilize limited screen real estate provide the unifying theme scene throughout the Newton interface.

Design for a new product category presents a unique opportunity to define solutions in a manner that is both comprehensive and internally consistent, and early adopters tend to work within the constraints of the style. As competition increases, however, the lust for product differentiation inevitably leads developers to break with the integrity of the original formal language. Sadly, the results affect not just the offending products, but the very style itself, which disintegrates and becomes increasingly difficult for newcomers to understand (or even recognize).

239: The eclectic style of architect Michael Graves is exemplified by this design model for the Metropolis Phase One Office Building, Los Angeles.

The most effective styles are not limited to one or a few forms of expression, but can be applied to a wide range of artifacts. The eclectic post-modern style of architect Michael Graves, for example, has been applied with equal effectiveness to public buildings, industrial plants, private residences, interior spaces, furniture, packaging, product design and corporate identity. Graves' desire to break with the dull uniformity of Late-modern architecture

240: Forms, patterns, and colors based on the architectonic motifs seen in Graves' architectural work are applied with equal fluidity to a corporate identify program for Lenox china (a), furniture for the Kyoto Collection from Arkitektura (b), and the Big Dripper teapot from Alessi (c), all by Michael Graves.

led him to adapt Roman motifs to produce expressive, monumental forms. The same concise vocabulary of classical forms and a few subdued colors is apparent throughout Graves' work. Thus, many of the formal characteristics of a monumental office building (239) can be seen in his packaging and corporate identity (240-a) as well as in his desks, chairs, and accessories (240-b), and even in small scale, utilitarian objects such as the Big Dripper coffee maker (240-c). The unity of these diverse products is based not on superficial adornment or even a consistent color palette, but on the individual forms and the way they are related to one another in the assembly.

Stylistic movements that encompass a wide range of designed artifacts always depend on fundamental aspects of the ultimate form – from material selection, to method of construction, to finish and presentation. Each movement reflects a unique value system and approach to problem solving that inevitably shapes the solutions that emerge, regardless of the specific artifact in question. Thus it is that a piece of furniture produced by a Gerritt Reitveld can be more visually reminiscent of a painting by Piet Mondrian than of a similar piece of furniture by Michael Graves.

Each of today's GUI standards also embodies a distinctive style that must be applied across a range of software artifacts. Despite their broad similarity, each environment provides a unique set of formal, visual, and behavioral conventions grounded in the goals, values and interests of its designers and the characteristics of its anticipated users. Every GUI depends on a small set of visual primitives designed for comprehensive use throughout the software

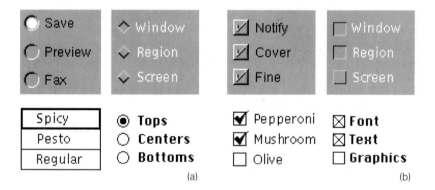

241: The largely conventional semantics of exclusive (a) and non-exclusive (b) settings in many GUI standards (clockwise from top left in each group: NeXTStep, OSF/Motif, Macintosh, OPEN LOOK) underscores the importance of consistent application throughout the environment.

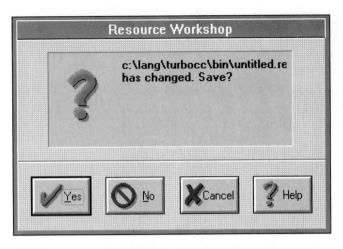

242: Non-standard graphical elements provided by Borland's Application Framework for Windows produce applications that break the consistency of the GUI environment. Despite its potential advantages, a graphical language such as the one proposed here will only create confusion and annoy users until comprehensive deployment throughout the environment is achieved.

environment. Because their semantics are largely conventional (241), elements must be used consistently to be understood by the user. Non-standard elements such as the large, graphical dialog buttons provided by some application frameworks (242) can be distracting if they don't appear in every application. A similarly graphical "Cancel" button in the Newton interface succeeds even without the accompanying label because it is designed for general application and is used throughout that environment (243).

243: In the Newton user interface, where space constraints are far more serious than in Windows, simple graphical abbreviations such as the "X" for "Close" are accepted as part of a small vocabulary of graphical primitives that becomes familiar through its ubiquitous application.

244: The graphical language of sketching and gesture is apparent throughout the PenPoint product identity. The fluid, informal style reflected in this sales collateral and documentation is appropriate for a product promising to replace the keyboard with the stylus. Design by Clement Mok designs, Inc.

Appropriateness

Successful styles develop a visual language based on formal and compositional elements reflecting the inherent qualities of the cultures within which they evolve. PenPoint (see screen in Figure 23) was the first GUI environment designed with support for handwriting recognition as a central feature. The loose, informal character of written language thus became an organizing visual theme for the product and its supporting documentation (244). In this setting, the concrete notebook-like character of the PenPoint interface provides a far more appropriate formal language than, for example, the abstract, geometrical forms produced by the De Stijl movement.

Styles emerge from a social and cultural milieu that is at once shaped by and reflected in the style. The stated goal of the Russian Constructivist movement, for example, was to enlist the arts and design in support of the new communist society in the early post-revolutionary years (Meggs, 1992). The monumental typography, dynamic layout, and heavy use of symbolism seen throughout Constructivist work (245-246) proceed directly from this political imperative. Constructivist designers used both overt and subtle relationships among elements to control the viewer's experience and emphasize critical elements to evoke the desired reaction.

245: The radical perspective and activist political agenda of the Russian Constructivist movement are reflected in these cover designs for the Soviet arts journal, *Left Front of the Arts.* Design by Alexander Rodchenko. © Estate of Alexander Rodchenko/VAGA, New York 1993.

Alexander Rodchenko's cover designs for *Left Front of the Arts* (245) typify the urgency and emotional appeal of Russian design in the early post-Revolutionary years. Each of these designs uses bold forms and sharp contrasts in size, color, and imagery to arrest the viewer's attention while the message is delivered. While contrast remains the dominant theme, the fundamental

246: The dynamism of the revolutionary era is reflected in El Lissitzky's cover for *Object* magazine. © 1993 ARS, New York/ADAGP, Paris.

Constructivist technique of creating tension by establishing visual relationships between contrasting elements is readily apparent as well. A similar tension can be seen in El Lissitzky's cover design for the journal, "Object," (246) features a characteristically asymmetric layout, with the visual weight moved high in the composition to ensure that the composition remains dynamic, if not mildly unsettling. Note the heightened level of visual activity introduced by juxtaposing vertically oriented and oblique elements. This would often be stylistically inappropriate in a user interface, but could be used to draw the attention when appropriate.

247: The bright, saturated colors, playful, concrete imagery, and ubiquitous sound effects provided by *KidPix* quickly grow tiresome for the adult, but they are an endless source of fascination to the child. Image courtesy of Alesha Marie Guyot, Sunnyvale, CA (See Color Plate 13).

Appropriateness as a design criterion for GUI applications ensures that "primitive" visual language elements – such as those seen in the menus and tool palettes of the wildly successful *KidPix* (247) – are used only in situations where they will enhance, rather than subvert, communication with the anticipated user. KidPix uses large, detailed icons, and bright, contrasting colors because the young children for whom it was designed have not yet learned to make the subtle perceptual distinctions required by a more sophisticated formal language. While this approach may be perfectly appropriate for a child, it quickly becomes tedious and excessive for more sophisticated users. A recent study showed, for example, that the highly concrete sound effects accompanying each action were less entertaining and more distracting for older users (Nielsen and Schaeffer, 1993).

Common Errors

The luxury of fixed stylistic conventions that are largely pre-determined by the target GUI standard is rare outside the GUI domain (the book is perhaps the closest analogy). In this section, as in the presentation of Techniques to follow, we will focus on errors in the application of style to GUI design problems rather than on the development of the styles themselves.

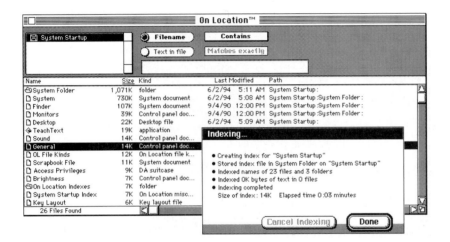

248: *Unwarranted innovation.* Design professionals learn quickly that constraints free the designer to focus their resources on those portions of the problem where innovation is most likely to lead to a successful product. The very essence of the GUI lies in a desire to eliminate the need to re-invent common components in every application. This not only makes the designer's job easier; it also lowers the barriers that slow user acceptance of the environment (not to mention the application). Despite these strong arguments for respecting established convention, deviation from the visual language of each GUI standard is fairly common. One of the first "mainstream" Macintosh applications to follow this path was the file indexing and retrieval product, OnLocation. It self-consciously rejected the Macintosh toolbox in favor of its own heavily rendered, pseudo–3D visual treatment. The reaction was predictably negative in the Macintosh community, where users are notoriously vocal in their demands for conformity to the Mac style. One columnist compared the program's unusual appearance to, "*a third-generation photocopy of the NeXTStep user interface* (Levy, 1989)." OnTechnology founder Mitch Kapor acknowledged the mistake and a version with the standard look and feel was eventually released. While creative excess can still be found in utility programs and smaller applications, such self-conscious disregard for the standard is increasingly rare in mainstream development organizations.

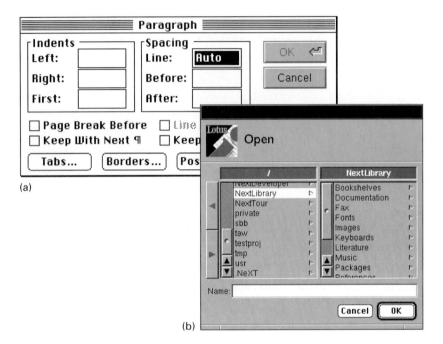

(a)

(b)

249: *Combining unrelated elements.* Combining elements or ideas from different GUI standards inevitably leads to confusion. The components are unlikely to use the same visual language and have certainly not been designed to work together in any case. A design program is a subtle construction in which complex internal relationships are reflected in the external appearance of each component. New elements simply cannot be added *a la carte* with any reasonable hope of success. Extensions to a style must be carefully designed to fit within the existing visual and conceptual framework. That "widgets" lifted directly from one GUI environment and deposited in another should fail should not be particularly surprising. The gray, three-dimensional NeXTStep buttons look awkward enough in the Macintosh dialog above (a), but the stark, two-dimensional, monochrome Macintosh buttons look even more out of place in the elegant three-dimensional, grayscale NeXTStep window (b). These examples are synthetic, but the same effect is being consciously repeated by Macintosh developers who demand a gray background, (just like Windows) even though appropriate control definitions are not yet available on that platform. Every designer is familiar with the inspired client's ubiquitous request: "make it just like that one (only with *my* logo on it!)" In visual interface design, even more than in other areas, this pressure must be resisted, since breakdowns in the visual language threaten the integrity of the entire environment.

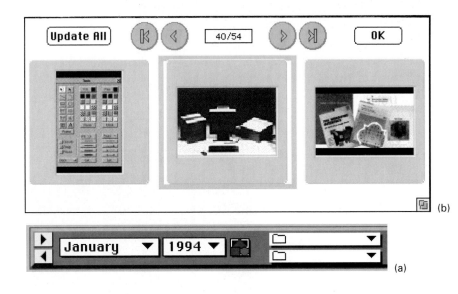

(b)

(a)

250: *Partial fulfillment.* Ever since the appearance of the widely acclaimed NeXT-Step user interface, GUI designers have searched for ways to incorporate the much beloved "pseudo-3D" look into their own products. While the motivation has always been sound – with critics and customers alike contributing to the deafening consensus that the 2D look was dated and even boring – the desire to add "3D" for its own sake quickly overtook any rational consideration of the functional and stylistic reasons for doing so. The goals were clear enough, but tight development schedules, and assumptions buried deep in existing toolkit architectures, limited the ease with which the new presentations could be retrofitted onto existing platform technology. On the assumption that anything was better than nothing, partial solutions (in which only some elements received the 3D treatment) were quickly incorporated into both Windows 3.0 and Apple's System 7. While these extensions were handled with restraint, applications quickly followed suit by freely intermingling two- and three-dimensional, colored and monochromatic controls. As in Figure 249, applications have often attempted to provide a 3D context without removing dependencies on existing 2D controls (a). In other cases, 3D controls are simply inserted into a 2D context (b), These "enhancements" simply undermine attempts at a coherent visual language and unnecessarily complicate the user's experience.

(a)

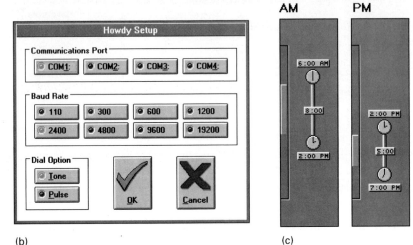

(b)

(c)

251: *Internal or external inconsistency.* Most applications eventually find areas in which they must break with the conventions of the GUI standard, if only to provide functionality that was never anticipated by the toolkit providers. Even then, however, it can be assumed that the rest of the application will be able to use standard components. There is every incentive, then, to design extensions to be visually and conceptually compatible with the standard – in the interest of internal consistency, if nothing else. Alas, application-specific extensions frequently differ from, but rarely improve upon the standard. Using "folder tabs" (the latest metaphor mania) because they are "easier" than scrolling, for example, adds little value if a supplementary scrollbar (a) is required to support more than a few categories. The strange juxtaposition of tabs and scrollbar is far less elegant than either mechanism alone. Similarly, using red and green "LED buttons" (b) in place of standard radio buttons blurs the distinction between settings and commands. The resulting array is difficult to read (particularly for users with color-deficient vision) and visually disorienting. The three-way scrollbars on the right (c) are even more unusual. They allow the user to independently manipulate the duration and start time of an interval. While their value in a scheduling application is clear, these visuals are so unrelated to anything else in the Windows environment that a user's initial response is typically, "What the heck *are* those things?"

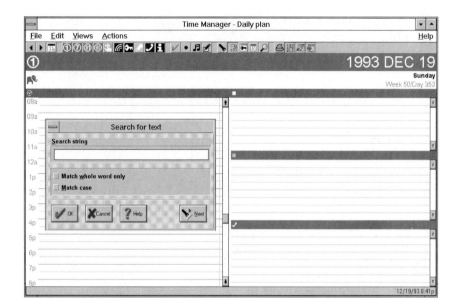

252: *Internal or external inconsistency.* GUI applications are *externally* consistent when they adopt the same visual language and behavioral conventions used throughout the environment. They are *internally* consistent if the same elements are used in the same way throughout the application itself. Because applications depend heavily on services provided by the environment, however, they may not be able to achieve even internal consistency if they are radically inconsistent with the rest of the environment. As this example shows, even a carefully designed application – for which a great deal of effort is expended on a custom presentation for the primary window – can experience "consistency leaks" in the form of secondary windows or dialogs that have not benefitted from the same stylistic treatment. In this case, the application framework on which the program is based provides the dialog for free, at the cost of consistency with the rest of the application (and the standard environment as well, for that matter). Moreover, any GUI-standard dialogs – such as File selectors, Print controllers, etc. – are likely to produce exactly the same problem for this application. While the importance of external consistency varies with the application type ("vertical" applications have more latitude than "horizontal" applications, for example, because they tend to have dedicated users), the users of any application will be distracted by serious internal discontinuities.

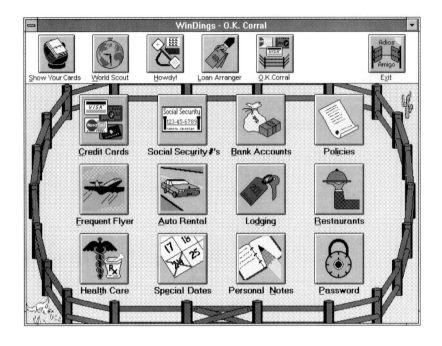

253: *Incompatible concepts.* Often the question of appropriateness is simply a matter of taste. Effective design always begins with *knowing the user* in hopes of understanding their needs, goals, and values. Only when you identify with the user will you recognize that an idea – or simply its presentation – is going to seem stilted, unnatural, or upsetting. Novel imagery, concepts, or metaphors should always have some degree of conceptual compatibility with those already present in the standard GUI environment, or at least with familiar concepts in the user's task domain. While most would agree that the Windows desktop leaves much to be desired as a complete operating environment, the Wild West imagery seen here seems a curious choice of metaphorical replacement. The associations between information management tasks and their representation in the OK Corral (e.g., "Show Your Cards" for the Rolodex) are extremely weak. In fact, beyond the pun-based function labels and the gaudy, fenced in work area, there is little to integrate the Wild West metaphor with the rest of the product. Note, for example, that none of the button labels inside the corral have any relation whatsoever to the cowboy theme. While the OK Corral may provide a playful diversion, it strains credulity to imagine a busy executive depending on this conceptual model for critical information management tasks.

Although style divorced from its *raison d'être* by time and circumstance is just an empty shell, some designers may see it as a tempting refuge when faced with the necessity for original thinking.

Steven Heller
Graphic Style

Techniques

The most important techniques for working with style in GUI environments do not address the creation of the style itself. Particularly in user interface applications, the style is largely pre-determined by the target GUI standard. Moreover, GUI styles are rarely "designed" self-consciously and intentionally, but tend instead to emerge organically from a series of successful existing solutions to comparable problems. In this review, we focus on three techniques aimed at developers working within the well-defined style typified by the standard GUI environment:

Mastery
Generalization
Evolution

• Mastering a Style
• Generalizing Across Styles
• Extending and Evolving the Style

Those charged with defining a new style face a more serious challenge. We suggest a thorough review of the Principles section above and an analysis of what works well and poorly in existing stylistic approaches. Experimentation and invention will of course have their role to play, but ultimately, the style must emerge of its own accord, with its appropriateness ensured through a convergence of the *worldviews* of user and designer.

254: Published style guides have recently become widely available for virtually every standard GUI environment, so there is no longer any excuse for remaining ignorant of the design conventions – and even more importantly: of the reasoning behind them – prescribed for your target environment.

Mastering the Style

In designing for standard GUI environments, choosing the "right" style is easy; the selection is implicit in your choice of GUI standard. Every mainstream GUI now provides a published style guide (254) documenting the conventions prevailing throughout that environment. Familiarity with the style guide may seem like an obvious first step, but our experience suggests otherwise: a surprisingly large percentage of the design errors in a typical application can be attributed to simple ignorance of the conventions of the target environment. The rules embodied in a GUI style guide are more than just "common sense" – they cannot be inferred without a full understanding of

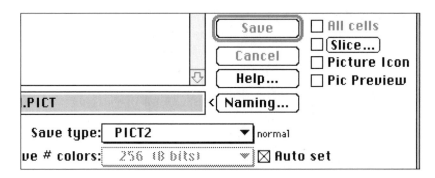

255: This detail from a popular graphics utility contains numerous violations (e.g., the use of a button in the Slice check box, the arrow to the left of the Naming button, the settings to the right of the pop-up menus) of the agreed-upon syntax and semantics of the Macintosh visual language.

the GUI standard's visual language and its underlying conceptual model. Nor can these rules be extracted inductively by looking at a few existing applications (even those provided by the vendor of the environment itself).

The first thing to do, then, is to read and understand the style guide for your "host" environment. Only after you fully understand the style – including its limits and its philosophical underpinnings – will you understand when to "violate" it and how to extend it to cover new situations in a logically consistent way. A designer who understood the Macintosh human interface conventions, for example, would never, as seen in Figure 255, use buttons as labels for check boxes or textfields. Novel constructions such as these quickly forfeit any promised efficiencies if users are forced to pause and re-familiarize themselves with the situation.

Most GUI standards define a number of higher-level idioms in addition to their basic controls. Controls are intended to be put together in specific ways in certain recurring situations. In the Microsoft Office conventions, for example, navigation through windows containing multiple panes or categories is supported using "tabbed" dialogs (256–a). The OPEN LOOK GUI addresses the same problem using an exclusive setting or – as in Figure 256(b) – an exclusive setting menu. The Macintosh environment favors scrolling lists of icons, with one icon representing each category (65). It is important to follow these local conventions when possible, because they support basic orientation and navigation tasks. Any advantages that might be gained by the introduction of a "better" approach will usually be dissipated by their unfamiliarity to the target user.

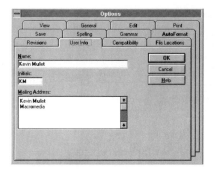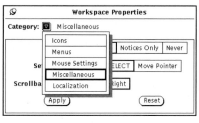

256: Different higher-level idioms are used to present the same functionality (display a given "page" in the dialog) in Windows and OPEN LOOK. It is important to know the standard approach in your target environment, especially when (as in this example) no direct support is provided by the toolkit.

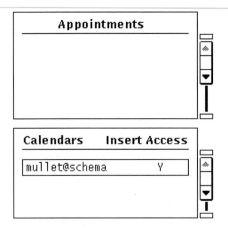

257: The toolkit doesn't always provide the right behavior for free, even if you use it "correctly". The interior labels on these OPEN LOOK scrolling lists conflict with the standard design for hierarchical lists, in which that part of the list is used to support navigation through the hierarchy.

Because they represent low-level platform technology, GUI toolkits are often so flexible that it becomes easy to produce non-compliant designs. Toolkit designers won't prevent you from doing the wrong thing, because they want to permit you to be *able* to do the right thing, when circumventing the standard becomes necessary. Non-compliant behavior may even be built into the toolkit itself, since the design and development of GUI standards normally take place in different engineering organizations. In the example above (257), scrolling lists developed for a particular OPEN LOOK toolkit introduce elements (the column labels at the top of each list) that clash with elements of the standard OPEN LOOK scrolling list. Learning when to – and when not to – use the built-in behavior is an essential step in the mastery of any GUI standard.

Many user interface professionals view GUI standards as unnecessary constraints on their design activities. We think this is precisely the wrong attitude. Standards free the designer from having to worry about a myriad of detail requiring hundreds of coordinated decisions. All of the time that would otherwise be spent worrying about what shape the buttons (or windows) should be (or what font, color, labeling style, etc.) can instead be spent refining the conceptual model, streamlining the interaction design, or testing the usability of the product.

Using a GUI standard correctly requires more than merely "complying" with the style guide. A GUI application should reflect the spirit rather than the letter of the law. The visual language in a GUI environment is a fragile convention that depends almost entirely on a consistent mapping of behavior to visual elements in all client applications. Your application will avoid causing problems if you keep four rules in mind:

Summary: Mastering the Style

1 Read the style guide(s) describing the environments for which your application is intended. Learn the overall conceptual model and the important details from the *user's* point of view.

2 Respect the visual language of the style. Understand the user interface toolkit(s) you will undoubtedly be using in terms of the *user-level* concepts and standard elements they are intended to support. Never use the standard elements for purposes at odds with the ones for which they were originally intended.

3 Learn the idioms of the target environment. Don't assume that the toolkit will take care of everything for you.

4 Pay particular attention to the usage and availability of user-customizable attributes (such as colors and fonts) in the target environment.

Simple ignorance of the standard is still the greatest impediment to success for many GUI developers. This is indeed a tragedy, since the documentation is so readily available (usually on the developer's own bookshelf). The concepts involved are not difficult, but they are not always just common sense either. Understanding the rules and rationale of a style is a prerequisite for every other aspect of working with that style, from applying it correctly and working across styles, to extending and evolving the stye, and even breaking it if necessary.

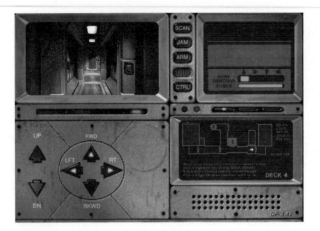

258: Immersive games – such as the CD-ROM adventure *Iron Helix* – simplify cross-platform design by "taking over" the display environment. Standard GUI elements are entirely replaced with custom controls.

Working Across Styles

With the noted exception of games, simulations and other "immersive" programming (258), everyone can agree that cross-platform applications should be as consistent as possible – all other things being equal – with the user's local environment. Today, however, the benefits of consistency with a particular GUI standard must be balanced against the increasing likelihood that a given individual will also be using your application on an entirely different platform – whether on a home machine, on a portable while traveling, or during collaboration with colleagues in an off-site work environment. Other factors that argue for cross-platform consistency in the application, even at the expense of cross-application consistency within an environment, include reduced documentation costs, reduced support costs, reduced training costs (for the user), and (potentially) lower development costs.

Successful cross-platform vendors have discovered the value of designs that lend themselves to implementation in multiple GUI environments (259). Standards can be bent when doing so produces real portability benefits. This approach allows developers to maximize consistency with the environment while sacrificing few of the benefits of consistency across platforms. While significant differences exist between GUI's, many of the same components reappear (albeit somewhat differently) in virtually every environment (260). Your Macintosh version may not be quite as "Mac-like" as a Mac user would like, but you may be forgiven if the product becomes available much sooner than would be possible with a "native" design.

259: Local policies for high-level (i.e., window level) structure should be followed wherever possible. Cross-platform translation is rarely this straightforward, but when it is, simple constraint-based geometry managers can remove much of the burden from the application developer.

Even so, it is important to recognize and respect important differences in the formal vocabularies of the various GUI standards. Common controls may have an entirely different appearance in each environment, and changing the standard presentation may lead to confusion and even errors. Layout considerations can be equally important, particularly when arbitrary, but well-learned mappings are in effect. In Windows, for example, the convention for dialog layout is to place the affirmative response to the left of the negative response (e.g., OK, Cancel), while the Macintosh convention (Cancel, OK) is exactly the opposite (261). Ignoring the local practice in this case can have catastrophic results, since dialogs are used to confirm most dangerous operations and even a momentary confusion can lead to data loss.

260: These functionally equivalent examples of the pop-up settings menu drawn from six GUI standards (top to bottom, left to right: NeXTStep, OSF/Motif, OPEN LOOK, Windows, Macintosh [new], and Macintosh [old]) are easily interchangeable for the developer, but are significantly different and potentially confusing to the user. Always use the correct presentation and style of interaction for each target environment when *any* functional difference is apparent.

261: The standard button order in dialog boxes is reversed between the Macintosh and Windows. Even in the presence of a clear default button indicator (and a safe default!), problems can arise for single-platform users if the designer chooses to standardize on one ordering across platforms. A tendency to "mouse ahead" – or simple force of habit – can cause damaging operations to be confirmed unintentionally, particularly in stressful situations.

The key to usable cross-platform design lies in isolating and preserving critical elements in the visible language of each platform and maximizing the cross-platform consistency of the remaining elements. Consistency of sequencing and arrangement is more important than visual identity in this case, even if this entails minor divergence from the locally optimal design. Ideally, a consistent control arrangement can be encapsulated within the structure of a platform-specific presentation context. When conventions are flexible, adopt the most general approach. Both Windows and Macintosh, for example, permit either horizontal or vertical arrangement of dialog response buttons. In this case, the horizontal arrangement at the bottom of the window is not only more portable to environments such as Motif or NeXTStep, but is also more space efficient and compatible with the spatial continuity of the dialog. Standard components, such as the File selector in Figure 262, can be augmented when necessary, but should rarely be replaced with entirely application-specific designs.

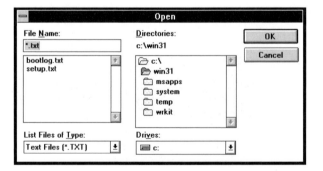

262: The "correct" functionality is normally encapsulated behind a high-level programmatic interface, so there is little incentive to standardize common dialogs (file selectors, print controllers, etc.) across platforms.

The nice thing about standards is that we have so many to choose from.

Anonymous

As cross-platform design becomes increasingly competitive, the need for cost-effective development techniques will continue to press designers toward "least common denominator" solutions. These should be avoided, since the kinds of things that need to be modified – such as labeling policies and button arrangements – usually provide critical orienting cues for the user. The right thing to do is to evolve the standards toward global consistency and create smarter toolkits (or toolkit extensions) that can handle the layout for you. In the meantime, keep these rules in mind when designing for multiple styles:

Summary: Working Across Styles

1 Develop a matrix of standard elements that covers the mapping of each GUI element to all of the target environments. Most environments include the same elements, but there are exceptions.

2 When a target environment doesn't support an essential component, consider altering or extending existing widgets (see *Extending and Evolving the Style*) to create an equivalent for each style.

3 Non-essential elements – such as menu and control mnemonics (the underlined characters in Figure 262) – should be supported in their native environments but should be omitted elsewhere.

4 In promoting consistency across platforms, focus on high-level *orienting* features such as the organization of menus and the layout of control areas. Keep the general arrangement of windows and dialog boxes as consistent as possible with the rest of the target environment, even if this means special-casing some of the code.

Success requires balancing the needs of the development organization with those of the user. There is much than can be generalized across environments, provided the basic user-level concepts and conventions are left intact.

263: The ledger representation seen in *Quicken* – the popular financial management application from Intuit – is an effective application-specific extension to the Windows environment. Because it occupies only the window's client area, the ledger does not interfere with other standard elements.

**Extending and
Evolving the Style**

No GUI standard is intended to preclude application-specific extensions and enhancements. On the contrary, the standard GUI provides a suitable context within which coherent application-specific extensions can be developed with minimal interference across applications. Stylistic innovations are, in fact, an important generative influence on the evolution of new or improved conventions. When extensions are necessary, however, it is important to ensure their visual and conceptual compatibility with the visual language and underlying conceptual model used by existing GUI components.

The Windows version of Quicken (263) demonstrates the latitude provided by a standard GUI. By affecting only the client area of a standard editor window, this application-specific extension meshes cleanly with the existing Windows document model. The functionality of the ledger is clearly communicated by the subtle banding of the alternating lines, which evoke the familiar visual pattern of a check record.There is no need to eliminate the standard window borders or button controls, to add a 3D view of the thickness of the pad, or to suggest the presence of a binder or checkbook cover.

Arbitrary divergence from existing visual language conventions can, in contrast, lead to serious breakdowns in communication. One toolkit-level

Most GUI standards
designed more effecti
cation. Your resource
high-level extensions
nents. Instead of sim
interaction technique
extension process:

1 Review the style g
capability. Never i
extended or re-use

2 Understand the in
will be predictabl
style.

3 Respect establishe
dimensionality an
wherever possible

4 Consider docume
perhaps even offe
and the rest of the

The need for applica
form designs. In vert
extensions can great
kits provide hooks f
Thoughtfully-design
itself, which often in
mentation, of a succ

264: Incompatible extensions, such as these "Menus with Pictures Beside Text" conflict with established visual language conventions (in this case, they conflict with both menus and toolbars in Windows).

extension to Windows, for example, offers "Menus with Pictures Beside Text" displayed in place of the standard menu bar (264). Even ignoring the dubious value of iconic menu labels, there are serious problems with this approach. Because there is no visual cue to suggest the presence of a menu, these elements are likely to be confused with the more familiar toolbar (which would appear in the same location). Users may even waste time searching for hidden menus in conventional toolbars.

265: Users are surprisingly attendant to subtle visual cues. Extensions that ignore or contradict the cues used elsewhere in the environment – such as the non-standard icons (which *look* like buttons) and pop-up menus in this window – will be temporarily confusing and permanently annoying.

Conclusion

8

To describe the problem is part of the solution. This implies not to make creative decisions as prompted by feeling but by intellectual criteria. The more exact and complete these criteria are, the more creative the work becomes.

Karl Gerstner
Designing Programmes

If you take only one idea away from this book, let this be the one. Problem solving and communication, not personal expression, is the key to effective visual design for graphical user interfaces. A clear visual organization is essential for effective communication. The techniques described in Chapter 4 provide the foundation for all communication-oriented visual design, and the ability to establish clear visual relationships among the elements of a composition is central to every one of them. This is the place to begin for those who wish to put our methods to an immediate test.

The techniques we've described can be applied by anyone–carefully and consciously at first, then subconsciously and even automatically–as you gain experience and a better understanding of visual phenomena. Of course the results will not be perfect on your first try, but you'll do better than you would without them. Patience, sensitivity, and a lot of practice are needed to become skilled in these techniques, but anyone can do it if they're willing to invest the effort.

Of course all design decisions can never be covered by a simple set of design rules and techniques. We hope these techniques will prove enlightening – perhaps even useful, but because we know you all have responsibilities unrelated to visual design, we strongly recommend you retain the services of a professional designer for all serious development work. Visual designers are probably the most cost-effective addition available to your development

254: Clear internal organization, spatial relationships among conceptually related elements, and restrained contrast are apparent in this advanced design concept for a network video phone tool.

team: they are relatively inexpensive and their impact on the quality of your product can be phenomenal, because practically everything they produce will be visible to the end user. There are also a plenty of consulting firms and independent designers to assist you on a contract basis.

We close with the observation that visual design is happening to your product even now, regardless of whether you've explicitly assigned someone to tackle the visual design decisions. We know you care about design issues, or you would have put this book down long ago. If your product team has a hole in it where the visual designer should be, consider this observation before you decide that professional design support is too expensive:

> Questions about whether design is necessary or affordable are quite beside the point: design is inevitable. The alternative to good design is bad design, not no design at all. Everyone takes design decisions all the time without realizing it - like Moliere's M. Jourdain who discovered he had been speaking prose all his life - and good design is simply the result of making these decisions consciously, at the right stage, and in consultation with others as the need arises.
>
> **Douglas Martin**
> *Book Design*

We couldn't agree more.

Acknowledgments

To find out more about the work of any of these leading international design consultancies, contact them at the following addresses.

11 Needham Road, London W11 2RP England
Phone: +44 01.229.3477; Fax: +44 01.727.9932

Pentagram

212 Fifth Avenue, New York, NY 10010 USA
Phone: +1 212.532.7000; Fax: +1 212.532.0181

620 Davis Street, San Francisco, CA 94111
Phone: +1 415.981.6612; Fax: +1 415.981.1826

300 Broadway, Suite 29, San Francisco, CA 94133 USA
Phone: +1 415.627.0790; Fax: +1 415.627.0795

MetaDesign

Bergmannstraße 102, D-1000 Berlin 61 Germany
Phone: +1 030.69.00.62-00; Fax: +1 030.69.00.62-22

1160 Battery Street, San Francisco, CA 94111 USA
Phone: +1 415.616.4800; Fax +1 415.616.4899

The Understanding Business

All product names are trademarks of their respective companies.

- Ami Pro is a trademark of Samna Corporation.
- Apple, the Apple logo, Macintosh, and LaserWriter are registered trademarks of Apple Computer, Inc.
- ASCEND is a registered trademark of NewQuest Technologies, Inc.
- Button Cube is a trademark of Software Workshop, Inc.
- deskMinder is a registered trademark of TECHSoft.
- FrameMaker is a registered trademark of Frame Technology Corporation.
- FreeHand is a registered trademark of Aldus Corporation.
- GO, PenPoint, are trademarks of GO Corporation.
- Hewlett Packard, HP, HP Visual User Environment, DeskScan II, Dashboard for Windows are trademarks of Hewlett Packard Company.
- Intellimation logo and Intellimation Library for the Macintosh are trademarks of Intellimation, Inc.
- Kodak logo is a registered trademark of Kodak Company.
- MacPaint and MacWrite are registered trademarks of Claris Corporation.
- Mercedes Benz logo is a registered trademark of Daimler Benz.
- Microsoft is a registered trademark of Microsoft Corporation.
- MS-Windows is a trademark of Microsoft Corporation.
- Motif and OSF/Motif are registered trademarks of Open Software Foundation Inc.
- NeXT, the NeXT logo, Workspace Manager, NextStep are registered trademarks of NeXT, Inc.
- Norton Desktop for Windows, Norton Disk Doctor for Windows are registered trademarks of Symantec Corporation.
- On Location is a trademark of ON Technology.
- Pepsi Cola logo is a registered trademark of PepsiCo.
- Quark XPress is a registered trademark of Quark, Inc.
- Quicken is a registered trademark of Intuit, Inc.
- Sheridan Personal Integrator, PTask, 3-D Widgets & MenuButtons are registered trademarks of Sheridan Software Systems.
- SmartIcons and SmartPics are trademarks of Lotus Development Corporation.
- Sony and the MiniDisc logo are trademarks of Sony.
- Star and Viewpoint are trademarks of Xerox Corporation.

- Sun, the Sun logo, Sun Microsystems, NeWS are registered trademarks of Sun Microsystems, Inc.
- SunOS and OpenWindows are trademarks of Sun Microsystems, Inc.
- SuperPaint is a registered trademark of Aldus Corporation.
- UNIX is a registered trademark in the United States and other countries, exclusively licensed through X/Open Company, Ltd.
- OPEN LOOK is a registered trademarks of Novell, Inc.
- WinDings and O.K. Corral are registered trademarks of Application Techniques Inc.
- WordPerfect is a registered trademark of WordPerfect Corporation.
- Zinc Interface Library is a registered trademark of Zinc Software Inc.
- Line art in Figure 207 used with the permission of Apple Computer, Inc.

About the Authors

Kevin Mullet holds a BS and MA in Industrial Design from The Ohio State University, where his graduate work on animated graphical displays combined coursework in experimental psychology and computer science with the existing design development curriculum. He is currently designing an advanced multimedia production environment at Macromedia, a leading provider of authoring tools for the Macintosh and Windows environments. Mr. Mullet worked previously as a human interface engineer at SunPro, the software engineering tools business unit of Sun Microsystems, Inc., where he designed graphical programming tools and visualization techniques, and at SunSoft, Inc., where he worked on a variety of OpenWindows products. He has consulted extensively on system- and application-level software design issues and is a leading expert on the OPEN LOOK Graphical User Interface. Before joining Sun, Mr. Mullet was Senior Designer at Aaron Marcus and Associates, a Berkeley, California-based design firm consulting in visual design research, user interface design, and electronic publishing. His research interests include visual and diagrammatic displays, visual programming environments, and algorithms for automating the layout of controls and displays.

Darrell Sano holds a BFA in Graphic Design from the University of Hawaii and a MFA in Graphic Design from the University of Illinois at Urbana-Champaign, where his work involved research and development for computer-based design education programs, including layout principles, pattern generation, and symmetry studies. Mr. Sano is currently a user interface designer at Silicon Graphics, Inc. Prior to joining SGI, he was an interface designer at SunSoft Inc., where he designed and prototyped advanced interface concepts for UNIX" and Mosaic Internet applications. Mr. Sano worked previously as an interface design consultant and has more than seven years of experience as a professional graphic designer and consultant on corporate communications, identity systems, and publication design. Mr. Sano's research interests include visual design systems for future interactive environments, designing interactive information and communication systems, and alternative representations and metaphors for graphical user environments. His design work has been recognized by the American Center for Design and has been published in the international design journals *Graphis* and *Novum Gebrauchsgraphik*.

Bibliography

Ades, Dawn
   The 20th-Century Poster: Design of the Avant-Garde, New York: Abbeville Press.

Albers, Josef (1963)
   Interaction of Color, New Haven: Yale University Press.

Aldersey-Williams, Hugh (1992)
   World Design, New York: Rizzoli International.

Alexander, Christopher (1964)
   Notes on the Synthesis of Form, Cambridge: Harvard University Press.

American Institute of Graphic Arts (1981)
   Symbol Signs, New York: Hastings House.

Apple Computer, Inc. (1992)
   Human Interface Guidelines: The Apple Desktop Interface, Reading: Addison-Wesley.

Ardalan, N., Bakhtiar, L. (1973)
   The Sense of Unity: The Sufi Tradition in Persian Architecture, Chicago: University of Chicago Press.

Baecker, Ronald M. and Buxton, William S. (1987)
Readings in Human–Computer Interaction: A Multidisciplinary Approach, Los Altos, CA: Morgan Kaufmann.

Baer Capitman, Barbara (1976)
American Trademark Designs, New York: Dover.

Banham, Reyner (1960)
Theory and Design in the First Machine Age, Cambridge: MIT Press.

Barratt, Krome (1980)
Logic and Design, Westfield, New Jersey: Eastview Editions.

Berlo, David K. (1960)
The Process of Communication, New York: Holt, Rinehart, and Winston.

Berst, Jesse (1992-a)
Windows Watcher, *Windows Magazine*, August 1992, 89–92.

Berst, Jesse (1992-b)
Windows Watcher, *Windows Magazine*, September 1992, 69–70.

Bertin, Jacques (1989)
Graphics and Graphic Information Processing, translated by P. Berg and P. Scott, Berlin: William de Gruyter and Co.

Bertin, Jacques (1983)
Semiology of Graphics, translated by P. Berg, Madison: University of Wisconsin Press.

Bothwell, Dorr and Mayfield, Marlys (1961)
Notan: The Dark-Light Principle of Design, New York: Dover

Bringhurst, Robert (1992)
The Elements of Typographic Style, Vancouver: Hartley & Marks.

Broos, Kees (1985)
ontwerp: Total Design, Amsterdam: De Beyerd, Breda.

Brown, Mark, and Sedgwick, Robert (1988)
A System for Algorithm Animation, *Computer Graphics,
SIGGRAPH'84 Conference Proceedings*, 18, 177-186.

Brown, Robert K., and Reinhold, Susan (1979)
The Poster Art of A.M. Cassandre, New York: E.P. Dutton.

Card, Stuart K., Moran, Thomas P., and Newell, Alan (1983)
The Psychology of Human–Computer Interaction, Hillsdale, NJ:
Lawrence Erlbaum Associates.

Carr, Stephen (1973)
City Signs and Lights, Cambridge: MIT Press.

Carroll, John M., Mack, Robert L., and Kellogg, Wendy A. (1988)
Interface Metaphors and User Interface Design, in Helander, M. (ed.),
Handbook of Human–Computer Interaction, Amsterdam: Elsevier
Science Publishers, 67–85.

Carter, Rob, Day, Ben, Meggs, Phillip (1985)
Typographic Design: Form and Communication, New York: Van
Nostrand Reinhold.

Cherry, Colin (1978)
On Human Communication–a Review, a Survey, and a Criticism, Third
Edition, New York: John Wiley and Sons.

Christ, Robert E. (1975)
Review and Analysis of Color Coding Research for Visual Displays,
Human Factors, 17, 542–570.

Cleveland, William S. (1985)
The Elements of Graphing Data, Monterey, CA: Wadsworth Advanced
Books and Software.

Cleveland, William S. and McGill, R. (1985)
Graphical Perception and Graphical Methods for Analyzing Scientific
Data, *Science,* 229, 828–833.

Cleveland, William S. and McGill, R. (1984)
Graphical Perception: Theory, Experimentation, and Application to the Development of Graphical Methods, *Journal of the American Statistical Association*, 79, 531–554.

Collins, Phil (1987)
Radios: The Golden Age, San Francisco: Chronicle Books.

Crosby, Theo, Fletcher, Alan, and Forbes, Colin (1970)
A Sign Systems Manual, New York: Praeger Publishers.

Diethelm, Walter (1976)
Signet Sign Symbol, Zurich: ABC Verlag.

Dondis, Donis A. (1973)
A Primer of Visual Literacy, Cambridge: MIT Press.

Dreyfuss, Henry (1972)
Symbol Sourcebook, New York: Van Nostrand Reinhold.

Droste, Magdalena (1990)
Bauhaus 1919-1933, Köln: Benedikt Taschen Verlag GmbH & Co. KG.

Dwiggins, William Addison (1948)
Layout in Advertising, New York: Harper and Bros.

Edwards, Owen (1989)
Elegant Solutions, New York: Crown Publishers, Inc.

Elemond Editori Associati (1991)
Swatch after Swatch after Swatch, Milan: Electa.

Fleig, Karl (1963)
Alvar Aalto, Zurich: Editions Girsberger.

Fletcher, Allen, Forbes, Colin, Gill, Bob (1963)
Graphic Design: Visual Comparisons, New York: Reinhold Publishing Corporation.

Friedmann, Mildred (ed.) (1982)
De Stijl: 1917-1931, Visions of Utopia, New York: Abbeville Press.

Frutiger, Adrian (1989)
Signs and Symbols: Their Design and Meaning, New York: Van Nostrand Reinhold.

Frutiger, Adrian (1980)
Type Sign Symbol, Zurich: ABC Verlag.

Furnas, George W. (1986)
Generalized Fisheye Views, *CHI'86 Conference Proceedings*, 16–23.

Gallo, Max (1972)
The Poster in History, Secaucus, NJ: The Wellfleet Press.

Garner, William R. (1974)
The Processing of Information and Structure, Potomac, MD: Lawrence Erlbaum Associates.

Gerstner, Karl (1986)
The Forms of Color, Cambridge: MIT Press.

Gerstner, Karl (1981)
The Spirit of Colors, Cambridge: MIT Press.

Gerstner, Karl (1974)
Compendium for Literates: A System of Writing, translated by Stephenson, Dennis Q., Cambridge: MIT Press.

GO Corporation (1992)
PenPoint User Interface Design Reference, New York: Addison-Wesley.

Gombrich, Ernst H. (1984)
The Sense of Order: A study in the psychology of decorative art, Ithaca, NY: Cornell University Press.

Grillo, Paul-Jacques (1960)
Form, Function, and Design, New York: Dover (Originally published as, *What is Design?*, Chicago: Paul Theobold and Co.).

Gropius, Walter (1965)
The New Architecture and the Bauhaus, Cambridge: MIT Press.

Hambidge, Jay (1948)
The Elements of Dynamic Symmetry, New York: Dover (originally published as, *The Diagonal*, New Haven: Yale University Press).

Hamilton, George H. (1967)
Painting and Sculpture in Europe 1880–1940, New Haven: Yale University Press..

Hanks, Kurt and Belliston, Larry (1980)
Rapid Viz: A New Method for the Rapid Visualization of Ideas, Los Altos, CA: William Kaufmann, Inc.

Hanks, Kurt and Belliston, Larry (1977)
Draw: A Visual Approach to Thinking, Learning, and Communication, Los Altos, CA: William Kaufmann, Inc.

Helander, Martin (ed.) (1990)
Handbook of Human–Computer Interaction, Amsterdam: Elsevier Science Publications.

Heller, Steven and Chwast, Seymour (1988)
Graphic Style: from Victorian to Post-Modern, New York: Harry N. Abrams, Inc.

Hemenway, Kathleen and Palmer, Steven E. (1978)
Organizational Factors in Perceived Dimensionality, *Journal of Experimental Psychology: Human Perception and Performance*, 4, 388–396.

Herdeg, Walter (1983)
Graphis Diagrams: The Graphic Visualization of Abstract Data, Zurich: Graphis Press.

Herdeg, Walter (1981)
  Archigraphia, Zurich: Graphis Press.

Hibi, Sadoa (1987)
  Japanese Detail Architecture, San Francisco: Chronicle Books.

Hochberg, J. and McAlister, E. (1953)
  A Quantitative Approach to Figural "Goodness," *Journal of Experimental Psychology*, 46, 361–364.

Hofmann, Armin (1965)
  Graphic Design Manual, New York: Van Nostrand Reinhold Company, Inc.

Hofmann, Armin (1989)
  Armin Hofmann His Work, Quest and Philosophy, Basel: Birkhäuser Verlag.

Hurlburt, Allen (1978)
  The Grid, New York: Van Nostrand Reinhold Company Inc.

Hurlburt, Allen (1981)
  The Design Concept, New York: Watson-Guptill.

Kepes, Gyorgy (ed.) (1966)
  Sign Image Symbol, New York: George Braziller.

Kepes, Gyorgy (ed.) (1966)
  Module, Proportion, Symmetry, Rhythm, New York: George Braziller.

Kepes, Gyorgy (ed.) (1966)
  Sign, Image, Symbol, New York: George Braziller.

Kobara, Shiz (1991)
  Visual Design with OSF/Motif, New York: Addison-Wesley.

Kubovy, M. and Pomerantz, J.R. (eds.) (1981)
  Perceptual Organization, Hillsdale, NJ: Lawrence Erlbaum Associates.

Kuwakama, Yasaburo (1989)
Trademarks & Symbols of the World, Rockport, Massachusetts: Rockport Publishers.

Laundy, Peter, and Vignelli, Massimo (1980)
Graphic Design for Non-Profit Organizations, New York: The American Institute of Graphic Arts.

Laurel, Brenda (ed.) (1990)
The Art of Human–Computer Interface Design, Reading, MA: Addison–Wesley.

Le Corbusier (1987)
The Decorative Arts of Today, translated by James Dunnett, Cambridge: MIT Press.

Le Corbusier (1964)
The Modulor, New York: Faber and Faber.

Levy, Steven (1990)
Mitch's Manifesto: One Man's Crusade to Rehabilitate Software Design, *MacWorld*, October 1990, 57-68.

Lindinger, Herbert (1990)
Ulm Design: The Morality of Objects, Cambridge: MIT Press.

Livingston, Alan and Isabella (1992)
The Thames and Hudson Encyclopedia of Graphic Design and Graphic Designers, London: Thames and Hudson.

Lucio–Meyer, J.J. de (1973)
Visual Aesthetics, London: Lund Humphries.

Marcus, Aaron (1992)
Graphic Design for Electronic Documents and User Interfaces, New York: ACM Press.

Margolin, Victor, (ed.) (1989)
Design Discourse, Chicago: University of Chicago Press.

Martin, Douglas (1989)
   Book Design, New York: Van Nostrand Reinhold.

McFadden, David Revere (ed.) (1982)
   Scandinavian Modern Design, New York: Henry A. Abrams.

McKim, Robert H. (1980)
   Experiences in Visual Thinking, Second Edition, Boston: PWS.

McLean, Ruari (1975)
   Jan Tschichold: Typographer, Boston: David R. Godine.

Meggs, Philip B. (1992)
   A History of Graphic Design, 2nd Edition, New York: Van Nostrand
   Reinhold.

Microsoft Corporation (1987)
   The Windows Interface: An Application Design Guide, Redmond,
   Washington: Microsoft Press.

Mitchell, William (1990)
   The Logic of Architecture, Cambridge, MA: MIT Press.

Modley, Rudolph (1976)
   Handbook of Pictorial Symbols, New York: Dover

Monmonier, Mark (1991)
   How to Lie with Maps, Chicago: University of Chicago Press.

Morgan, Hal (1986)
   Symbols of America, New York: Steam Press.

Morris, Charles W. (1938)
   Foundations of the Theory of Signs, *Iternational Encyclopedia of Unified
   Science Series*, 1(2), Chicago: University of Chicago Press.

Mouron, Henri (1985)
   A.M. Cassandre, translated by Michael Taylor, New York: Rizzoli.

Müller–Brockmann, Josef (1988)
Grid Systems in Graphic Design, Stuttgart: Verlag Gerd Hatje.

Müller–Brockmann, Josef (1983)
The Graphic Designer and His Design Problems, New York: Hastings House.

Myers, Brad (1990)
Taxonomies of Visual Programming and Program Visualization, *Journal of Visual Languages and Computing*, 1, 97–123.

Nadin, Mihai (1988)
Interface Design and Evaluation–Semiotic Implications, in Hartson, R. and Hix, D. (eds.), *Advances in Human–Computer Interaction*, Volume 2, 45–100.

Nichols, Karen Vogel, Burke, Patrick J., Hancock, Caroline (1990)
Michael Graves, Buildings and Projects 1982-1989, Princeton: Princeton Architectural Press.

Nielsen, Jakob (1993)
Usability Engineering, San Diego: Academic Press.

Nielsen, Jakob and Schaeffer, Lynn (1993)
Sound effects as an interface element, *Behaviour and Information Technology*, 12(4), 208–215.

Nielsen, Jakob (ed.) (1989)
Coordinating User Interfaces for Consistency, Boston: Academic Press.

Norman, Donald A. (1988)
The Psychology of Everyday Things, New York: Basic Books (paperback edition titled, *The Design of Everyday Things*).

Norman, Donald A. and Draper, Stephen K. (1986)
User–Centered System Design, Hillsdale, NJ: Lawrence Erlbaum Associates.

Palmer, Steven E. (1985)
The Role of Symmetry in Shape Perception, Acta Psychologia, 59, 67–90.

Passini, Romedi (1992)
Wayfinding in Architecture, New York: Van Nostrand Reinhold.

Pearce, Peter (1990)
Structure in Nature is a Strategy for Design, Cambridge: MIT Press.

Peirce, Charles Sanders (1931)
Collected Papers, Cambridge, MA: Harvard University Press (excerpted in Buchler, Justus, ed., *Philosophical Writings of Peirce*, New York: Dover, 1955).

Purvis, Alston W. (1992)
Dutch Graphic Design: 1918-1945, New York: Van Nostrand Reinhold.

Rand, Paul (1993)
Design: Form and Chaos, New Haven: Yale University Press.

Rand, Paul (1985)
Paul Rand: A Designer's Art, New Haven: Yale University Press.

Ruder, Emil (1981)
Typography, New York: Hastings House.

Rüegg, Ruedi (1989)
Basic Typography: Design with Letters, New York: Van Nostrand Reinhold.

Sexton, Richard (1987)
American Style, San Francisco: Chronicle Books.

Spencer, Herbert (1983)
Pioneers of Modern Typography, Cambridge: MIT Press.

Spiekermann, Erik and Ginger, E.M. (1993)
Stop Stealing Sheep & Find Out How Type Works, Mountain View, CA: Adobe Press.

Spoehr, Kathryn T. and Lehmkuhle, Stephen W. (1982)
Visual Information Processing, San Francisco: W.H. Freeman.

Sprigg, J., Larkin, D. (1987)
Shaker Life, Work, and Art, New York: Stewart, Tabori & Chang.

Stevens, Peter (1981)
Handbook of Regular Patterns, Cambridge: MIT Press.

Strunk, William, Jr. and White, E.B. (1979)
The Elements of Style, Third Edition, New York: Macmillan.

Sun Microsystems, Inc. (1989)
OPEN LOOK Graphical User Interface Specification, New York:
Addison-Wesley.

Sun Microsystems, Inc. (1990)
OPEN LOOK Graphical User Interface Application Style Guidelines,
New York: Addison-Wesley.

Tecce, Angela and Vitale, Nunzio (1990)
In Plastica, Naples, Italy: Electa Napoli.

Teichner, W.H. and Krebs, M.J. (1974)
Visual Search for Simple Targets, *Psychological Bulletin*, 81, 15–28.

Teichner, W.H. and Mocharnuk, J.B. (1979)
Visual Search for Complex Targets, *Human Factors*, 21, 259–275.

Tognazzini, Bruce (1989)
Achieving Consistency for the Macintosh, in Nielsen, J. (ed.),
Coordinating User Interfaces for Consistency, Boston: Academic Press,
57–73.

Treisman, A.M. (1985)
Preattentive Processing in Vision, *Computer Graphics and Image
Processing*, 31, 156–177.

Treisman, A.M. and Paterson, R. (1984)
Emergent Features, Attention, and Object Perception, *Journal of Experimental Psychology: Human Perception and Performance*, 10, 12–31.

Treisman, A.M. and Schmidt, H. (1982)
Illusory Conjunctions in the Perception of Objects, *Cognitive Psychology*, 14, 107–141.

Troy, Nancy (1983)
The De Stijl Environment, Cambridge: MIT Press.

Tschichold, Jan (1991)
The Form of the Book: Essays on the Morality of Good Design, Point Roberts, WA: Harley and Marks.

Tufte, Edward R. (1990)
Envisioning Information, Cheshire, Connecticut: Graphics Press.

Tufte, Edward R. (1983)
The Visual Display of Quantitative Information, Cheshire, Connecticut: Graphics Press.

Warncke, Carsten-Peter (1991)
De Stijl 1917-1931, Köln: Bendikt Taschen Verlag GmbH & Co.

Walker Art Center (1989)
Graphic Design in America: A Visual Language History, New York: Harry N. Abrams.

Wertheimer, Max (1958)
Principles of Perceptual Organization, in Beardslee, D.C. and Wertheimer, M. (eds.), *Readings in Perception*, Princeton: Van Nostrand, 115–135.

West, Suzanne. (1990)
Working with Style, New York: Watson-Guptill.

Wilbur, Peter (1979)
 International Trademark Design, New York: Van Nostrand Reinhold.

Wilbur, Peter (1989)
 Information Graphics, New York: Van Nostrand Reinhold.

Wong, Wucius (1972)
 Principles of Two-Dimensional Design, New York: Van Nostrand Reinhold.

Wrede, Stuart (1988)
 The Modern Poster, New York: Museum of Modern Art.

Wurman, Richard Saul (1991)
 USAtlas, New York: Access Press.

Wurman, Richard Saul (1989)
 Information Anxiety, New York: Doubleday.

Yoshida, M., Earle, J.V., Katzumie, M., Lehmann, J. (1980)
 Japan Style, Tokyo: Kodansha International.

Ziegler, Ulf Erdmann (1992)
 Nicolaus Ott + Bernard Stein: Vom Wort zum Bild und züruck, Berlin: Ernst & Sohn.

Index

interest 53
internal consistency 182
internal inconsistency 231
interpretant 171
Interpretation 174

K

kanban 27
KidPix 226
Kiljan, Gerard 10
Kodak 58

L

language system 2
layering 79, 82
layout grid 162
legibility 28, 81
level of abstraction 174, 208
leverage 46
Lissitzky, El 226
literal representation 25, 197
literal translation 33, 36
logograms 177
London Underground 23

M

Macintosh 4, 127, 240
Macintosh scroll arrows 86
MacPaint 27
MacWrite 27
MagicCap 36
Magritte, Rene 170
mailbox 189
maps 23, 38, 76
mastering the style 234, 237
mastery 233
Matter, Herbert 64
Meggs, Philip B. 12
menu accelerators 30
Mercedes Benz 21, 177
MetaDesign 76, 90, 95, 97, 118, 136, 154
metaphor 25, 33, 189, 232
metaphorical reference 196
metaphorical signs 190
Mexico City Olympics 182, 183
Microsoft Mouse 24
Microsoft Office 235
minimalist interfaces 24
Mitsubishi 177

modern art 8
modern design 14
modular units 158, 161
Mondrian, Piet 99, 218
Motif 240
movement 52
MTV Network 217
Müller-Brockmann, Josef 64, 98, 99, 126, 136, 138, 142

N

navigation 91, 155
near alignments 147
negative space 127, 129, 185, 206
New Typography 103
Newton 223
Newton Toolkit 220
NeXT 22, 216
NeXTStep 22, 44, 65, 77, 81, 104, 210, 240
Nihon Sun icons 210
nominal measurement scale 55

O

OK Corral 232
Olympic Games 85
OPEN LOOK GUI 59, 104, 128, 236
OpenWindows Snapshot tool 119
optical adjustment 122, 125
optical scaling 122
optical spacing 122
ordered perception 56, 82
organization 89
orientation 52, 54
OSF/Motif 85, 104
Oxford Museum of Modern Art 43

P

paper clip 46
Parthenon 61
PenPoint 25, 224
Pentagram 43, 84, 154
Pepsi Cola 205
perceptual grouping 95
perceptual immediacy 192, 206
perceptual layers 76
perceptual variables 79
peripheral vision 169
photorealism 34

U

U.S. Department of Transportation
(DOT) 39, 85, 136, 187, 205
U.S. National Park Service 133
understatement 19
UniGrid 133
unity 20, 89
Univers typographic family 81, 141
usability 19
USAtlas 219
user interface toolkits 7

V

value 54, 208
verbal representations 200
Victoria and Albert Museum 39
Vienna Secessionist 14
Vignelli Associates 133, 158
visual affordances 24
visual complexity 42
visual design 1
visual field 55
visual identities 39
visual interference 30
visual language 2, 38, 54, 152, 181, 183,
210, 213, 217, 224, 227
visual noise 29
visual programming environments 5
visual representation 187
visual structure 89
visual syntax 2
visual variables 54, 208
visual weight 87, 103, 208
VUE Workspace Manager 119

W

Westinghouse 177
white space 126
Windows 240
WordPerfect Office 47, 244
working across styles 238, 241

X

Xerox Star 190

Y

yin-yang symbol 115

Z

Zinc Interface Library 68
Zwart, Piet 10, 100